THE NYC ASIAN AMERICAN EXPERIENCE ON STAGE

EDITED BY ALVIN ENG

The text of this book is set in Garamond.

Publication of this book was funded by the National Endowment for the Arts.

NATIONAL
ENDOWMENT
FOR THE ARTS

Cover and book design: Jue Yee Kim
Cover photo by Tseng Kwong Chi © Muna Tseng Dance Projects, Inc. New York
All Rights Reserved

Published in the United States of America by The Asian American Writers'
Workshop, 37 St. Mark's Place, New York NY 10003-7801. Email us at
desk@aaww.org. The Asian American Writers' Workshop is a not-for-profit
literary organization devoted to the creation, development and dissemination
of Asian American literature.

Distributed by Temple University Press, 1.800.447.1656 | www.temple.edu/tempress

CONTENTS

I. Introduction / Acknowledgments

II. The Plays

III. The Verbal Mural

Culled From Interviews Conducted by the Editor With:

• Tisa Chang • Daryl Chin • Frank Chin • Ping Chong • Jessica Hagedorn • Wynn Handman
• David Henry Hwang • Aasif Mandvi • Chiori Miyagawa • Han Ong • Ralph B. Peña • Gary San Angel
• SLANT • Diana Son • Ellen Stewart • Muna Tseng

IV. Contributors

I INTRODUCTION/ACKNOWLEDGMENTS

ACKNOWLEDGMENTS:

Special Thanks To:

All of the contributors and their colleagues without whom this book would not exist.

Peter Ong, Andrea Louie, Derek Nguyen, Jeannie Wong, Elisa Paik, Nancy Yap, Quang Bao and staffs past and present at the Workshop for believing in and realizing this project through some pretty challenging circumstances.

Designer Jue Yee Kim and copy editor Nina Chaudry for going above and beyond...

Another special shout out to the Workshop volunteers and interns: Hung Dang, Jenny Lee, Marie Avetria, Carlos Gomez.

For invaluable feedback and support: Jin Auh, Daryl Chin, Jessica Hagedorn, Bonnie Rosenstock, Gary San Angel (my original conspirator on this project) and Wendy Wasdahl.

Muna Tseng for sharing her brother's gifts with us for the TOKENS? cover.

Finally, extra special thanks to you for reading this book.

INTRODUCTION:

Most times, a life in the theatre can be such a tenuous proposition at best that even the old "noo yawk" dis' of "that (one's life in the theatre) and a token will get you on the subway" doesn't hurt after a while. In fact, it becomes quite amusing...inspiring even. And in many ways, that is empowerment or "tough love New York City style"--finding the inspiration, resilience and ultimately love in and of your art and nurturing it while the rest of the city (if not the world) swirls around you at a trillion miles an hour with seemingly as many simultaneous cultural events in tow. In other words, you know you're up on the big stage, but acutely aware that you're not up there alone. The phenomenon of keeping your head period (not to mention above water) in this dizzying spin is what this book explores--from the unique perspective of "our neighborhood," the New York City Asian American theatre world.

Today, the New York City Asian American theatre is bigger than ever with at least four active producing companies, numerous performing/dance troupes and the occasional (read, one) Asian American play in a "mainstream" venue's season. Yet given all of this artistic growth (and this growth is indeed, an achievement to be applauded), we are still arguably as commercially insular as ever. While there always seems to be that break-out spark or two of a successful production, that long-awaited day where Asian American theatre becomes another seamless stitch of the supposedly class-free quilt of misfits that is New York City theatre has yet to dawn. So here we are, some thirty years on, still searching for the light of day while being obscured by the foreboding shadows of the same problems that have always plagued our neighborhood. In this murky twilight, one can't help but contemplate "When is a neighborhood a ghetto?" or "How can I be ghettoizing myself when I'm just...being myself?"

Which brings us back to the title of this book, TOKENS? THE NYC ASIAN AMERICAN EXPERIENCE ON STAGE. Yes, a token gets you on the subway, and the subway is the common denominator for New Yorkers in all of the city's greatly varying neighborhoods. But while that token can take you on a trip to anywhere in the city, it does not allow you to stay there. At that point, one feels a strange sensation that is akin to being branded with a permanent asterisk. It is a state of being (or non-being) that Leonard Cohen so eloquently describes as being "there, but ain't exactly real, or it's real, but it ain't exactly there." But one thing is for certain: In that instance, you stand alone, and your token is reduced to tokenism. It is this peculiar isolated cry in the urban wilderness that is at the heart of New York City Asian American theatre and all ten plays in this compilation--regardless of whether its characters, theme or premise are "Asian American." Some plays deal with this issue head-on and aim for the gut, some aim for the funny bone, while still others take it to a very different plane that mirrors this point of view without reflecting our physicality. So for the next 4-500 pages, we stand alone together, and our shared struggles become a celebration. A celebration of savoring and documenting our world while overcoming all varieties of obstacles that come with being a part of the New York City Asian American theatre at this tricky turn in the road and of the clocks to a new century where we know not of what lurks around the corner.

As the saying goes, "there's a million stories in the Naked City and this is 'one' of them," albeit composed of ten plays and a "Verbal Mural" of an oral history. Yes, it's admittedly a playwright-centric point of view, but the play is the thing, and these plays, all by New York City-based Asian American theatre artists, were all written and produced during the 1990s, and all but two of them take place in New York. And while reading a play is a completely different experience than seeing a play, reading these scripts will give you a great visceral snapshot of what Asian American theatre was like in New York City in the 1990s, from internationally renowned artists to newly formed ensembles. The "Verbal Mural" features reflections on all of the issues brought up in this introduction and much much more in the form of straight talk from a rich cross section of the playwrights and producers who, for all intents and purposes, founded and maintained "our neighborhood" over the last thirty years of the 20th century (and most of them still live and work here).

Alas, if you're new to these parts, you could think of this book as a talking, walking tour of an area of the city you've only known peripherally. But if you're very familiar with this turf, here's a chance to catch up with new and old friends and be privy to what they really say about the 'hood "in private." But old hand or newcomer, you'll notice that like all neighborhoods, the New York City Asian American theatre is changing... in many unexpected ways.

As neighborhoods in New York and the world begin to change and merge over the next century, will "hyphenated Americans" like "Asian Americans" (a name borne in defense of cultural pride and in defiance of a "mainstream neighborhood" that ignored them) become a relic of the 20th century? In turn, will a token (OK, by then a MetroCard) become a rite of passage to a new, diverse, super cyber highway or will it remain a rite of way down that same ol' grimy, pothole-laden dead end street?... Just as there are a million stories in the Naked City, there are also a million questions, and TOKENS? THE NYC ASIAN AMERICAN EXPERIENCE ON STAGE is one of them.

So yeah, this book may not get you onto the subway, but it will certainly give you a hell of a ride... All aboard!

ALVIN ENG
New York City,
Summer of '99 (the last one of the 20th Century)

II THE PLAYS

TRYING TO FIND CHINATOWN

by David Henry Hwang

This play is an expression of the way in which I believe ethnicity is sometimes a matter of self-identification. I was a jazz violinist for many years and essentially anchored my identity in that world. Similarly, I had met a Seattle stage director who was racially Caucasian, but had been adopted as an infant by Japanese American parents. As our nation becomes increasingly diverse, traditional definitions of race become blurred, and, in the ideal world, we will choose our own identities.

DAVID HENRY HWANG

TRYING TO FIND CHINATOWN was commissioned and received its premiere at the Actors Theatre of Louisville (Jon Jory, Producing Director), as part of the 20th Annual Humana Festival of New American Plays, in Louisville, Kentucky, on March 29, 1996.

Written by David Henry Hwang
Directed by Paul McCrane

Set Design: Paul Owen
Costume Design: Kevin R. McLeod
Lighting Design: Brian Scott
Sound Design: Martin Desjardins
Original Violin Music Composer: Derek Reeves
Dramaturg: Michael Bigelow Dixon
Stage Manager: Julie A. Richardson.

Cast:
BENJAMIN: Richard Thompson
RONNIE: Zar Acayan

Characters:
BENJAMIN, Caucasian male, early 20s
RONNIE, Asian American male, mid 20s

Setting:
A street corner on the Lower East Side, New York City. Present.

Note on Music:
Obviously, it would be foolish to require that the actor portraying "Ronnie" perform the specified violin music live. The score is recorded on tape and played over the house speakers, and the actor can feign playing the violin using a bow treated with soap. However, in order to effect a convincing illusion, it is desirable that the actor possess some familiarity with the violin, or at least another stringed instrument.

Property List:
Electric violin with bow (RONNIE)
Violin case, open, with change and dollar bills (RONNIE)
Coins (BENJAMIN)
Dollar Bills (BENJAMIN)
Scrap of paper (BENJAMIN)
Pack of cigarettes (RONNIE)
Lighter or matches (RONNIE)
Hua-moi (BENJAMIN)

Trying to Find Chinatown

Darkness. Over the house speakers, fade in Hendrix-like virtuoso rock'n'roll riffs—heavy feedback, distortion, phase shifting, wah-wah—amplified over a tiny Fender pug-nose.

Lights fade up to reveal that the music's being played over a solid-body electric violin by RONNIE, a Chinese American male in his mid-20s, dressed in retro-'60s clothing, with a few requisite '90s body mutilations. He's playing on a side-walk for money, his violin case open before him, change and a few stray bills having been left by previous passers-by.

Enter BENJAMIN, early-20s, blonde, blue-eyed, looking like a Midwestern tourist in the big city. He holds a scrap of paper in his hands, scanning street signs for an address. He pauses before RONNIE, listens for a while. With a truly bravura run, RONNIE concludes the number, falls to his knees, gasping. BENJAMIN applauds.

BENJAMIN: Good. That was really great. *(Pause)* I didn't...I mean, a fiddle...I mean, I'd heard them at square dances, on country stations and all, but I never...wow, this must really be New York City! *(He applauds, starts to walk on. Still on his knees, RONNIE clears his throat loudly.)* Oh, I...you're not just doing this for your health, right? *(He reaches in his pocket, pulls out a couple of coins. RONNIE clears his throat again.)* Look, I'm not a millionaire, I'm just... *(He pulls out his wallet, removes a dollar bill. RONNIE nods his head, gestures towards the violin case, as he takes out a pack of cigarettes, lights one.)*

RONNIE: And don't call it a "fiddle," OK?

BENJAMIN: Oh. Well, I didn't mean to—

RONNIE: You sound like a wuss. A hick. A dipshit.

BENJAMIN: It just slipped out. I didn't really—

RONNIE: If this was a fiddle, I'd be sitting here with a cob pipe, stomping my cowboy boots and kick-ing up hay. Then I'd go home and fuck my cousin.

BENJAMIN: Oh! Well, I don't really think—

RONNIE: Do you see a cob pipe? Am I fucking my cousin?

BENJAMIN: Well, no, not at the moment, but—

RONNIE: All right. Then this is a violin, now you give me your money, and I ignore the insult. Herein endeth the lesson. *(Pause)*

BENJAMIN: Look, a dollar's more than I've ever given to a...to someone asking for money.

RONNIE: Yeah, well, this is New York. Welcome to the cost of living.

BENJAMIN: What I mean is, maybe in exchange, you could help me—?

RONNIE: Jesus Christ! Do you see a sign around my neck reading, "Big Apple Fucking Tourist Bureau?"

BENJAMIN: I'm just looking for an address, I don't think it's far from here, maybe you could...? *(RONNIE snatches the scrap of paper from BENJAMIN.)*

RONNIE: You're lucky I'm such a goddamn softy. *(He looks at the paper.)* Oh, fuck you. Just suck my dick, you and the cousin you rode in on.

BENJAMIN: I don't get it! What are you—?

RONNIE: Eat me. You know exactly what I—

BENJAMIN: I'm just asking for a little—

RONNIE: "13 Doyers Street?" Like you don't know where that is?

BENJAMIN: Of course I don't know! That's why I'm asking—

RONNIE: C'mon, you trailer-park refugee. You don't know that's Chinatown?

BENJAMIN: Sure I know that's Chinatown.

RONNIE: I know you know that's Chinatown.

BENJAMIN: So? That doesn't mean I know where Chinatown—

RONNIE: So why is it that you picked me, of all the street musicians in the City—to point you in the direction of Chinatown? Lemme guess—is it the earring? No, I don't think so. The Hendrix riffs? Guess again, you fucking moron.

BENJAMIN: Now, wait a minute. I see what you're —

RONNIE: What are you gonna ask me next? Where you can find the best dim sum in the City? Whether I can direct you to a genuine opium den? Or do I happen to know how you can meet Miss Saigon for a night of nookie-nookie followed by a good old-fashioned ritual suicide? *(He picks up his violin.)* Now, get your white ass off my sidewalk. One dollar doesn't even begin to make up for all this aggravation. Why don't you go back home and race bullfrogs, or whatever it is you do for—?

BENJAMIN: Brother, I can absolutely relate to your anger. Righteous rage, I suppose, would be a more appropriate term. To be marginalized, as we are, by a white racist patriarchy, to the point where the accomplishments of our people are obliterated from the history books, this is cultural genocide of the first order, leading to the fact that you must do battle with all of Euro-America's emasculating and brutal stereotypes of Asians—the opium den, the sexual objectification of the Asian female, the exoticized image of a tourist's Chinatown which ignores the exploitation of workers, the failure to unionize, the high rate of mental illness and tuberculosis—against these, each day, you rage, no, not as a victim, but as a survivor, yes, brother, a glorious warrior survivor! *(Silence)*

RONNIE: Say what?

BENJAMIN: So, I hope you can see that my request is not—

RONNIE: Wait, wait.

BENJAMIN: —motivated by the sorts of racist assumptions—

RONNIE: But, but where...how did you learn all that?

BENJAMIN: All what?

RONNIE: All that, you know, oppression stuff, tuberculosis...

BENJAMIN: It's statistically irrefutable. TB occurs in the community at a rate—

RONNIE: Where did you learn it?

BENJAMIN: I took Asian American studies. In college.

RONNIE: Where did you go to college?

BENJAMIN: University of Wisconsin. Madison.

RONNIE: Madison, Wisconsin?

BENJAMIN: That's not where the bridges are, by the way.

RONNIE: Huh? Oh, right....

BENJAMIN: You wouldn't believe the number of people who—

RONNIE: They have Asian American studies in Madison, Wisconsin? Since when?

BENJAMIN: Since the last Third World Unity hunger strike. *(Pause)* Why do you look so surprised? We're down.

RONNIE: I dunno. It just never occurred to me, the idea of Asian students in the Midwest going on a hunger strike.

BENJAMIN: Well, a lot of them had midterms that week, so they fasted in shifts. *(Pause)* The Administration never figured it out. The Asian students put that "They all look alike" stereotype to good use.

RONNIE: OK, so they got Asian American studies. That still doesn't explain—

BENJAMIN: What?

RONNIE: Well...what were you doing taking it?

BENJAMIN: Just like everyone else. I wanted to explore my roots. And, you know, the history of oppression which is my legacy. After a lifetime of assimilation, I wanted to find out who I really am. *(Pause)*

RONNIE: And did you?

BENJAMIN: Sure. I learned to take pride in my ancestors who built the railroads, my Popo who would make me a hot bowl of jok with thousand day-old eggs when the white kids chased me home yelling, "Gook! Chink! Slant-eyes!"

RONNIE: OK, OK, that's enough!

BENJAMIN: Painful to listen to, isn't it?

RONNIE: I don't know what kind of bullshit ethnic studies program they're running over in Wuss-consin, but did they bother to teach you that in order to find your Asian "roots," it's a good idea to first be Asian? *(Pause)*

BENJAMIN: Are you speaking metaphorically?

RONNIE: No! Literally! Look at your skin!

BENJAMIN: You know, it's very stereotypical to think that all Asian skin tones conform to a single hue.

RONNIE: You're white! Is this some kind of redneck joke or something? Am I the first person in the world to tell you this?

BENJAMIN: Oh! Oh! Oh!

RONNIE: I know real Asians are scarce in the Midwest, but...Jesus!

BENJAMIN: No, of course, I...I see where your misunderstanding arises.

RONNIE: Yeah. It's called, "You white."

BENJAMIN: It's just that—in my hometown of Tribune, Kansas, and then at school—see, everyone knows me—so this sort of thing never comes up. *(He offers his hand.)* Benjamin Wong. I forget that a society wedded to racial constructs constantly forces me to explain my very existence.

RONNIE: Ronnie Chang. Otherwise known as, "The Bow Man."

BENJAMIN: You see, I was adopted by Chinese American parents at birth. So, clearly, I'm an Asian American—

RONNIE: Even though you're blonde and blue-eyed.

BENJAMIN: Well, you can't judge my race by my genetic heritage alone.

RONNIE: If genes don't determine race, what does?

BENJAMIN: Perhaps you'd prefer that I continue in denial, masquerading as a white man?

RONNIE: You can't just wake up and say, "Gee, I feel Black today."

BENJAMIN: Brother, I'm just trying to find what you've already got.

RONNIE: What do I got?

BENJAMIN: A home. With your people. Picketing with the laundry workers. Taking refuge from the daily slights against your masculinity in the noble image of Gwang Gung.

RONNIE: Gwan who?

BENJAMIN: C'mon—the Chinese god of warriors and—what do you take me for? There're altars to him up all over the community.

RONNIE: I dunno what community you're talking about, but it's sure as hell not mine. *(Pause)*

BENJAMIN: What do you mean?

RONNIE: I mean, if you wanna call Chinatown your community, OK, knock yourself out, learn to use chopsticks, big deal. Go ahead, try and find your "roots" in some dim sum parlor with headless ducks hanging in the window. Those places don't tell you a thing about who I am.

BENJAMIN: Oh, I get it.

RONNIE: You get what?

BENJAMIN: You're one of those self-hating, *assimilated* Chinese Americans, aren't you?

RONNIE: Oh, Jesus.

BENJAMIN: You probably call yourself, "Oriental," huh? Look, maybe I can help you. I have some books I can—

RONNIE: Hey, I read all those Asian identity books when you were still slathering on industrial-strength sunblock. *(Pause)* Sure, I'm Chinese. But folks like you act like that means something. Like, all of a sudden, you know who I am. You think identity's that simple? That you can wrap it all up in a neat package and say, I have ethnicity, therefore I am? All you fucking ethnic fundamentalists. Always settling for easy answers. You say you're looking for identity, but you can't begin to face the real mysteries of the search. So instead, you go skin-deep, and call it a day. *(Pause. He turns away from BENJAMIN, starts to play his violin—slow and bluesy.)*

BENJAMIN: So what are you? "Just a human being?" That's like saying you have no identity. If you asked me to describe my dog, I'd say more than, "He's just a dog."

RONNIE: What—you think if I deny the importance of my race, I'm nobody? There're worlds out there, worlds you haven't even begun to understand. Open your eyes. Hear with your ears. *(He holds his violin at chest level, does not attempt to play during the following monologue. As he speaks, a montage of rock and jazz violin tracks fades in and out over the house speakers, bringing to life the styles of music he describes.)* I concede—it was called a fiddle long ago—but that was even before the birth of jazz. When the hollering in the fields, the rank injustice of human bondage, the struggle of God's children against the plagues of the devil's white man, when all these boiled up into that bittersweet brew, called by later generations, the blues. That's when fiddlers like Son Sims held their chin rests at their chests, and sawed away like the hillbillies still do today. And with the coming of ragtime appeared the pioneer Stuff Smith, who sang as he stroked the catgut, with his raspy, Louis Armstrong voice—gruff and sweet like the timbre of horse hair riding south below the fingerboard—and who finally sailed for Europe to find ears that would hear. Europe—where Stephane Grapelli initiated a magical French violin, to be passed from generation to generation—first he, to Jean-Luc Ponty, then Ponty to Dedier Lockwood. Listening to Grapelli play "A Nightingale Sang in Berkeley Square" is to understand not only the song of birds, but also how they learn to fly, fall in love on the wing, and finally falter one day, to wait for darkness beneath a London street lamp. And Ponty—he showed how the modern violin man can accompany the shadow of his own lead lines, which cascade, one over another, into some nether world beyond the range of human hearing. Joe Venutti. Noel Pointer. Sven Asmussen. Even the Kronos Quartet, with their arrangement of "Purple Haze." Now, tell me, could any legacy be more rich, more crowded with mythology and heroes to inspire pride? What can I say if the banging of a gong or the clinking of a pickax on the Transcontinental Railroad fails to move me even as much as one note, played through a violin MIDI controller by Michael Urbaniak? *(He puts his violin to his chin, begins to play a jazz composition of his own invention.)* Does it have to sound like Chinese opera before people like you decide I know who I am? *(BENJAMIN stands for a long moment, listening to RONNIE play. Then, he drops his dollar into the case, turns and exits R. RONNIE continues to play a long moment. Then BENJAMIN enters D.L., illuminated in his own spotlight. He sits on the floor of the stage, his feet dangling off the lip. As he speaks, RONNIE continues playing his tune, which becomes underscoring for BENJAMIN's monologue. As the music continues, does it slowly begin to reflect the influence of Chinese music?)*

BENJAMIN: When I finally found Doyers St, I scanned the buildings for Number 13. Walking down an alley where the scent of freshly steamed *char siu bao* lingered in the air, I felt immediately that I had entered a world where all things were finally familiar. *(Pause)* An oldwoman bumped me with her shopping bag—screaming to her friend in Cantonese, though they walked no more than a few inches apart. Another man—shouting to a vendor in Sze-Yup. A youth, in white undershirt, perhaps a recent newcomer, bargaining with a grocer in Hokkien. I walked through this ocean of dialects, breathing in the richness with deep gulps, exhilarated by the energy this symphony brought to my step. And when I finally saw the number 13, I nearly wept at my good fortune. An old tenement, paint peeling, inside walls no doubt thick with century of grease and broken dreams—and yet, to me, a temple—the house where my father was born. I suddenly saw it all: Gung Gung, coming home from his 16-hour days pressing shirts he could never afford to own, bringing with him candies for my father, each sweet wrapped in the hope of a better life. When my father left the ghetto, he swore he would never return. But he had, this day, in the thoughts and memories of his son, just six months after his death. And as I sat on the stoop, I pulled a *hua-moi* from my pocket, sucked on it, and felt his spirit returning. To this place where his ghost, and the dutiful hearts of all his descendants, would always call home. *(He listens for a long moment.)* And I felt an ache in my heart for all those lost souls, denied this most important of revelations: to know who they truly are. *(BENJAMIN sits on the stage sucking his salted plum, and listening to the sounds around him. RONNIE continues to play. The two remain oblivious of one another. Lights fade slowly to black.)*

END OF PLAY

SAKINA'S RESTAURANT

By Aasif Mandvi

Sakina's Restaurant was developed intermittently over the course of five years. It started in the fall of 1992 with me deciding to write a one-man show and writing characters in my living room and performing them at the Duplex Cabaret Space in Greenwich Village. I then moved uptown to Wynn Handman's acting studios at Carnegie Hall. During the time that Wynn and I developed the characters I would bring to his acting class, I not only began to piece together the beginnings of a show but I began to realize what the show wanted to be. Instead of turning into another Eric Bogosian as I had originally thought I would, I found myself writing characters from within the South Asian community, and especially my family. My need to write these characters was never a conscious decision, it's just what came out. I had no statement that I wanted to make about immigrants or South Asians in America, all I wanted to do was write characters from my ethnic background that were real and that had never before been seen on the American stage. The parents in Sakina's Restaurant are really my parents, the rest of the characters contain aspects of my sister and me.

In 1994, I took these characters to Kim Hughes, and the two of us spent many many late nights rehearsing wherever we could (even in the conference room of her office job). Azgi was born by way of improvising with Kim on my idea that we needed a narrator to bring all these characters together. We first performed Sakina's Restaurant at the West Bank Downstairs Theatre on 42nd Street. I was terrified, Kim was giddy...The show was a success!! The audience loved it, they got it. It was then that I believed that maybe there was room for a show like this, about these people, about me. Kim and I continued to rehearse and develop the show in conference rooms, storage rooms, basements and now and then, even our apartments. We also continued to workshop it on and off over the course of the next three years at various venues around New York and in other cities. The character of Azgi continued to become more realized and the parables which were originally written for another project entirely found their way into the show and became one of the central themes.

In 1997 Wynn decided he wanted to do the show at the American Place Theatre, and we did the show there as a fundraiser. It was the first time the show was performed to an entirely South Asian audience, it was also the first time that I realized that the characters transcended my family and my experience of them; they were reflections of a community. There was a level of recognition in the audience that I had never experienced, even though the show had played successfully to many audiences before.

Sakina's Restaurant opened at the American Place Theatre on June 24, 1998. It was a beautiful day, and, for me, the culmination of a dream. The road to realizing this play has been long, glorious, frustrating, cathartic, overwhelming, joyous and spiritual. It has been a true and rare gift in my life to have had the opportunity to perform, share and move people with these characters. They are my friends, they are my family, they are my children, they are my voice, I hope you enjoy them.

AASIF MANDVI

SAKINA'S RESTAURANT had its World Premiere at the American Place Theatre, New York City, where it ran from June 1998 through January 1999.

Written and Performed by Aasif Mandvi
Directed and Developed by Kim Hughes

Scenic Design: Tom Greenfield
Lighting Design: Ryan E. McMahon
Sound Design: David Wright
Production Stage Manager: Richard A. Hodge

For My Parents

Sakina's Restaurant

Lights up.

We see AZGI standing with his suitcase center stage.

AZGI: Hello, my name is Azgi. I like Hamburger, Baseball and Mr. Bob Dylan. You know, I am practicing my introduction because today is a very important day for me, because today I leave my home here in India and I fly on an aeroplane! *(Motioning with his hands)* And I fly, and I fly and I fly, and then, I land!... *(Motioning with his hands)* And I land and I land and I land and I land, on the other side of the world in America. Oh, I am very excited. Practically the entire village has turned up in my parents' small house to celebrate my departure, can you believe?

(Turning up)

Ha waru me awuchu.

(Back to front)

OK, let's see. I have my passport, CHECK! My ticket, CHECK! You know, I am the first person in my entire family to even fly on an aeroplane... *(Nervous)* I hope no crashing. Oh, and the most important thing I have, a letter!... I read...

(He reads.)

"Dear Azgi,

(To audience)

That's me,

(Reading)

"America is a wonderful place, and as I told you in response to your letters, that since it was your dream to come here, I would help you as soon as Farrida and I could manage. Well Azgi, the time has come. I need help in my restaurant. I can sponsor you, it is hard work, but you can come and work for me, live with us, and get to see America, your dream is coming true."

Mr. Hakim is a very very important man, he own a restaurant in Manhattan! Here is address, 400 East 6th Street...NYC...USA...the World...the Galaxy...the Universe!!!!!!

(Turning up)

Ha waru me awuchu.

(Turning back, he sees his mother.)

Ma, Ma, don't cry. Why you crying, Ma? Listen, listen, You know what, you know what, when I go to America, I will write to you everyday. I will write to you so much that my hand will fall off. Ma, come on. Ma, you know what? When I go to America, I will write to you from the...from the...Top of the Empire State Building!! I will write to you from... from the bottom of the Grand Canyon!! I will write to you from everyplace I go, McDonalds! I will write to you!! Hollywood, Graceland, Miami, F.L.A. everyplace. I will even write you from Cleveland!! Cleveland, Ma! Home of the Indians!... Ma, come on, you know what you know what? When I go to America, one day I will be very rich! And then I will invite you and you can come and stay with me in my big house with my swimming pool, and my Cadillac—

(She hands him something)

What is this? A stone? You are giving me a stone! Ma, the poorest people in our village will give me more than a stone to take on my journey. How can I tell them that my own mother gave me a stone? The story of the river stone? The story of the river stone? I don't remember the story of the river stone. I don't remember, I don't remember—OK, OK, Bawa, I keep the stone. See? I'm keeping it, I'm keeping it.

(He mimes putting it into his pocket and then suddenly pretends to throw it away.)

Oh my God I threw it away!

I'm joking, I'm joking, Ma. It was a joke. Look, I keep it, OK! There it goes in my pocket, OK!

(Turning upstage and then turning back to face his mother)

Ma, I have to go.

(Music cue rises as AZGI slowly does Salaam to his mother, he kisses her hands and then her feet, he then picks up his suitcase and walks off towards America, he looks back at one point and holds up his hand as if to say goodbye. The lights fade and we hear an aeroplane fly through the air. When the lights come up accompanied by the song "Little Pink Houses" or any other appropriate song AZGI is standing on a busy New York Street, he mimes looking at the buildings around him and attempts to speak to people on the street, all of whom give him a very clear cold shoulder, he tries to say hello to people on the subway and the same thing happens until one solitary person speaks to him this it turns out is a bum, AZGI somewhat disappointed gives the man a dime and then is subsequently pick pocketed. He despondently hangs up his coat on the rack upstage and turns to face the audience and a brand new American day.)

(Noticing audience)

Oh, hello, how are you? Here I am! I made it! Oh my God this New York is a crazy place. But welcome to Sakina's Restaurant. This is my new job. I am the Manager here...OK I'm not really the manager... I am the OWNER!!!... No, no, no I am not the owner, I am the waiter here but you know it is such a good job—

(He hears someone off stage.)

Oh, excuse me,

(Speaking offstage)

Yeah?... Oh, OK.

(He begins to set up tables.)

You know Mr. and Mrs. Hakim were waiting for me at the airport when I arrive. I think it is very nice of them to let me stay with them until I find a place of my own. Their two children, Sakina and Samir, are also very nice but they are completely American. Samir, he is only ten years old. He is always playing with his Game Boy. He say to me, he say, "Azgi how are you doing?" I say, "Samir, how am I doing what?" Then everybody start to laugh. Sakina, their daughter, she is older, she is going to be getting married soon. She say to me, she say, "Azgi, don't you worry you will soon Catch On."

I just smile and nod my head and say, "Yes, yes, yes, you are absolutely right," even though I have no idea what any of these people are talking about. But I have found that in America, if you just smile and nod your head, and say "Yes, yes, yes, you are absolutely right," people love you!!!

I have not made any friends yet, because I am here in the restaurant, working, working, working. Mr. Hakim the owner, he is my very good friend, you know when I told him my dream one day to be a American Millionaire, he say to me he say *(Mimicking Hakim)* "Azgi let me tell you something very profound." *(To audience)* So I listen to you know, he say, "In America, Azgi, any ordinary idiot can be RICH, but not any ordinary idiot can be RESPECTED. I am not any ordinary idiot." *(Confused)* I think about this, and then I smile and nod my head and I say, "Yes, yes, yes, you are absolutely right." Mr. Hakim says I will go very far.

When I told Mrs. Hakim my dream to be an American Millionaire, she looked at me and she said, "Azgi, you are smart. Don't be fooled. America can give you nothing that you don't already have." And then she said, "When I was a young girl, I had a dream, just like yours, my dream was to be a classical Indian dancer." I said, "Oh yeah? Show me how you used to dance." She said, "No, I don't dance anymore, but when I first came to America and Sakina was just a baby I used to dance every-day," and then suddenly she close her eyes and she start to do like this—

(He moves his hips.)

I didn't know what to say. I said, "Mrs. Hakim!" But then she say to me, she say, "Azgi, let me teach you how to dance," I say, "No, No, No, I cannot learn, I can only watch," she say "No! you can learn, let me teach you how to make a bird, so I try you know. *(He begins to move his hands in the style of an Indian dance that represents a bird.)* I make a bird, make a bird, make a bird, make a bird... and bird fly away, bye bye bird! Gone!—OK, OK, OK, I do it for real, I'm sorry I was just kidding, *(Seriously now with real intent to learn)* I make a bird, make a bird, make a bird, make a bird, hey I'm pretty good, and then I do like this *(He shakes his hips)* and like this and—"Hey Mrs. Hakim you know what, I'm pretty good at this. I think if I had studied like you, I could have been a dancer myself." *(He gets into the dancing.)* I do a little bit of this and a little bit of this—

(A light change happens simultaneously with a sound cue that sends AZGI into slow motion as he continues to dance, the dance becomes more spiritual as he slowly wraps himself with a pink scarf that he picks up from under the stage, and as soon as he does the lights change and we are in the presence of)

FARRIDA: *(She is surprised by her husband who has snuck up on her.)* Oh my God! You frightened death out of me. Why you have to sneak up like that? OK Hakim, please don't be ridiculous, I don't dance like that, I don't dance like this. *(She wiggles her butt)* I am a very good dancer, OK Hakim you know what, by making fun of me, you are the one who looks ridiculous.

Embarrassed?—Embarrassed! Why should I be embarrassed?—I am not in the least embarrassed. I just think that there is a thing like that called manners, when you don't just sneak up on someone when they are doing something, and then you don't know what I am doing, what if I am doing something I don't want you to see. OK, very funny, ha ha ha. It is not called embarrassment. It is called politeness.

(She picks up her rolling pin and begins to roll out chapati. Throughout most of this piece she is intermittently rolling out chapati as she speaks to her husband.)

Well, there are many things about your <u>new wife</u> that you don't know. I am a very talented and mysterious woman. I can do much more than cook your food.

(He tries to make a sexual advance.)

Chul, chul, Hakim, come on stop, *Are'* come on, you are being absolutely crazy. Oh my God, you see how you get, you see how you get. You see what happens to you—you work in that restaurant 15 hours a day, and then you come home and all you are thinking about is Hanky Panky. Before you eat Hanky Panky! Before you wash your hands and face Hanky Panky! OK, Hakim you know what? I won't cook, I won't clean, I won't do anything, me and you we'll just do Hanky Panky, Hanky Panky, Hanky Panky!

(He pinches her and she turns around and tries to whack him with the rolling pin, he however ducks and she

misses him.)

You are a lucky man!

—That was before, that was a long time back, that was before we came to America. In India, how many friends I had, how much family, anybody to help. Now do you know what I do, do you know? —I cook, I clean, I take care of Sakina, and at the end of the day when she finally goes to sleep, I have five minutes for dance break which you interrupt with Hanky Panky.

—What you brought?—What present? Go away you didn't bring any present for me—Really! You brought present for me? Show no. *Are'* Show no—Come on, you can't bring present and then not show. OK. OK. OK. I close my eyes you show me? You promise, you promise, OK *(She covers her eyes.)* Guess? Guess? I can't guess, come on show no!... OK, OK I guess, I guess... no no no I want to guess.

OK you brought something to eat. No, something to wear? No!—Something for Sakina? No—Something for apartment?—YES!—New curtains!! You brought new curtains!!

(She has taken her hands away from her eyes.)

OK, OK, OK, I'm closing my eyes.

(She puts them up again.)

I can't guess anymore. C'mon, I'm looking—Ready, 1, 2, 3—

(She removes her hands from her eyes on the count of three, and she stands there staring in confusion at the sight before her.)

What you brought? What is this? A FERN? You brought a fern?—Why you brought a fern?—Oh my God, Hakim, Flowers. Flowers. Flowers means roses, flowers means tulips, flowers does <u>not</u> mean fern!—My God, what a romantic Rock Hudson I married! No, no, it's very nice. It's very nice. We'll put it in the window, people will come by and say, "Oh look, this lady's husband, he bought her a bush!"

(He wants her to teach him to dance.)

No, no, I can't teach you—Please Hakim, I can't teach you to dance. Besides, Hakim, that is a woman's dance. If a man dances like that, people will think he is a you know what!? You go, you dance with your fern.

(He seems to insist.)

OK OK I'm sorry, come here you want to learn, come here, OK do like this, like this, make a bird, make a bird, OK? OK, now you are a dancer.

(FARRIDA pulls on her scarf, so as to give the illusion that he is trying to pull her to him.)

No, I don't want to kiss you. I don't want to, because I don't want to. Hakim, please don't argue with me, I just don't want to. Because, just because, because you smell like cigarette! Are you happy now?—Then how come I am smelling cigarette in your mouth right now, when you told me after last time that that was your last pack and now I can smell that you are smoking again.

No, no, I don't want to dance with you, I want to know why you broke your promise. Relax. Relax. How can I relax Hakim, when you told me, you told me with your own mouth. You said, "Farrida, because I love you, I will stop smoking," and what did I say? You don't remember, I will tell you what I said, I said, "No. No. You will not, because I know you, and I know the kind of man you are" and what did you say? What did you say? You don't remember, you don't remember what you said, OK I will tell you what you said. You said, "*Khudda ni Kassam.*" Do you remember? *Khudda ni Kassam Hakim.* And you are a bloody liar! You lie to me, you lie to God, you lie to anybody.

Mane' tara sathe waat aj nai karwi, tara moma si gundhi waas aweche'.

—How can you say that? If you loved me, I would not smell cigarette in your mouth right now— Teach me to dance. You can't even do one bloody thing for me!

Dramatic. Dramatic. How can I be dramatic? You see me. You see my life. You see my life since I came to this country.—Can you imagine? Me. Me. Hakim, I was the girl in India who was always on the go! Movies, theatre, museum, money to burn. Where have you brought me? Where have we come, to this cold country where nobody talks to anybody, where I sit alone in two rooms all day long waiting for you come home. No friends, no one to talk to, nowhere to go. If I go anywhere, these Americans don't even understand what I am trying to speak.

Look at me, Hakim! I am not even the girl that you married. This is not me, this was not supposed to be my life. I gave up everything for you. For your dream, America! Land of Opportunity! For you, yes. For my baby, yes. For me, no. No opportunity.

—How can you say that, how do you know? Even if we do make it, what happens do we just go on smoking and dancing forever.

(Soft music begins to play, signifying that Sakina has woken up.)

See now, Sakina woke up.

(She looks offstage to talk to the apparently crying child.)

Na ro bacha Mummy aweche. Na ro.

(She turns back to Hakim, but he is gone.)

That's alright, Hak—you go, I'll take care of her.—You go, smoke your cigarette.

(She turns upstage.)

Na ro, Mummy aweche. Na ro bacha Mummy aweche, Na ro Na ro.

(FARRIDA walks upstage and we see her slowly take the scarf from around her neck and it becomes the baby SAKINA. The scarf is eventually unraveled and we are back in the company of AZGI, as he addresses the audience.)

AZGI: Once upon a time, an eagle and a lark sat on the branch of a giant tree. The eagle pushed out its giant chest and spread its powerful wings, and told the lark of its many adventures. "I have seen the world," said the eagle, "I have seen it seven times over. I have flown over temples and palaces, oceans and valleys, I have swooped down into valleys and I have flown so high that the sun has risen and set below me." The tiny lark had no such adventures of which to speak and it wracked its brain for a story to tell. Finally, it did the only thing it knew how to do. It began to sing. A tiny song, but as it did the tree, the field, the hillside and the entire valley, lifted up out of the earth and rose to heaven.

She doesn't dance anymore. I suppose that eventually she forgot that she could.—Or maybe she simply decided it was not worth trying to remember.

Dear Ma, another day in Sakina's Restaurant. I work, and I work, and I work and I work—but I never dance.

(AZGI is suddenly in the restaurant. He mimes a conversation with a table, tries to clean their dirty silverware, he goes to another table and picks up their plates, he rushes over to the kitchen and screams at ABDUL the cook, who is working behind the line.)

ABDUL!—I need two puri's on table 5! I need two lassi's on table 6, and this lamb curry is COLD, COLD, COLD! Food, Abdul, is supposed to be HOT, HOT! Not COLD! How come you don't seen to understand that?????

(AZGI runs to speak to one of his tables. To first table.)

I am very sorry. In all the time that I have worked in this restaurant, food is NEVER cold, NEVER! He is heating it up right now. I will bring it out in two minutes and you just keep enjoying your... water.

(He moves to the second table.)

Hello, how are you? My name is Azgi, I will be your waiter, How can I help you? Oh yeah, it is kind of spicy, but we have a scale. You see, you can order how spicy you would like one, two, three, four, five. You decide, He'll make it—What?—you want number five?

(AZGI is a little concerned.)

Sir don't take number five, Take number two—No, no, number two is better for you, it's very good, you'll like it very much.—Please sir, don't take number five. Sir I am trying to save your life OK. *(getting angry)* Look, look in my eyes, OK, number two is better for you. OK, you think about it, I will come back OK.

(He runs upstage again.)

ABDUL!—Where is my lamb curry????

(The lamb curry seems to have appeared on the line.)

A-ha!

(He runs over to the first table with the imaginary lamb curry. It is very hot and burns his hands.)

There you go. OK? piping hot—What happened? Why you look so sad? Not lamb?—CHICK-EN—Oh my God!—No, no, please sit down. Where you going? Please don't leave, sit down, I am very sorry, this is a terrible mistake, I will bring out chicken in just two minutes, please don't leave, whatever you do don't leave.

(He runs over to the second table.)

OK, OK, look I tell you what, number three, number three is plenty hot. You don't need number five. LISTEN MAN!! I AM FROM INDIA!!! And even in India nobody asks for number five! It's not a real thing that you can eat, it's just for show. I am not screaming, you are screaming! Look, look, now your wife is crying! I didn't make her cry, you made her cry! OK, OK. Fine, Fine, you want five, fifteen, one hundred five!! I give you OK!

ABDUL!—Listen on dup forty-one, I put number five, but you don't make it number five, you make it number two, OK? And this lamb curry is supposed to be chicken curry—Because I am telling you, that's why. Because I am the boss right now, OK. Listen you give me any trouble no, I will have Mr. Hakim fire you!!!—Oh, yeah? Oh, yeah? Come on, Come on Abdul. *(He puts up his fists.)* I will take you right now! I will kick your butt so hard that you will be making lamb curry for the tigers in India! Oh, yeah? Come on, Big Guy, come on, Big Guy, come on—

(Suddenly AZGI is faced with ABDUL who grabs him by the collar.)

—BIG GUY!

I am joking, man. I am just kidding around, why you take me so seriously?—Please don't kill me.

(Turning)

Every night I have the same dream. I am a giant tandoori chicken wearing an Armani suit. I am sitting behind the wheel of a speeding Cadillac. I have no eyes to see, no mouth to speak and I don't know where I am going.

Mr. Hakim, he come up to me, he say, "Azgi, Azgi, Azgi, you have to calm down, man." He say to me, he say, "Success, Azgi, is like a mountain. From far away it is inspiring, but when you get close, you realize that it is simply made of earth and dirt and rocks, piled one on top of the other until it touches the sky." Mr. Hakim, he is a smart man, but I wonder to myself when God was building the mountain and piling the rock, one on top of the other, was he working or playing?

(He begins to ponder this thought, and then suddenly he smiles and goes over to the first table.)

Hello, my name is Azgi...I am working...and playing.

(He goes over to the second table.)

Hello, my name is Azgi...I am working and playing...how are you?

(He goes over and looks in the direction of ABDUL, and blows him a big kiss.)

ABDUL...I love you man!!!

(Phone rings, AZGI turns and looks at the audience.)

Phone!

(He picks up the phone.)

Hello, Sakina's Restaurant. Azgi speaking. How may I—Oh, oh, Mr. Hakim? No. No. He is right here. I will get him—

(AZGI heads around behind the coat rack as if on his way to find HAKIM, when he comes around the other side, with tie in hand.... he is HAKIM.)

HAKIM: *(Into the phone)* Hello, Sakina's, How may I help you?—Oh, hello Bob! I am very fine.

Business is good, business is good you know can't complain, how about you?—Huh? Dinner for three? Tonight? Oh you must be going to have a big celebration—Usual table? OK—8 p.m. Very good. Oh congratulations, you must be very proud of him. Actually, we are also very proud of our Sakina because—

(He is embarrassingly interrupted on the other end of the line.)

Oh, OK Bob. No no that's fine. I understand. Time is money. Got to go. OK Bob, we'll see you later. OK, we'll see you then, bye bye...bye bye...bye bye.

(Hangs up, and then resumes putting on his tie and grooming himself in mirror and singing a Hindi song of choice. During this, he hears an imaginary knock on the door.)

Come in.

(He turns to see his daughter.)

Hey, hey, hey, hey! Come inside here, close the door, come here. What is this dress?—Oh, I see, I see.

(He talks to his daughter. His distress with his daughter is translated into his ineptness and frustration with his tie that he is trying to secure.)

You think you are too smart, huh?—You think you are too smart.—You think you can go anywhere, do anything, wear anything. You think you have become an American Girl!—You think the world should not care now how you behave, what you wear, how you dress, nothing! You have got all these fancy ideas from all your American friends. You are laughing with all your American friends you are saying, "Oh my parents are introducing me to an Indian man, nice professional Indian man, going to be a Doctor, how foolish of them, right? How foolish they are." All your American friends are laughing. They are saying Hey, Sakina, life is not like that.—Life is easy, marry who you want to marry, Black guy, White guy—who cares, right? Who cares? In America, everything is OK! No right, no wrong, no good, no bad, everything is COOL! As long as I feel good about myself, who cares, right?—Who cares how my father feels, or my mother feels, or my grandfather feels or my grandmother feels. Who cares! It is my business, my life, this is a free country! Am I right?

(Phone rings.)

Hello, Sakina's, how may I help you?—Tonight, dinner for two, Martin...can you spell that? M...A...R *(He notices that SAKINA is leaving and he tries to get her to come back in the room while continuing with the customer on the phone.)* T...I...N. No I got it, I got it, yes we do, yes we do, free popadoms, yes all night long, as many as you want, OK we'll see you then, yes I am excited as well, OK then, bye bye...bye bye...bye bye.

(Hangs up)

Sakina!—Sakina!...Come inside—Close the door. I'm talking to you. Crazy girl, running away.

(He turns to the mirror, notices his tie is completely screwed up and he is a little embarrassed. He reties it.)

"Oh Dad!" You are saying, "Dad! Dad! Dad! What do you know about life in America? You are from India! In America you have to learn to relax, because everybody in America is very RELAXED and very COOL!" Well, let me tell you something, I have seen all of your cool and relaxed friends, and you are not fooling anyone—you will <u>never</u> be an American girl. You can TRY. Oh yeah, you can TRY. You can wear your BIG HAIR, like American hair, and you can wear makeup like American makeup, you can even wear this cheap dress and show off your breasts and your legs and disgrace your whole family—but you will always be an Indian girl, with Indian blood, and these Americans, oh they are very nice, very polite on the face, have a nice day. Have a nice day. Welcome to K-Mart, Very Nice.—They will look at you and say, "Oh, she is so pretty, she looks like Paula Abdul."—But let me tell you something, the minute you steal one of their good ole boys from them, suddenly you will see how quickly you become an Indian again.

(Phone rings. He speaks in Gujaratti.)

Hello Sakina's Restaurant how may I help you? *Aaa Cam cho bhai, are koi divas miltaj nathi...aje, chullo, na na badha ne layaowjo, na khai takhlif nei, chullo pachi milsu...*OK bye bye...bye bye...bye bye.

(Hangs up and faces his daughter.)

We love you, Sakina, you are our daughter. But I will never agree to what you are doing with your life.—Why do you think we came to this country?—For YOU! Why do you think I have this restaurant?—For YOU! Why do you think I am working twelve hours a day?—For YOU and your brother. So that you could grow up in the richest country in the world, have all the opportunity, all the advantages and become something. We are saving every penny for your college, why? So you can run around with American boys...NO!! So we will be proud of you. Indian children make their parents proud of them. Can your American friends teach you that?—Can they teach you about your Culture? Your Religion? Your Language? Can they tell you who you are?... Go ask them. I know, I know, I know it is all fun and games right now, but what will happen? You will marry one of these American boys, have American children, and then what? Then everything will be forgotten—Everything will be GONE.—*Tu kai samje che me su kawchu tane`. Tara Mugaj ma kai jaiche`.*

Answer me, no? No No No No, Not in English. Speak to me in Gujaratti.

(He waits, and she does not respond. She is unable to.)

Can't...! Won't maybe. Look at you, look what you have become. You will not go to this dance tonight. I will show you, I will get rid of this "I want to be American" nonsense—

(Exploding in anger.)

I DON'T CARE! I DON'T CARE, I DON'T CARE IF THIS IS THE BIGGEST DANCE IN THE COUNTRY OR THE WORLD OR THE ENTIRE FUCKING AMERICA!! DANCING IS IMPORTANT, *(He dances around mocking her.)* BUT I AM NOT IMPORTANT!

(The phone rings. He composes himself and answers the phone.)

Hello, Sakina's how may I help you?—Yes, Bob, how are you?—Oh I am very sorry. Oh, no problem, that's perfectly alright, we'll see you another time. I hope she feels better, thank you for calling Bob. Bye-bye, bye-bye, bye-bye.

(Hangs up, and looks back at SAKINA.)

Tell Azgi that the Cohens have canceled, and go help your mother...in the kitchen.

(Phone rings, he watches her leave and then answers.)

AZGI: *(On phone)* Hey Ma, it is me, Azgi. Yeah, Azgi, I'm calling from New York. You know what, Ma? Next month Sakina is getting married, and tonight she is having a Bachelorette party, and I have been invited. I am very excited to be a Bachelorette. Hey, yeah, listen to the music.

(He holds up receiver.)

That's the music ma, You won't believe this party ma, so many people, Ma...I have to go, Ma. I love you, bye.

(He hangs up the phone and comes downstage dancing. He then dances downstage and then talks to the audience.)

Sakina told her parents that if she had to marry who they wanted her to marry, then she was going to have the kind of bachelorette party that she wanted to have. She invited 75 people, all of them would drink, including myself, and then she had a rock and roll band, and just to make sure that her parents would completely disapprove, she paid $200.00 for a "MALE STRIPPER." I told her, "I said for two hundred dollars in India I would run around naked for ONE WEEK!"—She said, "Oh, yeah?"

(The music that has been underlying the previous speech, suddenly becomes very loud and AZGI begins to strip. He speaks as his clothes are seemingly ripped off his body. He is incredibly embarrassed.)

No NO I cannot strip, No I do not do that kind of thing, I am very modest, I am from India, please do not do this, OK OK I tell you what I do this much OK? *(He simply opens a shirt a little.)* La la la la...That's all I can so thank you very much *(His shirt is ripped off him.)* Noooo!!! Because I was the only man, they decided to turn me into a Bachelorette.

(At this, AZGI suddenly runs over to the hat stand and takes the tube dress that has been hanging there. The

dress is slipped over his neck as if it were being done to him by the women at the party.)

No, no, please. I cannot wear this, this is a dress! I am very embarrassed. Please not a DRESS, anything but a dress!

(His protests of genuine embarrassment are unheeded by the women, who after the dress, proceed to finish off the transformation by squeezing a hair band onto his head much to AZGI's amazement and distress.)

AAAAAAAAAAAAAAAAAAAAAAAAAAAAHHHHHHHH!!!!!!!!!!!!!!!!

(AZGI stands center stage wearing a tube dress and a hair band.)

Once upon a time a man asked God for a new face because he was tired of the one he had, so God granted the man his wish. The tragedy of this story is that now every time the man looks in the mirror, he doesn't know who he is.

(AZGI moves over to the table stage left and sits down. We are now in the presence of SAKINA. She primps and preens in a large hand mirror, until she is suddenly surprised by the presence of TOM who is sitting across the table.)

SAKINA: Oh my GOD!!! *(Embarrassed)* I didn't see you come in... Wow you look great, I got your message. I can't stay long...'cus I gotta get upstairs by 7:30.—Well we're having this religious festival at our house and all these people come over and we make this food called Biriani and...Never mind, I just gotta get back upstairs by 7:30 to help my mom get ready for it. *(Pause)* So, what's up?—I'm just surprised to see you because last time we talked you were like, "Sakina we are broke up"...and then you hung up the phone. What?—That's not true!— Is that why you came here, to tell me that? *(She turns and takes a deep breath and then turns back to him.)* No I'm fine, I'm fine, first of all Tom, first of all, Stacey and I are the ones who started this band and Stacey and I are the only ones who can—

(She looks up at the imaginary waiter.)

Hi!—No, I'm not eating...no neither is he, thanks, OK?—Thanks.

(Waiter leaves.)

And Stacey and I are the only ones who can kick anyone out of this band, which is not even a band yet, because Stacey still needs to learn how to play the piano and so you are kicking me out of a band that does not even exist yet!—No, no, no, no, the manager manages the band, Tom. He does not kick people out of the band, that is not his job.—What?—She said that?—She said that! Stacey said that, Tom, look at me, look at me OK, Stacey is my best friend since the 8th grade, and if she said that, Tom, we are totally not friends anymore, so you better not be lying—Oh, my God! I can't believe she said that, I told her why I had to miss those practices, I totally said I have to miss three practices because I have to hang out with that Indian guy that my parents want me to marry—I had to hang out with him—I can't believe she said that, I don't understand, I explained the whole thing to her.

(TOM gets up to leave.)

Where are you going— That's it, that's all you had to say, now you're just gonna leave?

(She reaches for him.)

Wait! Would you please just sit down? *(She stands)* Please, Tom. *(She bends over and becomes cute and coy in order to lure him back to the table.)* Please, just for two minutes, please just sit down. *(He sits back down.)* Hi, What is going on here Tom?—What do you mean, what do I mean?—I mean you come here to tell me that my best friend is kicking me out of my band, and then last week you're like we have to break up 'cus "I need more space," and then this week I find out that you're dating Julie Montgomery, and I'm calling you every day this week and your Dad is like, "Tom? Tom went to the Library"—and I'm like, Tom at the library?...I don't think so—no, I don't think I'd be jealous of her. Because, because, because she's a racist pig, that's why. I can't believe you would even date her.—I was hoping you came here to tell me of her untimely death.—I don't care if I'm not Black. It's still disgusting.—I didn't say that, I just said she's a racist pig and I wish she'd die. You can still date her.—Everyone knows she is, everyone in school knows have you ever heard her mouth?—"Nigger. Nigger. Nigger."

(She suddenly looks around hoping that no one heard her.)

She even called me that word...What's so funny?—You're laughing, yes you are, Oh my God you're sick, Tom. This is retarded, I'm leaving. *(Gets up to leave as waiter returns. She speaks to the waiter.)* Hi!—Yeah I have to leave, I have to go upstairs and *(Directing it at TOM)* THROW UP! What?—I don't care if she's sorry, Tom, my problem is you, my problem is—What? *(Realizing that waiter has taken her seriously.)* No I don't need any PEPTO. It's just HIM, I'm sorry thanks...no no I'm fine, thanks. *(Waiter leaves. She turns back to TOM)* My problem is not her, my problem is YOU. I'm starting to like not know you anymore.—You explained it to her? You explained it to her. OK, fine this should be great, *(Sitting back down)* What, Tom, did you explain to her?—

(She listens and then hears something that makes her suddenly furious.)

Ah ha,—and then?—and?—OK shut up! No really Tom shut up! Tom, Tom, Shut up! Shuuuuuuuuuuuuuuuut uuuuup!—Listen to me. I am NOT IRANIAN!—I am INDIAN! INDIAN! INDIAN! What do you mean? How could you not know that? Look around, Tom. We dated for TWO MONTHS, Tom, TWO MONTHS! In that TWO months, I brought you to THIS Indian Restaurant like a million times. Where you ate all the "OOOOH, it's SO GOOD!" INDIAN FOOD that my Mom put in front of your face. And remember that party I took you to in Brooklyn with all those INDIAN people, wearing INDIAN clothes celebrating INDIAN Independence Day and then you turn around and tell Julie Montgomery, "Hey, Sakina's not a nigger, she's IRANIAN!" Well there it is isn't it, everything is a big mistake to you. Our whole relationship was a big mistake, remember that one?—Oh, my God! I can't believe you, I already explained the whole thing to you. It doesn't mean anything,—I am NOT going to marry him. Because I'm not that's how I know—no no no. My parents can't make me. It's not some kind of medieval thing. It's just part of the culture, that's all. It's just a custom, they are just trying to make sure that I am secure in my life, that's all, they're not American, they're not like your parents—I'm not saying that—Your parents are great! I'm just saying that my parents have a different attitude about things and if you can just accept that and not make a big deal about it?—Well there it is isn't it!! If everyone doesn't think like you, talk like you, believe what you believe, then it's all just dumb, right?

(He takes her hand, music comes on.)

What are you doing? No I can't kiss you...because we are in my Dad's restaurant... What? *(She suddenly starts giggling based on what he has said, she slowly moves toward him, and as the music gets louder she and TOM engage in a big sloppy wet teenage kiss, she pulls away and realizes that she is chewing "his" gum, she takes it out of her mouth.)* What? Why?—No, you're gonna make fun of him. Because you always make fun of him. OK, if I show you, you promise not to laugh?—Do you promise? Say it. Say I promise not to laugh...or make fun of him...OK

(She reaches into her purse, she pulls out of her purse a photograph and puts it on the table.)

When I was seven, my dad, yeah he gave me this picture of this guy that they betrothed me to, and I just kept it.—Because, because, I didn't know I was gonna meet anybody.—When you're young and geeky with a funny name and your Mom makes you wear harem pants and braids everyday it's hard to imagine that you're ever gonna meet anyone.—I don't suppose you can even relate, Mr. Free Throw wins the Junior Championship—So it was a good feeling to have a picture of a guy who was like mine, and even though I was different, so was he, and so we were, like a team.—Jeez, I feel totally stupid. I don't even know why I'm telling you this.—

(He gets up to leave.)

Where are you going? Where are you going?—No No I will tell him, I couldn't tell him last time, I'm gonna tell him next time.

(She snaps the picture up as he reaches over to tear it up.)

Hey!!! I think before I tear up his picture, I should tell him that I am not going to marry him, I think that would be courteous. Would you please come back!! Why is this such a big deal to you?— I'm gonna tell him. Come back, Please come back. Fine! Fine, Tom! Just leave! Just leave the way you always do! *(Pause)* WAAAAIT!!!!

What you don't understand Tom is that it doesn't make any difference, it's just the way it is. You can kick me outta the band, you can date a racist pig, Stacey can be a total bitch, my parents can cry, and I can even tear up this picture and it doesn't make any difference. *(Pause)* OK OK OK OK OK, *(She picks up the picture)* Fine...fine...fine.

(As music builds SAKINA attempts to tear up the picture, but it becomes obvious that she cannot. She holds the picture to her chest, and TOM walks away. she turns and undresses into AZGI again. As the music plays, AZGI picks up the strewn clothes and hangs them up, he then puts his shirt on again as the lights come up.)

AZGI: *(Noticing audience)* Oh Hello!!! Oh you know, Sakina's wedding was wonderful. So many people. She looked beautiful, she looked so beautiful, she looked like a gift. The Groom? He also looked very handsome. In fact, the two of them together, they looked perfect. A little uncomfortable, but perfect. The Groom, he is a medical student and he is also a very religious Muslim man. In fact, even at his own wedding he was studying for his final exam the next day and praying that he would not fail. Can you believe?? By watching him, I also start to pray...But the only thing I could think of to pray after watching him was, "Please God, don't let me spend my whole life just praying and studying, praying and studying, praying and studying..." Oh for their honeymoon, they are going to travel across America. Oh, it sounds very exciting. They will see everything, the Hollywood and the Redwood, they will ride on Wide Open Ventura Highways, and they will see The Grand Canyon, and the Mississippi. I told the groom, I said, "If I could, I would follow you. I envy the adventure you are going to have." And he looked at me, and said, "Azgi, if I could, I would follow you, I envy the adventure you are going to have."

(A sudden light change, AZGI suddenly doubles over in anguish.)

ALI: Shut up! Shut up!—I have to walk, I have to clear my head, and I have to come back. I have to walk, I have to clear my head, I have to come back, I have to walk, I have to clear my head, I have to come back. I have to WALK! I have to clear my head, I have to come—

(Suddenly he looks up as if someone has opened a door and he is staring into their face. He is visibly nervous, his mouth is dry and his hands are sweaty.)

I only have fifty dollars, I don't know if that's enough or not. Oh, that's fine, whatever you do for fifty dollars is fine. I don't know if I want the complete package anyway. It's probably safer that way, in regards to diseases and such. *(Realizing his faux pas)* I'm sorry, I'm not saying that you have any diseases. Oh no I ruined the mood. I'm sorry, it's just that I'm a Pre-Med student, so I'm always thinking about diseases. I don't do this kind of thing normally—NEVER!! Never before actually, I don't know if that matters to you, but it matters to me, and so I just thought I would share that with you.

(Pulling money out of his pocket and handing it to her)

Look, I'll just give you the money and you can put it over there on the dresser, or in your *(Noticing that she put it in her underwear)* There! This is very unlikely for me to be in a place like this—I've actually been trying to deepen my religious faith lately. I'm a Muslim, you know. Do you know what that is?... Yes, it's a type of cloth. What is your name?—Angel?—Really? *(He laughs.)* No, no, I'm sorry. I was just thinking that that's an ironic name for someone who does what you do for a living.—What? No, no, I'm sorry, I'm not a jerk. I'm sorry that was rude, Look I think you're very attractive. In fact, that's even the reason I followed you in here from the street...was because of the way you look...or at least who you look like. Well, you see, you look amazingly like this girl Karen who sits next to me in my Human Anatomy class, and who I cannot stop thinking about, and earlier this evening I was trying to study for my exam tomorrow, but I can't seem to concentrate because I can't stop thinking about Karen, and then when I think about Karen all the time, I think about my parents beating their chests when they realize I've failed all my exams. So I decided to take a walk and pray for some concentration, and that's when I saw you, and you—well, you look exactly like her, and you looked at me, and you smiled, and so when you started thinking to myself that you must be a sign...a sign from God!! That since I'll never be with Karen, I could be with you, and then I could go home and be able to study, and pass my exam and make my parents proud of me!!! *(He suddenly breaks down into tears.)* I'm sorry, I'm really sorry, I think I've made a terrible mistake. You see I just realized that God would never, never lead me to a place like this. I must be losing my mind. I have to study, I have to go! I need some sleep! I have to study, I'm really sorry. I have obviously wasted your time, I'm really sorry but I have to go. *(He leaves, there is a long pause then he returns.)* I think I should probably just get a refund. I don't know what your policy is as far as refunds go. I'm sure that it doesn't come up very often.—What?—Uh, thank you, that's very kind of you— Well I think you're very attractive yourself—No, I can't do that actually, No I can't, No I really can't—Well, because I'm engaged...or at least "betrothed" which is actually more like...engaged!— She's a very nice girl, Sakina!! Would you like to see a picture? I have one,—No of course not. What I'm trying to say is that she really is the perfect girl for me, comes from a very similar family, same religion, same tradition, same values, these things are important, you know. Besides, Karen is just a distraction. I mean, she's American. In the long run she would never accept Indian culture, she would never understand the importance of an Islamic way of life, she would probably want to have pre-marital sex which is something that as a Muslim I could never do. I know that probably sounds ridiculous under the circumstances, but it's true!!! It's not just a religion you know, it's a way of life and I have dedicated my entire spiritual life identity to the complete submission to the will of God. That's what Islam means. So you see, I can't just be running around having sex *(He thrust his pelvis forward unconsciously.)* like a rabbit *(He does it again, with more vigour.)* It would be a SIN!! And that is why I have to leave. What? What is my name?

(He pauses.)

AL!—Really!—OK, OK. It's not Al the way you are thinking of it, like short for Alan or Alvin or something. It's actually the short form of a very religious name, a name I can't even say right now, otherwise it would be a sin—I think. I probably don't even deserve this name.

(We begin to hear the song, "No Ordinary Love." This plays throughout the rest of the piece.)

What are you doing?—No I really don't think you should...REMOVE THAT!!!

(He hides behind his hands so as not to look at her but then he slowly looks.)

You want me to call you Karen?... OK!? Karen, Karen, Karen, Karen...

(She unbuttons his pants and begins to perform oral sex, the rest of the lines are delivered while he is receiving a blow job.)

Oh, my God, this is not me, this is not my life. Oh, shit!

(Looking down)

I'm sorry, I'm trying not to swear. It's hard, you know, to do the right thing, you know.—I'm always asking for forgiveness, because I believe that God understands and he is forgiving, and he knows how hard it is, to do the right thing all the time, even when you want to, more than anything else, and if you fail and you disappoint people, you can just try again, right? And you can have the intention to try again even while you're failing...failing! I don't suppose there is really any chance of me passing this exam tomorrow. I mean, If I'm going to be punished for this, and I'm sure I will be, that will probably be the punishment, because when you're trying to do the right thing and make people proud of you, Satan wants you to fail. And then you end up being a huge disappointment. Well, if I'm not going to be a doctor, I wonder what I will be?—Maybe I will be a bum!—And Sakina will say, "I can't marry him, he's a BUM!!!"

(He is getting quite worked up at this point as he gets closer to orgasm.)

And I will say, "GOOD!!!! BECAUSE THIS BUM WOULDN'T MARRY YOU WHEN HELL FREEZES OVER!" AND HER PARENTS WILL SAY, "HOW DARE YOU TALK TO OUR DAUGHTER LIKE THAT!!! AND I WILL SAY I JUST DID!! AND MY PARENTS WILL SAY, HOW DARE YOU TALK TO HER PARENTS LIKE THAT, YOU ARE A GREAT DISAP-POINTMENT," AND I WILL SAY, "MOM, DAD EAT

(He orgasms.)

SHIIIT!!!!!"

(He falls to his knees in shock, and slowly as if almost in slow motion he doubles over on the floor, unconsciously going into the Islamic position of prayer. After a few seconds, he regains his composure and attempts to stand and button up his pants.)

Thank you Angel, I mean Kar-... I mean Angel.

(He takes off his glasses.)

AZGI: Once upon a time a hunter wandered into a forest, armed only with a bow and arrow, in order to find food for his family. After some time he came upon a clearing, and in the middle of the clearing stood a goat. The hunter, excited by this, raised his bow and arrow in order to kill the goat, but just as he did, the hunter noticed that the goat was crying. The hunter, intrigued by this, asked the animal why it wept. And the goat answered "I weep because God spoke to me and he told me all the secrets of the Universe." The hunter asked the goat to share the secrets with him, and so the goat did, and after he was done the hunter realized...that now, he could never return home.

(Music and lights change, as AZGI slowly sits center stage and contemplates. Suddenly his meditation is broken by a sudden light change and computerized sound, he gets up and finds the sound is coming from and discovers SAMIR's Game Boy)

(Looking off)

Samir!! Samir!! Hey how come you leave your stuff lying around man, I got to clean up!!

(noticing audience)

OH, HELLO!

You know Samir he leaves his stuff just lying around you know, I have to clean up, *(Getting interested in the Game Boy.)* This is a very exciting little game though, apparently the idea is you see if you can just get your little man to the top of this mountain without getting hit by the falling rocks, then you get to go in the space ship and fly away...it's very good *(Playing)* Come on Jump! Jump! Come on you crazy man, come on, Jump! Jump!—

(Looking off.)

HELLO! Oh Samir, yeah there you are, I found your hat and your Game Boy because you leave your junk her in the restaurant and then I have to pick up your stuff—No, no, no, you can't have it, because I'm almost up to the space ship.

(Listening and playing at the same time.)

Sakina? Oh yeah, she sent a postcard? From her honeymoon? Oh yeah? Good for you, good for you.—To me!! To me!! She sent a postcard to me? Oh yeah let me see, let me see!! Come on it's my postcard man. OK, I give you the Game Boy, you give me the postcard, OK? I put it down, you put the postcard down, ready

(He puts the postcard on the table, SAMIR obviously doesn't and AZGI chases him around the restaurant)

Hey!! Hey!! You see how you are? Give me that postcard, come on Samir. Come on, give it to me! Hey!

(He chases SAMIR around the stage trying to get the postcard. At a certain point in the chase AZGI puts on the hat and becomes SAMIR, he squirms around trying to keep a hold of the postcard and then he throws it offstage and runs over to the Game Boy)

SAMIR: *(Playing with his Game Boy.)* It's on the floor—*(picking up the Game Boy)* Hey Cool! You're almost in outer space. You know what, you know what, you know what Azgi? My sister, she is gonna go all over the country for her honeymoon, and you know what, she said that she would send me a postcard from each place she went, but you know what the best part is, Azgi? You know what the best part is? When she goes to Disney World she is gonna send me an autographed picture of the Ninja Turtles...Cool right! Cus that's where they live!!! And we were supposed to go to Disney World last year, but we didn't go, cus my grandmother died and then we had to go to India, *(He pretends to puke)* that Sucked!!! And you know what? You know what? You know what? I got into this huge fight with my cousin Mustafa. Cus you know what, you know what, you know what,

(Light change.)

Dad!!! No I didn't punch him, I didn't punch him, I didn't punch him, no listen, I was showing Mustafa this really cool game, but he didn't wanna play, so then I said...let's play anyway! But he was being a spoil sport and messin up the game, and not playin right, so then I said, "FINE! I'm gonna play Ninja Turtles on my Game Boy," and when I was doing that he wanted to play too! All of sudden! But I said, "No way, Jose!" So then, so then, so then, Mom called me to come upstairs and look at some pictures of Dadi Ma when she was alive and she was really young and you were sitting in her lap and you were just a little baby—Dad Dad Dad, Do you remember that? Dad, do you remember when you were a baby? ....Do ya? *(Realizing he cannot change the subject so easily.)* SO THEN! I said that he could hold my Game Boy for just five minutes. JUST FIVE MINUTES! But then, when I came back he wouldn't give it so I had to give him a Ninja Kick in the head!!!

(He demonstrates a Ninja Kick to the head.)

That's all that happened, yeah but I didn't punch him, I didn't punch him, I didn't punch him, he said I punched him, I didn't punch him. So I don't have to share with a crybaby and a liar if I don't want to. But Dad it's my Game Boy, that I brought all the way from America remember? Remember, you said nobody could touch it, not even Sakina "cus it was the only thing that would keep me shut up," remember you said that? Huh?—So that just means he's a crybaby that's all. I don't have to share with a crybaby—No,—No,—But I'm not even sorry.

(His father slaps SAMIR on the behind. This is done by SAMIR turning himself with his right hand and slapping his own behind with his left hand. Every time that SAMIR is slapped in the remainder of this piece, it is done using this method.)

Hey!!! How come you're hitting me, he's the one who STOLE my Game Boy, how come no one is hitting him? What?—NA-AH—WHY?—Dad no!! That's totally not fair!—No, no, no, I don't want another stupid Game Boy. I just want the one I have. This was my birthday present from Jim's dad, you can't just give my birthday present to any stupid Indian kid that wants it just cus they don't have any cool toys here.—No, I don't want another one, why can't you buy HIM another one?—I'm sick of this. You know what, Mom already gave him my Ninja Turtle high tops, she already gave him those, yeah the ones with the lights in 'em that go "Kawabunga!" when you jump in 'em, she already gave him those. You're just gonna give him all my stuff.—I hate coming to India, I hate coming to this stupid country—No, no, no, he's not my brother, he's stupid! He smells!!—He can't even speak English! (*He is slapped again.*)

Didn't hurt (*Slap!*)

Didn't hurt more!!! (*Slap!!!*)

(*Crying*)

Alright! Alright! It hurt!! How come you always hit me when I tell the truth, huh? Yes you do, yes you do, yes you do, everyone in this country is stupid!! And they just want all my cool stuff, cus they don't have any cool stuff of their own, and they're just jealous, cus we get to live in America, and they're stuck here in ugly, smelly old India, and I never, ever, ever wanna come back here ever, and I don't ever wanna go anywhere with you and Mom ever again cus you're just liars! Liars! Liars! Liars!... And you abuse your children too!—Yes you do, yes you do!—You said we were gonna go to Disney World this year, and we were gonna see the Ninja Turtles like all my friends did.—Yeah, well, I don't care. I hate Dadi Ma too!!! I hate her for dying and ruining everything!

(*This time SAMIR is slapped on the face. After the slap SAMIR stands in shocked silence as he is about to burst into tears, in that moment he witnesses his father starting to cry. He has never seen this before and is therefore frightened and confused by what he sees.*)

Dad? Are you alright? Dad, I'm sorry! I'm sorry I said that about Dadi Ma.—Listen, you know what, Mustafa can have my Game Boy, alright?

(*He takes off the hat also, and hands it to his father.*)

He can have all my stuff. (*SAMIR reaches out with his hat and Game Boy but his father does not take them.*)

Dad! I'm sorry that your mom died. (*SAMIR begins to cry, slowly he backs upstage and he places both the Game Boy and the hat on the nearest table. He is again AZGI. The lights change and the area where FARRIDA had studios in a pool of light, AZGI enters it as himself.*)

AZGI: "This is not me, this was not supposed to be my life,"...she said (*Moving to the Hat and the Game Boy*) "I thought we were gonna go to Disney World!!!"...he said. (*Moving to where SAKINA had sat.*) It doesn't make any difference, it's just the way it is...she said. (*Moving to HAKIM's area*) Everything will be forgotten, everything will be gone...he said. (*Moving to where ALI had stood.*) "Well, maybe I should just get a refund," he said.

Everyone speaking my voice. Everyone except me, Ma. Where did I go? What happened to the top of the Empire State Building? What happened to the bottom of the Grand Canyon? How did all my adventures and romances end up on other people's postcards?

"I DON'T REMEMBER THE STORY OF THE RIVER STONE"... I SAID... Once upon a time, there was a boy, and this boy was standing by a stream, and by his foot he found a stone. He picked up the stone because he believed it was the most perfect stone he had ever seen. He immediately threw the tiny stone into the stream because in his young heart he believed that as soon as the stone entered the water and sparkled beneath the sunlight, it would become a diamond. As soon as the stone entered the stream, it began to flow with the current, faster and faster and faster and faster, the boy ran along side the stream watching his tiny stone, tossing and turning in the water, always moving, always dancing until...it disappeared and he could no longer see it. The boy panicked. He ran to the end of the stream, where he discovered that his tiny stone had been washed ashore amidst hundreds and thousands of rocks and stones and pebbles, all of which had taken the same journey down the same stream. The boy searched frantically for his perfect stone, picking up one stone after the next after the next, after the next but he could not find it. He searched day after day, week after week, month after month, year after year, until the boy became a man. And then one day he stopped searching, because he realized that the reason he could not find it was because he had never really known what it looked like.

(He pulls out the tiny pebble from the beginning of the play from his pocket. He looks at it and closes his fist around it, he turns and walks upstage as the music crescendos.Blackout.)

END OF PLAY

Swoony Planet

By Han Ong

In 1991, after working for two years at the Mark Taper Forum in Los Angeles (reading scripts, taking calls, arranging files), I was let go, a casualty of downsizing. But the artistic staff, who knew of my work as a playwright and who also knew that I had no other means of supporting myself, decided to offer me a commission for a play. Out of this, what I termed my "severance package," came SWOONY PLANET, which I handed to the theater in 1992. I was twenty-four when I directed a bare-bones workshop production at the Taper. Nothing came of that workshop, though there had been polite murmurs of interest from the Taper and from a scant few quarters. And so, SWOONY PLANET collected dust in my files until 1994 when I stuffed it into a box bound for New York City. I was going to try my luck not as a writer, but as a citizen, though aspirations toward writerly glamour did hover in my considerations of moving. Once in New York, though, the play's fate did not change. It continued to collect dust...until 1996 when I was approached by the Ma-Yi Theater Company and well-known set designer Loy Arcenas, who was looking to branch out as a director. I handed SWOONY PLANET over to them. At that time, I didn't think too much about it. SWOONY was simply an "old" play, one which hadn't been seen in New York, and I was glad that there were still some people interested in putting my work up.

A few months later, Loy Arcenas got together a group of his friends and acquaintances to read SWOONY in the basement of his upper west side building. He wanted, as did Ralph B. Pena and Jorge Ortoll of Ma-Yi, to "hear" the play. I came. I listened. And at the end of the evening, the feeling that kept slowly mounting as I heard the actors speak, became unstaunchable. There was no pushing it back any longer: I was shocked that I had written this thing. I felt... I felt awakened by the same sense of possibility that I suddenly remembered having suffused me as I sat down to write SWOONY. I was twenty-four then, more stupid-smart than I am now, more heedless of other people's opinions about what "worked" and what didn't, and, as to the prevailing canon of "classics", I almost always unsuccessfully restrained a chortle and a raspberry. That was the spirit in which SWOONY was written but the play had subsequently collected dust for so many years that I subconsciously and erroneously took that for a judgment of its merits, and so, during that night of being reacquainted (with my younger self, most of all), I was, well, nicely reminded that, heck, I was a writer. And I needed to be reminded because New York turned out to be a big bust. I had been suffering the dejection of seeing a good production of a play of mine (THE CHANG FRAGMENTS, directed by Marcus Stern, at The Public) stupidly received, and was living underneath a solo storm cloud of being a failed writer. And so, hearing again the ambitiousness that I once had, the show-offy language I was once capable of, I felt...alive. And it'd been a long time since I last felt that way.

I wish that there was some big spectacular movie ending to all this—that we opened and were a huge success, my bad luck forever reversing itself, etc.—but

all that happened was very simple and very quiet. A few months later, in the
spring of 1997, Ma-Yi put up the workshop. We ran for two weeks, not inviting
the critics, and playing to a small crowd. But Loy did a beautiful job and I was
nonetheless pleased. And among the wonderful actors were two who were old friends
from that other, L.A. life, and who had played in the workshop I had directed
long ago: Natsuko Ohama and Harvey Perr, reprising their roles as, respectively,
Kirtana and Kumar. The collegiality and mutual respect of the whole group was
another new, inspiring factor, and basking in it, I was able to finish the third
part of the trilogy of which SWOONY was the first: VIRGIN.

Oh, wait. Two months after the workshop closed, in June of 1997, I got a call
informing me that I was being awarded a MacArthur "Genius" Fellowship. Now I have
no way of knowing if the MacArthur panel had been alerted about SWOONY and had
seen it (since their proceedings are kind of hush-hush), but I would like to
believe that they did, and that it became a point in my favor. I would like to
think that they could see, as I couldn't until much, much later, the difference
between collecting dust and being dust. And so, maybe, there is a kind of movie
ending after all. And maybe, the trilogy might even be coming soon to a theater
near you...

HAN ONG

Swoony Planet (Play One of The Suitcase Trilogy)
by Han Ong

Produced by Ma-Yi Theatre Company
Ralph B. Peña - Artistic Director
Jorge Ortoll - Producer
Linhart Theatre, New York
April 1997

Designed and Directed by Loy Arcenas

Lighting Design: Blake Burba
Sound Design: Fabian Obispo
Production Stage Manager: C. Renee Alexander
Assistant Director: Andrew Sachs

Featuring:
Thomas Ikeda
Mia Katigbak
Forrest McClendon
Natsuko Ohama
Harvey Perr
Kaipo Schwab
David Teschendorf

Swoony Planet was originally commissioned and given an initial workshop by the Mark Taper Forum, Los Angeles, CA.

No set at all.

Any environ that parallels abandoned factories shelled-out churches.

This play is dedicated to Jessica Hagedorn

Swoony Planet
(Play One of The Suitcase Trilogy)

1. *Airport. Bench. Smoke all around. Clouds. A GUARD enters. (An actor who will later play LEONCIL-LO.) Addresses the smoke.*

GUARD: Excuse me

(Obscured by the smoke is KIRTANA, Indian (Asian) woman, mid 30s. She becomes visible in increments, as the smoke slowly dissipates.)

KIRTANA: Please go away

GUARD: There is no smoking here

KIRTANA: I'm not smoking

GUARD: What's all this then

KIRTANA: A woman preceded me to this spot
Why don't you go ask her

GUARD: Four hours ago
Someone was here four hours ago
Since then
You've remained stuck here Alone
For four hours

KIRTANA: I'm collecting myself

GUARD: For four hours?
What's left that still needs
collecting after four
hours? I'll help you
catch it

KIRTANA: This is a public place
It says public
An arrow points here saying, Public
Besides I don't see a crowd

Why should I be cleared out

GUARD: You're a security risk

KIRTANA: You're a cow
You beat your wife
Clear her out of the bathroom
each night after work don't you
so you can rush in there
can't wait to rush in there
to scrub clean the soil
that sticks to your skin
underneath that uniform

GUARD: This is my job

KIRTANA: HOW
You lousy cow
HOW am I a security risk

GUARD: I look at you—

KIRTANA: Your eyeballs wheel
everywhere for a wife substitute
I get the picture

GUARD: And you are a woman—

KIRTANA: Hooray
You are per CEPtive

GUARD: —who's alone
so that's strike one
in this type of environment
where interstate smuggling
is on the rise

KIRTANA: Go away
Please go away

GUARD: Am I breaking you down
Because—
          Good

Because the sooner you get out of here
the safer you'll
            we'll all be

KIRTANA: Please
Just a few more hours

GUARD: Where are you from?
India?

KIRTANA: *(A return to pissed)*
YOU should talk

GUARD: I was born here

KIRTANA: Well hip hip hooray
I'm from
Iowa, I came from Iowa if you wanna know

GUARD: And before that India right

KIRTANA: And before that I have no memory

GUARD: You're a traitor then is that what you are

KIRTANA: Immigrant
How could you possibly claim to have been
born here you don't even speak
the language

GUARD: Traitor that's what we call people like you
I speak English
For you, English says see under:Traitor

KIRTANA: Move off
If I'm a traitor what does that make your parents

GUARD: They were born here

KIRTANA: Well believe me
you are DESCENDED from Traitors

GUARD: If I were your husband—

KIRTANA: Well you're not
I'm a woman who's alone
but not defenseless
I have claws and teeth—

GUARD: You ARE from India
Well if I were your husband
I'd come pretty quick
to collect you
before the jungle reclaims your
manner

KIRTANA: Are you DEAF
I'm husbandless
I don't need one
And if this is your way of applying
for the post, well then
FUCK OFF BUDDY

(Lights dim on them. GUARD leaves. KIRTANA remains.)

2. *Simultaneous: From Stage Left enters MARTIN. White. 40s. From Stage Right enters ARTIE. Filipino-American. Early 20s. MARTIN in white undershirt and white boxers. ARTIE in yellow undershirt and yellow boxers. Each has in both hands a shirt and pants, white. They come in. Stand on opposite sides, facing forward flanking KIRTANA. Tight light on each. Each line they speak is punctuated by an arm being fitted into a sleeve, leg into pant, buttons being buttoned etc.—gestural like dance—movements to lay over this sequence of dialogue:*

MARTIN: When you were young

ARTIE: When I was younger

MARTIN: I used to look at you

ARTIE: You keep looking at me still

MARTIN: And I would open my mouth

ARTIE: You'd open your mouth
Martin I know all of this

MARTIN: Before you go just listen to me
My mouth would open

ARTIE: Into an O

MARTIN: It would curve up

ARTIE: Then down
A little cave
Your words like bats flying out
each one blind

MARTIN: Not the words
But their destination
Which was you

It would curve up
Then down
And I'd say looking right at you

ARTIE: What would you say Martin

MARTIN: I'd say Daddy

I'd peek at you through bars of a crib

ARTIE: I was never in any crib Martin

MARTIN: And I'd say, Call me Daddy
And one day

ARTIE: And one day

MARTIN: You did

ARTIE: All of a day

MARTIN: All of a <u>year</u>

ARTIE: And you said

MARTIN: An entire year hearing
your mouth curve up then down
your voice a junior
saying exactly what I said
saying Daddy

ARTIE: And you said

MARTIN: And I said
all full of joy

ARTIE & MARTIN: Now we're alike

(At this line, ARTIE & MARTIN have finished dressing and do indeed look alike. White pants, white long-sleeved shirt. Except MARTIN has a band of black around his waist, leather belt, which doesn't fit him anymore.)

MARTIN: Alike enough to be father and son

(Struggles with belt. Won't fit. Gives up.)

MARTIN: Jesus Christ

(Removes belt. Lifts it up in one hand towards ARTIE.)

ARTIE: I don't want it

MARTIN: The body fucks up
sneaks up on you
and then one day looking right in the mirror
from crib to middle age in just one glance
That's what a father is for
Take it

ARTIE: I don't want your belt

MARTIN: To tell about the tyranny of the body
That's what a father is for
To give a well-notched belt
each puncture letting a little air out
until

ARTIE: The belt's not my style Martin

MARTIN: Until you float up a little less each year
To make you earthbound
That's what a father is for

ARTIE: Martin
The belt may be the right belt
The story behind it may be the right story
          (Beat)
But you're not the right Father
Somebody else's but not mine
          (Beat)
I'm sorry

(Lights fade on MARTIN. Back up on KIRTANA at the Airport Bench. ARTIE walks to KIRTANA.)

3.

ARTIE: Taken?

KIRTANA: You wanna sit?

ARTIE: I'd like that yes

KIRTANA: Sit

(ARTIE sits.)

KIRTANA: This is Illinois

ARTIE: Are you talking to me

KIRTANA: Do you live here

ARTIE: Not for long

KIRTANA: It's not a big place is it

ARTIE: Big enough to have an airport

KIRTANA: But not too big

ARTIE: Actually quite sleepy

KIRTANA: Restful

ARTIE: *(Beat)* Sleepy

KIRTANA: I've been too awake
So this sounds completely
to me
Some sleep
is more than I've had in the last three days
The plane took three days

ARTIE: Really? Where did you get on

KIRTANA: They keep telling me three hours
but I'll swear to you

it's been three days with no sleep
Iowa We started surrounded by corn fields all yellow and green and by the time the plane tipped this
way all we could see looking down was miles and miles of black

ARTIE: What was black

KIRTANA: Razed grass I think
and structures going up
and it seemed to bode great speed
something far ahead I can't catch up with
like my son
(Sees GUARD approach)
Listen
There's a man coming this way
who's been hitting on me all night
I wanna stay a bit longer
Don't let him clear me out OK
Pretend you're my son

ARTIE: What

KIRTANA: Call me Mom
Say you've come to meet me
and take me home
He won't bother you

GUARD: This is a final warning

KIRTANA: (To ARTIE) That's the man

GUARD: Who is this

KIRTANA: He's my son
(To ARTIE)
That's who's been assaulting me

GUARD: Wait a minute now
Nothing's happened that hasn't been only verbal

ARTIE: Leave my Mom alone

GUARD: This is your Mom?

ARTIE: Didn't you hear what I said

                            I said, Leave my Mom alone

GUARD: A woman alone in an airport is a recipe for trouble

KIRTANA: How
(To ARTIE)
I asked him to be specific and he couldn't say anything

GUARD: That's not true I told you, Interstate smuggling

KIRTANA: I'm not afraid of guns

GUARD: Easy enough to say

KIRTANA: I know what it's like to be in the middle with guns pointed
from both sides
I've been living that way for months

GUARD: It's never the same—

ARTIE: —you don't seem to understand
this is not an invitation to debate
Leave my Mom alone—

GUARD: —A real gun is something else
So's real blood
particularly when it spills onto the whiteness
of airport floors
Never more sobering and redder than then

ARTIE: I really don't see what good all this talk of blood's doing

GUARD: ' It's my job
to keep it off the floor

ARTIE: Well my Mom's blood isn't on the floor is it?

GUARD: Take her home

KIRTANA: He'll take me home
(To ARTIE)
Let's go home Farouk

GUARD: (To ARTIE)
That's your name?
What kind of crackpot name's that*

ARTIE: I'm calling the cops

GUARD: I am the cops

KIRTANA: (In response to *) It's a king's name

GUARD: (To KIRTANA) A son with a king's name and
Unafraid of guns:
Get down from the clouds where you live lady
(To ARTIE)
Take her home
Lock her up

KIRTANA: (To ARTIE)
Take me home Farouk
Don't ever let me go
(Whispers the following in ARTIE's ear)
Say it back to me
Come on
Say it and he'll leave us

ARTIE: (Not quite sure of all that's transpiring)
I'll take you home Mom
and lock you up

KIRTANA: And you'll never go

ARTIE: And I'll never go

KIRTANA: Give us a kiss

(He kisses her. Slowly)

GUARD: (To KIRTANA) I wish I had a mother like you

ARTIE: (To GUARD) You can fuck off now

GUARD: (To KIRTANA) That's not a mother's kiss You don't fool me
(Exits)

KIRTANA: Do you have a mother?

ARTIE: I have a mother yes

KIRTANA: She's lucky having a son like you

ARTIE: I'm better in the abstract

(*LIGHTS* dim as an airplane flying overhead is heard.)

4. *Lights return. Same place. Empty. Enter JESSICA. Filipina-American. Early 40s. Cigarette in hand.*

JESSICA: I'm looking for my son
                        (Looks around)
Anyone?
                        (No one)
The thing about hands is
Hands knead
and in the absence of a son (who's
the right kind of dough)
they grope elsewhere
Cigarettes for instance

(GUARD enters.)

GUARD: There's no smoking here
Are you coming or going

JESSICA: Neither

GUARD: Listen it's three AM
and you're not the first crazy lady
I've had to help so if
you've got no business—

JESSICA: I'm looking for my son

GUARD: This is an airport
not an orphanage
And there's no smoking here

JESSICA: He's flying out

GUARD: There you go
He's gone
Will you put out that cigarette

JESSICA: A hand needs a cigarette
I don't do it for the smoke

GUARD: I don't care ma'am

JESSICA: *(Throws cigarette on floor, grinds it with undue emphasis with her feet.)*

I'm sorry
I'm not myself

(Lights fade.)

5. *In the darkness, a song. Sung live by all performers, who are off-stage.*

SONG
Half the world
is packing a suitcase
The other half's
tossing in bed

The first half dies
with no proof or trace
no memory of dinner talk
any remnant of grace
no azure stroll
never a leisurely pace
instead a bolt a run
perpetual longing for Place

Half the world
is packed tight in Samsonite
The other half's
clobbered by sleep

This half lives
underwater not flying by air
that avenue of dreamtime
the long-uncut hair
of the past stretching yards
and years back to where
we once had an estate
                    once had a guard dog
                    once had a sun
                              constant in heat
This half may be rooted here
but all the while
it breathes
the air of
another year
another currency
another God
miles away

Half the world
is doing is making

is acting the act
The other half
is watching is waiting
and forever holds back

(Lights fade up. All characters (7) emerge into a line-up, an inverted triangle whose final point is ARTIE, closest to the audience. The song is sung once more, this time accompanied by the percussion of the singers stomping on the ground, or beating out a rhythm on their chests, or clapping. It should end with a series of claps, or stomps, or beats, speeding urgently then a sudden stop. Everyone deserts the stage, but ARTIE.)

6. *Lights fade tight on him to suggest nighttime.*

ARTIE: It's a motel room in Arizona
                                          That much I know
Some numbers splay across a wooden door
Fixing me to:
                 this room
                 this specific shoebox in the world
                 This is where I am
                 not lost at all
That much I know
                 (Beat)
That I am here
                 (Beat)
Here is Arizona
And I've come so far
                 so fast
                 (Beat)
And I'm still packing my suitcase
And tossing in bed
Packing my suitcase
And tossing in bed
Packing my suitcase
And tossing at sea: those twin feats one must learn
                           to master without a father's precedent
                           without benefit of example
                           in the great
                           American magic act
            (Beat)
Here goes
Watch this trick
Now you see me

(Lights out)

ARTIE'S Voice: Now you don't

7. *Lights. Agency. Two chairs, facing each other. On Right, KIRTANA. On Left, notebook in hand, pen too, JESSICA.*

KIRTANA: You do see

JESSICA: There are freeway systems in this country
is what I'm saying
And they complicate things beyond comprehension

KIRTANA: He ran away as teenagers do
Nobody beat him

JESSICA: No one's saying you did

KIRTANA: Fifteen

JESSICA: Nobody's going to blame you

KIRTANA: Seduced by the promise of neon and
a constant buffet of hamburgers.

JESSICA: It's foolish to think that
the finger will be pointed at
you here
There are other agencies
the church for example
in which blame is placed
            blame is always placed
on the parent
              the source of all wrongdoing
It's something we don't abide by
in this agency
We counsel

KIRTANA: And track right?

JESSICA: We <u>help</u> track
to the best of our abilities

KIRTANA: I've come very far
            come carried by good word of mouth
                          so many mouths talking about this
place you don't know

JESSICA: And they say what? Good things?

KIRTANA: A magic act, they say

JESSICA: The success
when it's come
has come against great odds

KIRTANA: But not—
                    Not insurmountable
People leave tracks
have fingerprints

JESSICA: People do leave tracks—

KIRTANA: Some larger than others yes
And a boy like Farouk
          like no other

JESSICA: But you take a look out any window in any city
and you'd be hard pressed
to second-guess destinations
I mean
I've been here years
                    half a lifetime
and I'm still not used to it
this ludicrous tic-tac-toe of cars
Wheels are like—

KIRTANA: Feet He's left footprints

JESSICA: A little yes
But he escaped—

KIRTANA: Not escaped. Left

JESSICA: OK Left
And wheels are the perfect conduit for that
Invented for just that purpose
And yes there are license plates to be written down
Sightings
But those things when they happen are the exception
And wheels

The thing about wheels is that
they're better than brooms
Footprints may have been laid down
But wheels sweep them so clean you'd hardly know
anyone had been there
They guarantee
Often they guarantee exits so speedy—

KIRTANA: You're not painting a good—

JESSICA: No not good
Practical
We don't operate on false hope

KIRTANA: *(Beat)*
But where else can I go
If you fail me who else

JESSICA: There are detective agencies—

KIRTANA: They cost

JESSICA: I know
But sometimes they're better equipped
for—
Complications come
in the form of
in many forms
some we're not equipped to handle

KIRTANA: Such as

JESSICA: In the instance of abductions

KIRTANA: He'll escape
I know he will

JESSICA: This has happened to him before?

KIRTANA: Back in India
His father's parents
vindictive
people

They took him away from me
And he came back
Ran halfway across the country
(And it's not—
                    there are hills and haters of children—
                                                            not
a simple matter of running track)
He came back to me
                    (Beat)
And now he's gone

JESSICA: *(Beat)*
We'll find him

KIRTANA: I know you will
It's our particular fate
Jar the symmetry
Fifteen
and
He'd look at television: Mom we jar the symmetry

JESSICA: You have a local address?

KIRTANA: I'm staying at a motel
The 6 of Hearts

JESSICA: Why don't you go back to Iowa
It could be—

KIRTANA: Weeks, months
Have you heard of the Bob and
Cowboys' Grill?

JESSICA: Yes

KIRTANA: I waitress there
You can put that down
on the form
When no one's looking I sneak some
Indian spices into
whatever's brewing
One day it was beef stew
And the manager

JESSICA: Bruce

KIRTANA: You know him?

JESSICA: The entire female population
has been warned to stay miles away
He hasn't—

KIRTANA: No, no
He's been very kind
Very kind and very stupid Thicklike

JESSICA: And nothing else

KIRTANA: He kept bragging about
the beef stew, calling it
Great American Food
saying how you will never go bankrupt
selling American people
American food (and sure
enough, that batch of beef
stew sold out quicker than
any other before it) but little did he know
those spices
scumming around the top
were mine
all mine
(Beat)
How about you
You're from somewhere else too

JESSICA: Manila
I grew up there
This agency is founded entirely by immigrants

KIRTANA: Manila is
the Philippines?

JESSICA: PI

KIRTANA: What's that

JESSICA: Philippine Islands

KIRTANA: is Marcos?

JESSICA: Was
Not that I keep up
I don't anymore

KIRTANA: You have no family back there

JESSICA: They're all dead

KIRTANA: I have relatives in India

JESSICA: Do they know about your son

KIRTANA: *(Shakes No)*
They're the same as dead
More my husband's family than mine actually

JESSICA: And you're not married now

KIRTANA: I never divorced him
just left
Escaped, to use your word
A suitcase in one hand, a knife in the other,
my boy on my back, we camelled our way
out of there
(Beat)
Are you married

JESSICA: Twelve years

KIRTANA: Is he Filipino too

JESSICA: *(Shakes No)*
American
I meant
I promised I'd stop doing this

KIRTANA: What

JESSICA: Substituting that word for white
My husband is white
It's something my mother did too

even after years of living here
Mom <u>you're</u> American now, I said
but she never quite took to it

KIRTANA: You shouldn't beat your head over
just a word

JESSICA: Yes but—

KIRTANA: There are more important things
(Beat)
Such as a son
(Beat)
Farouk

JESSICA: Is that his name

(KIRTANA nods.)

8. *MARTIN and JESSICA. Patio. Sounds of crickets. Night. Shadows of leaves play.*

JESSICA: He crept in

MARTIN: Crept in how
We invited him

JESSICA: Just snuck up on me

MARTIN: What piece of news was he gabbing on about
You shouldn't have screamed

JESSICA: Look at you Martin
Always the diplomat
He asked what had happened over the weekend

MARTIN: The robbery

JESSICA: The break-in, he kept screaming, tell me
And I said—

MARTIN: —furniture stolen—

JESSICA: —gave him an itemized listing

MARTIN: So why'd you scream

JESSICA: —no suspects, I said
and he kept saying, Any person you know who might
have access to the house, and then and there
I should have known to
stop the conversation dead
but instead I said Carol

MARTIN: That's why you screamed

JESSICA: I said, Carol our housekeeper
and then he asked if we'd put Carol
through some police check

MARTIN: He wouldn't say something like that
He's got this one-of-a-kind brain
that processes (it's what

we use him for)
numbers and diagrams
Where others see crisscrossing
lines of no conceivable use
he sees their application
how to translate them into freeways

JESSICA: The same thing had happened to his
family and they'd done a check-up
on their housekeeper and wouldn't you
know she'd been siphoning loot for
years, at which point that
wife of his
little bird in Chanel
yellow and white teeth
began to crack jokes

MARTIN: What jokes

JESSICA: How can they expect it'll go over well
with me these jokes—Do they think
I'm some sort of
us-not-them kinda gal expecting me to throw
my head back and laugh
The one thing
about you Americans—

MARTIN: We Americans: not that refrain again

JESSICA: you have beautiful teeth but you
reveal them in the aftermath of an ugly joke
Yes we invited him
but we certainly
gave no indication he
had podium rights

MARTIN: You go to work
and see these people
for whom you've developed—

JESSICA: I go to work. Yes.
I bring no one home
And if I did

Not one of them would
think, Carol

MARTIN: —and relative to that kind
of partisanship,
between needy and
sponsor
which is
this cult of
suffering you've built up

JESSICA: A family, Martin

MARTIN: —is nobody can compete
You think
because we're doing
well and belong to this
set—

JESSICA: The smart set

MARTIN: —we become automatically guilty—

JESSICA: Since when*

MARTIN: —as if we were
causing them
misfortune
(in response to *)
Since you mentioned it
two nights ago

JESSICA: You talk
because you're missing a son

MARTIN: He's a friend—

JESSICA: I don't want him back

MARTIN: —and he's a—

JESSICA: I said

MARTIN: And I'm telling you what
                        What do you expect me to tell you

JESSICA: I'd rather be robbed
than entertain people like that

MARTIN: I'd much rather do anything but be robbed again
How much more violated do you
want to get Their grubby
hands through our drawers
MY clothes
picking and choosing as if
I were dead
You want a family?
What do you have
One broken lock
And a son out the door.
And now you
don't want friends

JESSICA: The right kind of friends

MARTIN: What do you end up with?
An even emptier house

9. *Hill. BUGLE BOY, young black man. He sings a song, in dim spotlight. Behind him, a field of stars.*

SONG (<u>Outskirts of Town</u>)
Wind blows through
making tin cans rattle
Losers pass through
making each woman tattle
Why don't you
and I take shelter
away from the townsfolk
with their radio and rumor
run out to the tracks
gleaming their poorman's humor
Darling can you
and I try marriage
and be mindful of us only
as we weave and we wear the exile's gown
Sweetheart let's you
and I cast our luck
with hearts that are lonely
who bear and who grieve on the outskirts of town.

(Lights fades on him. He remains there. A silhouette against stars.)

10. *Tight lights on faces: ARTIE, Upstage Left. Standing. JESSICA, Downstage Right. Seated. A phone conversation. Phone receivers may or may not be used. They are both on one half of the stage, as the other half's being occupied by BUGLE BOY.*

JESSICA: You said you'd call earlier

ARTIE: I'm calling now

JESSICA: What's that music Where are you

ARTIE: Arizona

JESSICA: What kind of bar

ARTIE: Mom I'm a fag

JESSICA: Don't get snippy with me

ARTIE: Just stating a fact

JESSICA: You want a fact exchange
This is mine: He ran out on us

ARTIE: I'm still gonna see him

JESSICA: He ran out on you

ARTIE: I know you don't want me to

JESSICA: It's not that I don't

ARTIE: Where you work
You have
Access to information

JESSICA: Access?
This is a man who hasn't called
hasn't written for sixteen years!

(No response)

What's this going to accomplish?

(Lights up on BUGLE BOY. ARTIE is in both scenes.)

BUGLE BOY: *(Points up)*
What's that
Three points that end
No eight
Eight points that tip into
a blade

ARTIE: *(To Jessica)*
What's that star
composed of eight points
which come to a blade

JESSICA: I don't know

ARTIE: Aurora Borealis?

BUGLE BOY: That's not it

JESSICA: Head in the stars
That's where you are

ARTIE: Mom
I gotta go

JESSICA: He's beautiful in the distance

ARTIE: Who

JESSICA: Your Dad
(He doesn't even deserve the name
Martin's been talking about you)

BUGLE BOY: The bear
It's the bear

ARTIE: *(To BUGLE BOY)*
Ursa Major
(To JESSICA)
He's not my Dad

JESSICA: No your Dad shines so much

brighter because he vanished
before you could find him out
for the fraud that he is
That's what I've been
telling Martin:
Abandon him and then
he'll start thinking highly of you

BUGLE BOY: That doesn't sound right

ARTIE: I gotta go

JESSICA: Will you call me

ARTIE: When

JESSICA: As soon as you get to California

ARTIE: I can't promise anything

(Light fades on JESSICA.)

BUGLE BOY: Will you come with me

ARTIE: Where

BUGLE BOY: *(Points)*
See that rainbow down there
Carnival's in town
Only time anyone would
be caught dead here

ARTIE: What do I call you

BUGLE BOY: I told you

ARTIE: But it's—

BUGLE BOY: Bugle Boy

ARTIE: Strange name

BUGLE BOY: My father gave it to me

ARTIE: Thinking what

BUGLE BOY: Is there supposed to be a story behind everything

ARTIE: Fathers and sons

BUGLE BOY: What do you do

ARTIE: Mainly I listen

BUGLE BOY: You get paid to listen

ARTIE: Then I sift
Then I write down
What do you do

BUGLE BOY: Certainly not a writer
What do you write
                You write about your people

ARTIE: Who's that

BUGLE BOY: Privilege

ARTIE: I'm not

BUGLE BOY: You don't work

ARTIE: I'm not rich

BUGLE BOY: What kind of muscles does that give you Writing
Not calves

ARTIE: You're checking out the wrong part

BUGLE BOY: What should I be looking at

ARTIE: *(Lifts hands)* Veins

BUGLE BOY: I like a body to read in the dark
I like to run my hands through skin
and run into
a scar Scars And say This body is not
a stranger to work

                    or discomfort
What I don't like is smoothness
                    and ease
Because it's a world I don't
think I'll ever know
And besides those things
make you flabby
And that's one thing I
don't intend to be

ARTIE: I've earned veins in the right places
And <u>you</u>

BUGLE BOY: Veins in my name That's one

ARTIE: Tell me the story

BUGLE BOY: I didn't know till my Dad
screamed at me one night:
I called you Bugle Boy direct from
the Bible expecting you to be
                              some sort of angel
                              some herald
of Good News from now on but all your grown-up life
                                              ever since you were thirteen
all you kept trumpeting was a rap sheet

ARTIE: What kind of rap sheet

BUGLE BOY: Petty thievery

ARTIE: Cars?

BUGLE BOY: It's a country dependent on freeways
Cars don't sound petty to me do they to you

(Beat)   I've killed a couple of dogs in my time
Mailman's prerogative
(Beat)
So you wanna come with me

ARTIE: Where

BUGLE BOY: Carnival
A magician who gives late shows

ARTIE: And after that

BUGLE BOY: My place

ARTIE: Where's that

BUGLE BOY: On the outskirts of town

11. *Blue light isolates KIRTANA, standing center.*

KIRTANA: At the University of Bombay where I went
before giving up
thought to be by my husband's
side, a professor told me
You are where history is
going to be made
How absurd thinking yourself
important enough to stencil into books

But I think now
(It's all I do now is think)
Meera Kherjee, the star debater
of the University of Bombay, not
only smart but glamorous, so ripe
for history-making, is
today behind a fat
tyrant she married, a permanent
lock on her lips. From debate to
complicity: no limit to the
perverseness of God's game
plan. And me.
Here in America. History. My footprints so lonely.
So at night to console myself I say,
                                        But you're making history
                        I say,
                                repeating after the professor,
                                                        Despite ourselves
                                                        We are history

We lie in bed and toss
Our days are bad and our clothes a mess
still we're history
(Beat)
I say that at night and yet I know inside this heart
I would give up History in a minute in exchange for some
Company
my son back at my side

12. *Carnival: red, yellow, green lights. MAGICIAN (actor who'll later play KUMAR) enters. Stops Center. ARTIE and BUGLE BOY enter Upstage, crouch flanking facing MAGICIAN.*

MAGICIAN: *(Facing audience; takes off top hat)*
In this hat
ladies and gentlemen
my first trick
a rabbit out of my hat
(Beat)
Did I hear a snicker
For what is this
snicker ladies and gentlemen
(Cocks ear)
Lack of originality? Did I hear
someone say, LACK OF ORIGINALITY?
Well let me defend myself: Magic need
not be original The only demand
on Magic is that it be
MAGICAL
I used to be a bus conductor
would you have guessed
all day long I strode the same
narrow corridor which cuts
through the bus's middle yelling
                         All aboard
punching tickets and yelling
                    Come one come
                    All aboard the Homebound Express
                    (what a beautiful word,
                    homebound)
I varied
I tried to vary
              these little choruses everyday
Some days I'd shout
(Singsong)
                    Hey there ho there
                    we're all going home
                    after a hard day's work
                    Clap hands
(He claps.)
                    Clap hands
(He claps.)
Day in day out running after

ORIGINALITY that's what
I'd do
     And did you think I'd get some show of thanks for this? Nooooo
And now you ask me for
ORIGINALITY? After history
has proven to me its
uselessness has proven it
unappreciated? Puh-leeze

A rabbit out of a hat
That's what you're getting so
Shut Up or Get Out
        (Waves fingers; incantating)
Yabba dabba doo
Yabba dabba dee
A rabbit a rabbit
        (Reaches into top hat, pulls out a rose)
What the
        (Keeps pulling out rose after rose after rose; into top hat)
Where the fuck are you
        (Rose after rose after rose; to audience:)
OK
You asked for originality
You got it
No rabbit just flowers
Are you satisfied
ARE YOU SATISFIED!

DESPITE MYSELF I'M ORIGINAL!

(Lights fade on MAGICIAN, who exits, and rise on ARTIE. He rises, wobbles. BUGLE BOY goes to him.)

BUGLE BOY: Steady

ARTIE: The earth just tilted

BUGLE BOY: You felt the earth tilt

ARTIE: More people with luggage*
got off a plane and we
tilted some more
(At * MARTIN enters. With him is a small scale architectural model of a strip mall, which he rests on the floor in the exact spot where the MAGICIAN was earlier.)

BUGLE BOY: You're just swooning

ARTIE: *(Ironic)* Cause I'm in love with you?

BUGLE BOY: Cause you're in love with me
but you don't know it yet

(They exit.)

13. *JESSICA enters.*

MARTIN: You walk around believing you
have a target glued to
your forehead and
think people will
come and bash you in
Ghosts ringing our
doorbell at night now
he's not coming back
It's in his blood

JESSICA: I am not afraid of change

MARTIN: I've been watching you—

JESSICA: You keep watching me

MARTIN: How you rearrange the furniture
preparing for what is it

JESSICA: I've let him go

MARTIN: And this latest
it's <u>change</u> too—

JESSICA: Change flows two ways: forward and
back Which is this, you
haven't even bothered
asking yourself
I never thought
It'd get this complicated

MARTIN: Well it is

JESSICA: It doesn't have to be

MARTIN: Bullshit

JESSICA: The wrong friends, the right friends

MARTIN: What you do is civics, not economics

JESSICA: What I do feeds more
than what you do ever will

MARTIN: It's progress
Where do you stand
With the future or with the past

JESSICA: A wheat field into a mall?
We drive by there every day
A daily reminder

MARTIN: You want the geography to be
impervious to progress just so
we can have a scenic drive

JESSICA: Who are the financiers

MARTIN: What've you got against
the Japanese

JESSICA: I'm a professional sympathizer I have
more than enough sympathy to spare

MARTIN: But not for them

JESSICA: Money

MARTIN: The root of all evil

JESSICA: Doors open when they land
while for my people—

MARTIN: How proprietary

JESSICA: They would love to be thought of
as mine—

MARTIN: Do you teach them to be afraid
like you Your heart skipping
a beat everytime we drive
onto a freeway

JESSICA: —they live here

while the Japanese
leave and don't have to sustain I do

I'm the one who has to sustain

MARTIN: A mall
is not a nuclear plant

JESSICA: It attracts listless—

MARTIN: We give them jobs

JESSICA: —aimless youth

MARTIN: Because you're depressed you want
everything around you to spin in
the same circle No change
possible until you're good and ready

JESSICA: You'll end up with a ghost mall How can
we drive past some dead thing by
the side of the road every day   As if we needed
any more reminders

(They stand silent.)

14. *ARTIE and BUGLE BOY bring a bench in. Set it so that it covers the architectural miniature from view. Train station. JESSICA and MARTIN remain. ARTIE, with backpack, and BUGLE BOY, stand side by side, in front of the bench. Sound of a train. Theylook Left.*

BUGLE BOY & MARTIN: I guess that's it

ARTIE: Here it comes
You have my address*

JESSICA: I guess so

(JESSICA and MARTIN exit. Each on opposite sides.
*BUGLE BOY pats breast jacket pocket .In response to *).)*

ARTIE: Will you call

BUGLE BOY: You're not the kind who should be given
a head start   You'll bolt and then
you'll outrun me

(Beat)   I'll call

ARTIE: Do that

BUGLE BOY: On the road

ARTIE: Handing out telegrams in shorts
to show off calve muscles

BUGLE BOY: Hitchhike your way
to California using veins as bait

ARTIE: Can't get too far on that

BUGLE BOY: Why not

ARTIE: Veins aren't too popular around here

BUGLE BOY: Do I get a kiss

ARTIE: Sure

(BUGLE BOY looks, sees no one, kisses.)

ARTIE: You look then you kiss

BUGLE BOY: You take what you can

ARTIE: And then you run?

(The space between them widens. Mainly it's BUGLE BOY who moves, walking off Right. They wave and mouth the following lines, all drowned out by the boom and hiss of a train pulling in:)

ARTIE: Bye

BUGLE BOY: Take care

ARTIE: I'll see you

BUGLE BOY: Promises promises

IF THERE IS TO BE A BREAK, IT SHOULD OCCUR HERE.

15.

Restaurant. Spill, from off-stage, red-blue off-on neon. Table. Two benches ,similar to train station bench, flank it. KIRTANA: in waitress uniform. JESSICA seated.

JESSICA: Kirtana regarding Farouk

KIRTANA: This is strictly social

JESSICA: This is social

KIRTANA: Unless of course you've news for me

JESSICA: No I'm afraid that's what I was announcing

KIRTANA: As soon as you get news I'm sure you'll tell me

JESSICA: Of course

KIRTANA: But till then we'll be social
We can be social can't we

JESSICA: Of course

KIRTANA: I'll be back with the food and then
you should tell me all about
your life How exemplary it's been

JESSICA: Far from it

KIRTANA: No don't say that Of course exemplary If
not you then who

(She exits, to return with two plates. Sets before JESSICA and herself. Sits.)

JESSICA: This is your concoction

KIRTANA: Beef I pollute all the stews now
Bruce has no idea why he's doing so well
Just pockets the money and pats
me on my bottom

JESSICA: You should sue

KIRTANA: No

JESSICA: You <u>could</u>

KIRTANA: And then what

JESSICA: And if you don't, what

KIRTANA: More waiting
Case after case tied up in the courts like
a long ball of yarn unwinding
To knit what
                    what kind of fabric

JESSICA: Someone steps on your rights
you have recourse to that

KIRTANA: It's called unemployment

JESSICA: You certainly
don't believe
this is all you have to look
forward to

KIRTANA: What marketable skills do I
possess to begin with

JESSICA: Nothing that training can't remedy

KIRTANA: Night classes

JESSICA: *(Detecting something askew in KIRTANA's voice)*
Yes?

KIRTANA: I've tried them

JESSICA: And what's wrong with night classes

KIRTANA: *(Beat)*
Full of backward geeks consigned
there by pathological social
ineptitude and failure   Impossible to
miss the scent of failure in all

those rooms Don't think I haven't
forced myself to try Night
after night just sitting
hoping to extract some hope from all this

JESSICA: And there is

KIRTANA: This is not what I came for
In just a few nights watching
a roomful of elderly students each
pouched heavy with dismay you
begin to understand this country
It only has time for winners And
What winners need more than
anything else is a batch
of geeks to make them look
winners in comparison
a batch to clean up after
parties and victory
celebrations So the skills those schools
teach, the skills they would
profit from teaching
are service industry ones
of smiling and serving soup

JESSICA: But I don't understand
How is what you're afraid of different
from what you're doing right now

KIRTANA: I went to the University
of Bombay   I want you to know that

JESSICA: No one's taking that away from you

KIRTANA: I'm telling you now I come
from a family of proud women
each one bearing pride in a
different manner, but all
equally proud nonetheless
I have pride in my accomplishments
(Beat)
Eat your stew
(Beat)

I'm sorry

JESSICA: This is wonderful

KIRTANA: I wanted to thank you

JESSICA: For

KIRTANA: Introducing me to that group

JESSICA: Are they good people*

KIRTANA: (Simultaneous with *)
Who'd have thought in the
middle of Illinois these
Indians

JESSICA: I'm glad you liked them

KIRTANA: I walked through this door
the room all of a sudden
parting in equal rhythm*
to take me in all full
of smiles asking after me
The kind of confidence I can only
associate with having been
born here not boat-tipsy in any
way not like me who's constantly afraid

JESSICA: (Simultaneous with *)
I've heard so much about them
but just haven't had the time
to check up

KIRTANA: A group of
people so tip-top they
could've been issuing from
a TV set
Except

JESSICA: Except what

KIRTANA: Well not except really but

There's this guy

JESSICA: Really

KIRTANA: Oh don't smile like that I feel silly enough

JESSICA: An Indian guy

KIRTANA: He wears this ten-gallon hat
and walks into rooms as if preceded
there by a ticker-tape parade
An Indian John Wayne

JESSICA: And

KIRTANA: He's bullish

JESSICA: He's asked you out

KIRTANA: We've gone out

(KUMAR, unseen, enters.)

JESSICA: On a date   Was this a first date

KUMAR: Speak of the devil

KIRTANA: What are you doing here
Walking so stealthy I couldn't
even hear

KUMAR: I thought we had a date

KIRTANA: I don't think so

KUMAR: So you've forgotten

KIRTANA: Maybe it's <u>you</u> who's confused

KUMAR: This was to be our
(Looks at JESSICA) second date

KIRTANA: We weren't talking about you Kumar

KUMAR: I'm Kumar

JESSICA: Nice to meet you

KUMAR: *(Kisses JESSICA on the hand)*
Very nice to meet you
Kirtana speaks highly of you

KIRTANA: <u>Spoken</u> Just that one time
Don't make it
sound like routine

KUMAR: Not yet

KIRTANA: Tell Kumar we weren't talking about him Jessica

JESSICA: I'm afraid we really weren't

KUMAR: My ears were buzzing

KIRTANA: Ear infection   A sign of old age

KUMAR: *(To JESSICA)* She's wonderful isn't she
Always a line for everything

KIRTANA: I've had to

KUMAR: There she goes again

JESSICA: So what is it you do if you
don't mind my asking

KUMAR: I'm into several ventures—

KIRTANA: Speculation   That's
how you described it   Your lips
biting into that word as if
tasting fruit

KUMAR: —real estate being one of them

KIRTANA: It's the perfect word
to characterize his

approach to life—Speculation—Isn't
that right Kumar

KUMAR: My approach to life?

KIRTANA: How you pursue things
romantic and otherwise
mere speculation   You convince yourself
of something long enough you begin
to believe it

KUMAR: Such as

KIRTANA: *(To JESSICA)*
Thicklike
Kumar I don't think we planned
something for tonight

KUMAR: I'm sorry then my mistake
so Should I come back

KIRTANA: Call first

KUMAR: No you're not the kind who
should be given any warning
because you'll bolt and
then you'll outrun me

KIRTANA: Believe me if anyone's bolting
it's not me   If you have to know
I'm practically glued here

KUMAR: So what is it keeps you
glued Certainly not a husband

KIRTANA: *(Acknowledging JESSICA)*
Friends

KUMAR: I have those   The problem with
them is they can only carry so far

KIRTANA: Maybe you have the wrong kind

KUMAR: I know who to surround
myself with One gift of mine

JESSICA: Maybe you should introduce me to some
of your friends

KUMAR: But despite all humaneness they
never seem to know what
to do for lonely nights spent
by yourself in big houses
lightning licking the surfaces
of windows making you feel
like a seven year-old

KIRTANA: Sounds like an advertisement
for a mother to me
(To JESSICA)
Doesn't it

KUMAR: What's wrong with wanting a mother
Perfectly natural tendency

KIRTANA: My hands are full

KUMAR: I don't see any rattles trailing
behind you

KIRTANA: It's the other way around

KUMAR: I don't understand

KIRTANA: You're not meant to
Call next time Kumar

KUMAR: Allright I promise

KIRTANA: You always do but your
promises have a way of never working out

KUMAR: Not the ones that matter

JESSICA: (Beat)
Such as

KIRTANA: Jessica

JESSICA: No this is a friend of mine
I'd like to know what intentions
you have Because you seem to have
strong ones and I'd like
to know As a friend

KUMAR: Honorable ones

KIRTANA: Honorable

KUMAR: You sound skeptical

KIRTANA: I haven't heard that word
in such a long time

KUMAR: No It's not a popular word

JESSICA: An Old World word

KUMAR: That's where I'm from

KIRTANA: But not entirely
Something not quite Old
World about you Kumar what
is that

KUMAR: Is that the part you like

KIRTANA: I don't know

KUMAR: But it's the part you don't
mind Because I know you <u>do</u>
mind from the way you
speak, curling your
lips the way you do Not that
I understand why Because I'm fit
if not fitter than most

KIRTANA: It's the part that won't
let me write you off
completely

KUMAR: An amalgam, yes

KIRTANA: Is that what they call it
these days

KUMAR: *(To KIRTANA)*
Just like you're one
(Beat)
I should leave now but before I
do can I say one other thing
A defense of what you called
my speculative
life which is not true at all
I don't believe in poverty
not for myself it's true
but I don't
I'm not hazy and unforthright either
which is what I understand
speculative to mean
Like I said
I know who to surround myself with—

KIRTANA: Kumar I'm sure Jessica isn't
interested in all this

JESSICA: No I am

KUMAR: Are you sure

JESSICA: Go on Please

KUMAR: You're quite sure?

JESSICA: I don't understand why
you should be so surprised

KUMAR: A history of indifference
from women which as I remarked
is beyond my understanding

JESSICA: You were married before

KUMAR: No never

A lifelong bachelor

KIRTANA: And you want me as a habit-breaker

KUMAR: *(Beat)*
Not when you put it like that no

KIRTANA: And how should I put it Kumar

KUMAR: I don't know Nicely maybe

JESSICA: Go on You were saying something

KUMAR: As an example of my—

KIRTANA: Unspeculativeness

KUMAR: —honorable
(Beat)
habits
What I've been doing
lately I've been trying to convince
these Vietnamese fisherman in
Texas whom the natives
are accusing of encroaching on
their territory, and with
these people who have no conception
of the importance
    the immense need for public representation
(because it's the public who'll vote
on whether or not their fishing
rights are extended) it's
key with these people to
talk, to
illustrate
by improvising ballpoint maps or using
cartoon representations
how this country works
and how if they are ignorant of how
it works they cannot therefore
demand
through legitimate means
what it is that is their due It's a very

jealous age we're living in They have no idea
and must be told
have to be educated
and that's what I do One example
of what I do

JESSICA: That sounds wonderful

KUMAR: But it's an uphill struggle
With these people
you can't be who I am

KIRTANA: Which is what

KUMAR: A dark-skinned
man Can't knock on
their doors and expect ears
to listen attentively,
beg for your
presence You have to
keep coming back and each day
they make damn sure you know
your presence is some form of
encroachment
Who better to cast their
lot with I'm in the
same boat But
Skin always in the way
(Beat)
Thank you for hearing me out
(To JESSICA)
It was nice meeting you

JESSICA: Nice meeting you I
hope we'll see each other again

KUMAR: Kirtana
KIRTANA: Kumar

(He exits.)

JESSICA: Is he who we were talking about

KIRTANA: (nods)
He took me out

JESSICA: Was this a date

KIRTANA: Not a date really   Well
OK a date   He's buying a house

JESSICA: Here?

KIRTANA: This is where he wants to
settle   Originally he's
from Kentucky but
he's buying a house
he wants to buy a house in Illinois
So he took me prospecting

JESSICA: And

KIRTANA: You're smiling   You keep smiling

JESSICA: Isn't this good news

KIRTANA: You've seen him

JESSICA: It's not good news

KIRTANA: He took me out to this wheat field
His hands were dancing wildly the whole time
                    conjuring things from the air and
                    saying, Here I'm gonna build a recreation
                              room and
                         here the study and
                         here the bedroom
and he held my hand
I mean I've only know him a few days but
he was holding my hand

JESSICA: And you didn't want him to

KIRTANA: It's not that I don't
want him to   It's just
I didn't feel

JESSICA: Give it time

KIRTANA: It's not about time
He took me to this wheat field and his hands were dancing
                              and the wheat was dancing
                              (a whole field of wheat
                              you should've seen how
                              beautiful it was Just
                              swaying
                              back and forth and I would
                              love to live there don't get
                              me wrong) but

JESSICA: But

KIRTANA: Everything else was swaying and dancing but I wasn't
(Beat)
I have this notion Don't think
me silly but I have this notion

JESSICA: Can I just say something

KIRTANA: No Please
I'm telling you this because I
want you to say something

JESSICA: It seems to me
I don't claim to be an expert on this but
it seems to me
that there are benefits to be had by companionship alone
that people put a premium on romance and then in the process
deprive themselves of other more basic
maybe more important things

KIRTANA: You and your husband

JESSICA: (Beat)
No I was lucky
I don't
know what I'm saying You're
right You have to dance
KIRTANA: My notion Can I tell you my notion

JESSICA: Please

KIRTANA: (*Turns her face out to audience, where the windows are supposed to be*) Oh look it's fall
already

JESSICA: I love the fall

KIRTANA: (*Face back to JESSICA*)
My notion is
That it seems to me that one of the inherent promises of
this country
            is that from time to time
                        on a <u>semi</u> regular basis in exchange for all the crap you get
                        one gets to swoon and I'd like
                        to be able to do that
I haven't swooned in so long and
I'd like to again
(*Beat*)
I came to America because you seem to have the patent on
swooning Does that
sound stupid

JESSICA: (*Shakes No*)
Not at all

KIRTANA: And with Kumar I just don't swoon
(*Beat*)
I just don't swoon

(*KIRTANA and JESSICA exit after a beat, taking their plates with them.*)

16. *Home for the Aged. ATTENDANT (played by MARTIN, male nurse's uniform on) enters, and throws white tablecloth over table. As soon as the tablecloth is in place and smoothed perfectly on, ARTIE enters. Backpack on.*

ATTENDANT: Under no circumstances are you to
frighten
scare
drop any bombs
He's very excitable

ARTIE: I don't want to scare him

ATTENDANT: And his name's Leoncillo
That's what everyone calls him

ARTIE: He goes by his last name

ATTENDANT: His bingo name

ARTIE: What's he look like

ATTENDANT: You'll see
And under no circumstances are you to say
we helped you find him or anything else

ARTIE: What's he look like
So I won't drop my jaw

ATTENDANT: This is an old person's home
What do you think he looks like
Why'd you come

ARTIE: Excuse me

ATTENDANT: He's not a nice man

ARTIE: I don't know him

ATTENDANT: If he gets nasty
(Points)
press that button by that column

ARTIE: Why's he here

a home for Jews

ATTENDANT: Why should you be surprised

ARTIE: Like I said, I don't know him
(*Beat*)
If you hadn't seen your father in
years wouldn't you—

ATTENDANT: If only that were so
Instead I've had to labor
under that sonofabitch's shadow
Sixteen years
that little weasel has had
me to marshmallow around
Can you imagine that SIXTEEN
YEARS doing little errands
scooping up after him
Boy oh boy was I glad when
he finally croaked   Except where I
used to wake up with this
intense feeling of aliveness every
morning plugging me up in every
part—this wish for him to just
shrivel up into the ground—now I
wake up empty and I don't know
if that's such a good thing
(*Beat*)
Go back home
I'm sure you have a nice
family waiting for you

ARTIE: You're not my father are you
Bring him in

(*ATTENDANT exits. Pause. ARTIE sits. Rests backpack on bench. ATTENDANT wheels LEONCILLO in to table. ARTIE gets up.*)

LEONCILLO: Who is this boy

ATTENDANT: It's your son

LEONCILLO: (*To ARTIE*)

Who are you

ARTIE: I'm Artie

LEONCILLO: Who

ARTIE: Arturo

LEONCILLO: *(To ATTENDANT)*
Get me out of here motherfucker

ATTENDANT: He just wants to have a talk with you
Not that that's possible if history's
to judge

LEONCILLO: *(To ARTIE)*
I DIDN'T DO ANYTHING
YOU GOT THAT

ATTENDANT: Well in that case you'll have nothing to fear

LEONCILLO: *(To ATTENDANT)*
How much is he paying you

ATTENDANT: It's not the money
Just payback for years
of having to put up
with your crap

LEONCILLO: How much is he shelling out
I'll triple it

ARTIE: I just want to talk

LEONCILLO: Who are you Who is this boy

ARTIE: I'm your son

LEONCILLO: Which one
I have hundreds

ARTIE: Jessica's son
What do you mean you have hundreds

LEONCILLO: I was a handsome motherfucker
Of course I had hundreds
(*To ATTENDANT, who's starting to exit*)
Where are you going

ATTENDANT: I'll be within distance

LEONCILLO: Ear to keyhole

ATTENDANT: It's a slow news day

LEONCILLO: Come back

(*ATTENDANT gone*)

ARTIE: I brought you something

LEONCILLO: Listen   You <u>could</u> be my son—

ARTIE: I am

LEONCILLO: —but what could I give you Now
Look at me
I used to be handsome and now
look at me

ARTIE: I just want to talk

LEONCILLO: What'd you bring me

ARTIE: (*Reaches into backpack; takes out box, which he gives to LEONCILLO*)
Here

LEONCILLO: (*Puts it to ear, shaking it*)
What's in here Candy?

ARTIE: Some chocolates

LEONCILLO: CHOCOLATES?! Don't you know I have
a weak heart

ARTIE: (*Unfazed; reaches hand out*)
I'll take it back

LEONCILLO: NO
I love chocolates

ARTIE: I can take it back

LEONCILLO: I said, I love chocolates

ARTIE: I won't be responsible for your death

LEONCILLO: Might as well go with a smile on my lips

ARTIE: Do you want to know anything about me

LEONCILLO: Like what

ARTIE: Like who I am

LEONCILLO: You're my son

ARTIE: Would you like some ID   You don't have to take it on faith

LEONCILLO: You look like me when I was young
God I hate you
You're a handsome motherfucker too aren't you

ARTIE: (Hands LEONCILLO his ID)
That's me

LEONCILLO: What is this

ARTIE: My driver's license

LEONCILLO: You drive?
What is this? Illinois

ARTIE: That's where we live

LEONCILLO: You're Jessica's kid?

ARTIE: Did you love her

LEONCILLO: Illinois She stuck it out huh
God I hate the midwest

        I loathe the midwest
Rednecks
How's she doing
                she been lynched and tarred

ARTIE: No

LEONCILLO: How's she doing

ARTIE: She's happy
She converted   Left Catholicism Just like you

LEONCILLO: I meant financially
is she happy

ARTIE: Very
Why'd you convert

LEONCILLO: Judaism suits me

ARTIE: How

LEONCILLO: HOW?

ARTIE: I'm curious

LEONCILLO: In the midwest CURIOUS boys stare at you
and say, You're our first
Asian.

ARTIE: Why Judaism

LEONCILLO: *(Beat)*
They know what it's like to be under Foot
(Beat)
It's founded by people who've had firsthand experience
of an exodus and
don't resent the modern-day version
At least I don't think they do

(Pause.)

ARTIE: Did you love her

LEONCILLO: Did she love me

ARTIE: I don't know I'm not her   I can't answer
Did you

LEONCILLO: I've planted so many little
flags in so many different
places Didn't have time
for love

ARTIE: Is that what I am A little banner

LEONCILLO: Like I said, You look like me

ARTIE: I'm not flapping for you
Do you see me flapping for you

LEONCILLO: What's all this then if not
one big flap You're the
flag I'm the sun

ARTIE: Can I have my ID back

LEONCILLO: *(Takes one more look at it)*
I take it back You're not so handsome

ARTIE: I don't care

LEONCILLO: *(Hands ID back)*
You got a girlfriend

ARTIE: I'm married

LEONCILLO: Got any kids

ARTIE: Four

LEONCILLO: You're fuckin' with me

ARTIE: How would you know

LEONCILLO: They got any ID

ARTIE: I killed them all

LEONCILLO: You killed them

ARTIE: Better than abandonment

LEONCILLO: You don't even remember me How could you feel abandoned
Listen Arturo

ARTIE: Artie

LEONCILLO: Artie
Do you want to get to know me <u>Now</u> get to know me?

ARTIE: Don't be ridiculous

LEONCILLO: Did you want to help hold my hand through sunsets

ARTIE: No

LEONCILLO: Did you want to spoonfeed me liquefied food

ARTIE: I came to see you
I came to see California

LEONCILLO: I traveled
Mainly I wanted out of the midwest
Jessica wouldn't
My feet itched And hers were golf shoes
                                        spiked into the ground

ARTIE: What are you explaining

LEONCILLO: I traveled so much
Too much I now realize
but that's the price you pay
logged so many lonely nights in exchange for—
                                        in exchange for what? I don't
even remember
                So as not to let this country catch up
lonely nights equal in number to yours
or maybe more
                probably more because I was older

                                        when loneliness and
                                          foreignness feel more
acute
All I have to show
All I have to show
                is a trunkload of bus and
                            train chits and
                            plane tickets all
punched telling: This man has gotten away from hooks
fists
and nooses

I still have it
that trunkload of tickets
Hoping one day for someone to show up
so I could give it away
It's yours Just say the word

ARTIE: What would I do with it

LEONCILLO: Burn it Make a fire
                  or Build a church
the only two choices left in this country
Do you want it

ARTIE: No
(Beat)
What are you trying to explain

LEONCILLO: Why I left You were going to ask me why I left

ARTIE: No she told me

LEONCILLO: Exactly like that?

ARTIE: But without the tickets

LEONCILLO: But you still want to know some other things

ARTIE: I'm not good at this
So I've written
(Takes out notebook from backpack)
down some questions

LEONCILLO: What's that

ARTIE: It's just a notebook

LEONCILLO: Your notebook

ARTIE: Yes

LEONCILLO: She asked you to take notes

ARTIE: It's mine

LEONCILLO: Not hers?

ARTIE: She has nothing to do with me

LEONCILLO: What do I get
If I pass this test

ARTIE: It's not a test

LEONCILLO: Everything's a test

ARTIE: The real test you failed years ago
This is just some post-failure survey

LEONCILLO: I need some incentive
For twenty-five years California was one
Big Incentive Blue sky
                White light
                Invisible Life
What incentive you got to give me

ARTIE: Sorry

LEONCILLO: I need an incentive

ARTIE: If you don't answer these questions
I take the candy back

LEONCILLO: The candy's mine

ARTIE: No I gave it too early

thinking you'd cooperate

LEONCILLO: The candy stays with me

ARTIE: I'm younger
                        stronger
I'm not in a wheelchair
If I want that candy back how much money you willing to bet
I won't get it

LEONCILLO: Is that a threat

ARTIE: I could push you
The wheels would do the rest

LEONCILLO: That's an incentive

ARTIE: *(Looks at notebook)*
First question
Did you think of me

(Long pause)

ARTIE: Did you think of me

LEONCILLO: *(Beat)*
I like watching TV

ARTIE: What kind of answer's that

LEONCILLO: No I didn't think of you
                        I watched TV
                        Plenty of TV to watch No time for memory
Next question

ARTIE: Question number two
Did you think of me

LEONCILLO: That's the same question

ARTIE: No It's question number two
I've crossed out question number one and
I'm looking at question number two

LEONCILLO: What's the difference

ARTIE: The difference is that there's a number two in front of this one
Question number two Did you think of me

LEONCILLO: I have no regrets
Next question

ARTIE: Question number three
If my name weren't Artie what name would you give me

LEONCILLO: *(Beat)*
Junior
I've always wanted a Junior

(Pause)

LEONCILLO: Is that it

ARTIE: Question number four
Would you recommend I go back to the Philippines

LEONCILLO: Why

ARTIE: Don't answer a question with a question
Question four Should I return to the Philippines

LEONCILLO: There's nothing there for you

ARTIE: Have you been back recently

LEONCILLO: You see footage on the news don't you

ARTIE: It's Western eyes It could easily be pejorative

LEONCILLO: Trust me
If there's any good I can do
It's to let you know that there is nothing back there for
you or for me
A book closed when we left You got that?
A book closed You can return and go through the same words
as I have but the story won't change Not even for you It's
the same sad poverty story

ARTIE: Is that why we left?

LEONCILLO: You should thank me

ARTIE: You should answer me

LEONCILLO: If you'd known you would thank me
Why do you want to go back

ARTIE: Maybe this isn't my country
(Beat)
Why did we come here?

LEONCILLO: Word of mouth
(Beat)
People look at you funny?

ARTIE: No

LEONCILLO: They call you names?

ARTIE: (Irritated)
Like what
(No response)
Not that I've heard no

LEONCILLO: They don't give you things you feel you deserve

ARTIE: But I can't say that their reasons are—
I just don't feel—I can't put my finger on it

LEONCILLO: The midwest is like that
makes you fingerless
nothing to point with to say, This is my own piece of land

ARTIE: Is that why you left

LEONCILLO: I've answered that
How many more questions

ARTIE: (Looks at notebook)
Question number six

LEONCILLO: What happened to Question five

ARTIE: You answered it

LEONCILLO: You didn't ask

ARTIE: I didn't have to

LEONCILLO: You think you're so smart

ARTIE: Question number six
I'm six Pretend I'm six
You have an entire day to spend with me
Where would you take me

LEONCILLO: Where would I take you?

ARTIE: Where would you take me

LEONCILLO: Where you wanna g.

ARTIE: Your choice not mine

(Long pause)

LEONCILLO: You're six

ARTIE: And I've never been out in my life

LEONCILLO: Stuck in the midwest

ARTIE: Well maybe once or twice But that's it

LEONCILLO: Stuck and six

ARTIE: I'm still six yes

LEONCILLO: And being six you need a lesson
                                    some kind of lesson

ARTIE: But fun at the same time

LEONCILLO: I thought this was my choice

ARTIE: Sorry

LEONCILLO: *(Beat)*
I would take you to the zoo
I would take you to two cages side by side to learn a
fundamental lesson of this country: On one side a white dove
                              on the other a crow
You know what a crow is

ARTIE: I know what a crow is

LEONCILLO: On one side a dove
on the other a crow
               Both motiveless and acting
               as instinct decrees
And outside these two cages are people
called Americans
And for the dove they applaud
And for the crow they cringe

That's why I would take you to the zoo

ARTIE: I don't understand You're telling me this isn't my country
and yet you're also saying
                  Don't go back to the Philippines

LEONCILLO: I'm not telling you this isn't your country
I'm telling you:
          Know your cage

ARTIE: Know my cage

LEONCILLO: Know your cage

ARTIE: To do what

LEONCILLO: Know your cage well
Memorize its dimensions
         its distinguishing traits
so that when you go to bed
in the instant before you pitch into black
that's what you see the clearest and
you'll know

if you run or
if you kill or
if you—What do you do

(Pause)

LEONCILLO: What is it you do

ARTIE: I want to write

LEONCILLO: if you run or
                 if you kill or
                 if you write
If and When you remember your cage
you'll know why you run and
                 why you kill and
                 why you write.

ARTIE: *(Beat)*
Have you ever killed anyone

LEONCILLO: Out of a countryful of sons
how come it was you who
showed up

ARTIE: You don't have to answer

LEONCILLO: There's a young Indian boy
here
changing sheets
Doesn't say a word I told him what
I've just told you
Thought
Of anyone here he'd still
have skin thin enough to
soak things up
Asked him what his name was
and he said Billy
But here they baptize him
Billy Sengupt
Bill Wallah
Billy EM Forster the Kid
anything to get a rise

But he doesn't move
Just goes on folding and cleaning
One day I thought
(just a passing fancy) I'd
adopt him Give him my name
He looked so nameless
(Beat)
But now that you're here

ARTIE: I don't want anything of yours

LEONCILLO: *(Beat)*
Yes I've killed someone

ARTIE: I guess that's it

LEONCILLO: I get to keep my chocolate

ARTIE: *(Nods; rising)*
One more thing
It's a request: Can I take your picture
(Takes out instamatic from backpack; hoists backpack on)

LEONCILLO: You gotta stand far back
Not a close-up

ARTIE: That's fine
(Backs off)
This far?

LEONCILLO: Farther

ARTIE: *(Backs off some more)*
How's this

LEONCILLO: Some more I'm vain I'm a vain man
It's true I don't mind saying it

(ARTIE keeps backing off until he disappears.
LEONCILLO begins to tear at his box.)

LEONCILLO: Chocolate Give me my chocolate
(Tears open box:

brings out ROSE after ROSE after ROSE after ROSE:
SIXTEEN in all)
What the hell—
(Pricks himself)
Ouch
OUCH
SOMEONE
I'M BLEEDING

17. *Lights cross fade dim white to ATTENDANT, Standing upstage center.*

ATTENDANT: Listen Billy
fold the sheets
Look at my hands
and do accordingly
fold
the south end
Layer on top of the west
a pie crust
kneaded into place

Now Billy
don't be afraid
of blue skin
how
cold
like some midnight bloom
and the veins
        Don't be afraid of veins
        because they're
        finally at peace
        If anything you should be
        afraid when they're still
        boiling like kettles
And remember to always
close their eyes
because the eyes
are the repository for
hardships little
crime-scene witnesses who
cannot help but look
agitated no matter how peaceful
the life led always some crime
lurking behind there somewhere the eyes refuse to
give in to Death They always lodge
the final protest And when
the relatives come
as they do the day after
obituaries are telephoned
always tell them when they
ask How did he die,
always tell them, Peacefully

Because that word will
carry them through
(Just a simple word but
you can't imagine how
long it'll carry them through
their lives)

It's a good trade to learn Billy
Don't be ashamed
When I leave here
besides a handful
there'll be you

Do as I do Billy
It'll be just like
in the old days fathers
passing trades to sons

Look it's done
The south end over the west
and then tie the knot
It'll never pooch
never loosen
Always remember that

18. *White lightfades to blue.*

•BUGLE BOY: It's not often you meet
someone like you
who's young
and confused
and wanting to do something
anything
so I tell myself
What are you afraid of
Bugle Boy
Open up
Open
and meet your match
Love
Love doesn't have to make
you flabby
I'm going
I'm getting there
I have your address

19.

KIRTANA: Farouk?
Your body's so small Farouk
I hope you have clothes beyond
those holed jeans you prefer
or I hope you're
in a warmer climate
Surfing Farouk
Surf back home to me

20.

JESSICA: Artie?

(MARTIN appears.)

MARTIN: I'm here

JESSICA: I was—

MARTIN: I heard you call me

JESSICA: I was

MARTIN: Here I am

JESSICA: That's all I wanted to know

MARTIN: Everything's all right
Let me take care of you
Why don't you just let
me take care of you

JESSICA: Go to sleep

(MARTIN walks out of the light. The blue light holds for a beat on JESSICA, then it widens.)

21. *JESSICA goes and positions two chairs, as in Scene 7: Agency. She sits in one. BUGLE BOY enters and stands by the other.*

JESSICA: He looks more skeletal each year

BUGLE BOY: He takes pride in that

JESSICA: Looking thin?

BUGLE BOY: Looking poor

JESSICA: Look at his closet: Nothing if
not the opposite But he goes
around wearing holed
articles instead   That's what your
generation likes

BUGLE BOY: I don't know what that word means

JESSICA: They want to project
indifference but one arrived
at by very meticulous means Holes
in exactly the right places

BUGLE BOY: The holes I
have I've worked hard to get rid of

JESSICA: You should talk some sense into him

BUGLE BOY: That's not what I'm here for

JESSICA: You mentioned you were friends

BUGLE BOY: I'm sick and tired of having to educate
people Of constantly being
expected to do that

JESSICA: I'm sorry

BUGLE BOY: And no, not friends I thought
we'd be friends to begin with,
but I don't think it's possible

JESSICA: Was it something I said

BUGLE BOY: I saw your
house Not inside But out Looking
at how the entire thing cuts against
the sky

JESSICA: An empty house

BUGLE BOY: He said he wasn't from privilege But the way he
held himself told a different story

JESSICA: You see where I work
This is it
Does this look like privilege to you
(No response)
Does it

BUGLE BOY: Charity work to quiet guilt

JESSICA: This is who I am
Not the house

BUGLE BOY: Your neighbors wouldn't help me
They peeked out from windows and
I expected sirens to
screech their way to where I was

JESSICA: Until recently they did the same to me

BUGLE BOY: What do they have to protect looking at me like that?
Sign of privilege to me

JESSICA: Why do you keep coming back to that
What's it to you

BUGLE BOY: It's not for me

JESSICA: It's not for me either

BUGLE BOY: I'll believe it once I see it
Thanks for your time

JESSICA: What do I tell Artie

(*KIRTANA enters.*)

KIRTANA: You lied to me

JESSICA: Kirtana

KIRTANA: I took in what you said
just staring at that wallpaper
all day long thinking about your
news—

JESSICA: What news

KIRTANA: —before realizing, It's not true
What you were trying to relay—

JESSICA: What NEWS Kirtana

KIRTANA: —when you were trying to relay—
You said possibilities

JESSICA: Our leads?

KIRTANA: Stop using that word Nothing further from the truth
All dead-ends, I'm telling you

BUGLE BOY: I'm going

JESSICA: No no please stay

KIRTANA: (*To BUGLE BOY*)
Don't trust them
They claim omnipotence here
but they lie
    They leak and
                sputter all the while claiming to be Magic

BUGLE BOY: (*To JESSICA*)
Tell Artie—
(*Beat*)
I don't know

JESSICA: That you came?

BUGLE BOY: Good luck with his veins

JESSICA: What's that mean

KIRTANA: It's not him Jessica

JESSICA: (To BUGLE BOY)
What's that mean

BUGLE BOY: He'll know

(BUGLE BOY exits.)

JESSICA: Kirtana

KIRTANA: It's not my boy

JESSICA: We have received reports of sightings

KIRTANA: Another Indian boy

JESSICA: This one's clearly a runaway

KIRTANA: Another Indian runaway

JESSICA: (Impatient)
Suddenly they've become legion is that it
Early on you said rare

KIRTANA: But not singular

JESSICA: You want a photograph taken would that
constitute concrete proof to you

KIRTANA: Do you have a photograph

JESSICA: It could be arranged

KIRTANA: You'll be wasting your time

JESSICA: Why are you purposely striking down

a possibility

KIRTANA: This is the <u>only</u> possibility you
can offer?

JESSICA: Not the only one—

KIRTANA: What others

JESSICA: —but it's the only one that's
turned into something definite
A track

KIRTANA: Look elsewhere

JESSICA: On what recommendation Yours?
We have sightings, witnesses
What do you have

KIRTANA: A mother knows

JESSICA: Are you afraid of being
reunited is that it

KIRTANA: Don't waste your time on Seattle

JESSICA: It's a <u>substantial</u> lead

KIRTANA: *(Disbelief)*
Male prostitution?

JESSICA: It's a possibility
which doesn't mean Yes
          It means Could

KIRTANA: My son's not a homosexual

JESSICA: Kirtana listen to me
You're not hearing what I'm saying

KIRTANA: No you said
          you clearly said in the last meeting, Mixed up
with male prostitution

JESSICA: If I did that was an unfortunate
choice of words
All I said
All I <u>remember</u> saying was, He's been spotted
in an area in Seattle that's populated primarily
by runaways

KIRTANA: And you said, Male prostitutes

JESSICA: And in these areas—

KIRTANA: Male prostitutes

JESSICA: —male prostitutes and drug dealers
To keep alive yes

KIRTANA: And that's supposed to make
me feel better

JESSICA: We don't paint—

KIRTANA: Not paint no You
scratch away

JESSICA: You asked us to find him
and we <u>did</u> <u>Maybe</u>
Just a name   A spotting
somewhere by witnesses who'd
seen a tacked-up Wanted sheet
with his photograph

KIRTANA: The fact remains—

JESSICA: You asked us to find him not render
him like some story book   We track
the <u>physical</u> body

KIRTANA: The fact remains Farouk is neither
homosexual nor a drug addict

JESSICA: *(Impatient)*
How would you know

KIRTANA: Why are you talking like this

JESSICA: Why are <u>you</u>

KIRTANA: I see pictures at night

JESSICA: We all do Kirtana

KIRTANA: Pictures of him floating in some river

JESSICA: Don't be SILLY

KIRTANA: A mother knows these things

JESSICA: You're saying to me what
                              That you'd much rather see him
dead in some river than
alive

KIRTANA: Not if he's in Seattle doing
what you claim   Not that kind
of life he might as well be dead

JESSICA: That's absurd You're a
sensible woman Always
you've struck me as being
this sensible person

KIRTANA: I've never told you
my history

JESSICA: History of what

KIRTANA: Premonitions that have come
true one by one I don't
know whose joke it was to
gift me with this   But I
never asked for it
(Beat)
I'm telling you, My
boy's in some river

JESSICA: Who put him there

KIRTANA: Murderers everywhere

JESSICA: You sit alone watching
the patterns of the wallpaper
all night after work
refusing to socialize—

KIRTANA: With whom
Who do I know besides you
and how do I know you won't
start resenting me
like this dog constantly hanging around

JESSICA: Kumar

KIRTANA: That's not what he wants
To socialize

JESSICA: And pretty soon you can't
tell the pattern of the
wallpaper apart from your life
You see murderers burning into
focus along the corners of the room

KIRTANA: I have to marshal facts at night now

JESSICA: But isn't that what I'm giving you

KIRTANA: Giving me what

JESSICA: Facts

KIRTANA: Facts

JESSICA: The solace of facts

KIRTANA: But not yours Your set
of facts don't provide
solace at all

JESSICA: He can be brought back
Rehabilitated

KIRTANA: That's not what we came here for
(Sits)

JESSICA: Do you want some tea

(KIRTANA shakes No.)

JESSICA: Go back and take the day off Get some sleep

KIRTANA: I quit

JESSICA: What do you mean you quit How
Have you got money saved up

(KIRTANA shakes no.)

JESSICA: What are you going to do

KIRTANA: There's always Kumar

JESSICA: He'll loan you money?

KIRTANA: I'll live with him

JESSICA: Since when

KIRTANA: It got so I wouldn't even
leave the restaurant after work
Just spend the night on the floors

JESSICA: Does Kumar know you want to
live with him

KIRTANA: Believe me he'll be ecstatic

JESSICA: Oh I don't doubt that
But does he know why

KIRTANA: A clean start No son I have
no son Jessica He doesn't need
to know a thing No better qualification
for a new wife than to be without history
Besides he doesn't want

someone to talk
               tell their story
He wants someone to listen
to <u>his</u>, ears always
buzzing after what he has to say

JESSICA: Do you love Kumar

KIRTANA: You want to know what I've learned

JESSICA: What

KIRTANA: One can't do without diversions Not
here Not have emotions
so unalloyed like—

JESSICA: One makes do*

KIRTANA: —like me
(In response to *)
Have you

JESSICA: I've made do yes

KIRTANA: But not entirely You have
this house Beautiful and large

JESSICA: Somewhere along the line
I can't even account for
it I lucked out

KIRTANA: Some lottery that I can enter
as well?

JESSICA: You already have
(Beat)
Do you love Kumar

KIRTANA: Does that matter

JESSICA: I thought it did to you

(From KIRTANA's bag, she takes out a cow-noise-maker.)

KIRTANA: This makes me laugh
(Dips it; It moos)

JESSICA: Do you love Kumar

KIRTANA: It's this country's main
business isn't it

JESSICA: Toys?
(Stretches her hand out as a gesture of asking for the toy.)

KIRTANA: (Hands TOY to JESSICA)
The manufacture of diversions Always
something else besides the wound
But never a cure,
just its diversion

JESSICA: It's good to laugh
(Beat)
Do you love Kumar

KIRTANA: You keep asking that

JESSICA: Because what you said
about swooning
                why you've held out
stayed with me

KIRTANA: (A sudden burst of adrenaline;
escalating quickly into mania)
Believe me
I'm SWOONING all right
I will not change
Do you hear that
This country changes you but
NOT ME It changes you for
the worse but not ME
Not my son either
He's not turning homosexual
Only because it's a new country
If there's anyone who'll change it's
this country
This country and not me

If the food's not to your liking, you change it
                    COOK IT YOURSELF
Right Isn't that right
If the wallpaper's not to your liking, rip it out
'You have recourse to that': Aren't those
your words? If this country lies
to you
(Snatches toy from JESSICA and begins to stomp on it)
If this country lies to you, fuck it
Then fuck it
(beat;
more calmly now)
I will not be moved
I will not be moved
I will not be moved

(Lights fade on everything but the crushed moo-toy, at center.)

22. *Dim lights Up Stage Center: See Scene 23. Stage Right: KIRTANA, smoking a cigarette. Stage Left: LEONCILLO, sitting in a wheelchair. Lights remain on the moo toy as well. Beside KIRTANA, a phone. Throughout the scene, she plays unconsciously with her hair. Throughout the scene, LEONCILLO coughs.*

LEONCILLO'S VOICE: You want to know what

ARTIE'S VOICE:I remember the carpet

LEONCILLO'S VOICE: Carpet

ARTIE'S VOICE:Green
Like grass chewed off
by horses
I want to know what it
is you remembered about

LEONCILLO'S VOICE: The plane

ARTIE'S VOICE:When we landed
When we first
What you felt

LEONCILLO'S VOICE: And you're writing this down

ARTIE'S VOICE:In my notebook

LEONCILLO'S VOICE: I remember cows
seeing them through porthole

ARTIE'S VOICE:Window

LEONCILLO'S VOICE: I'd never seen cows
I was so excited
What can I say
We're allowed moments of
stupidity But I was so excited
This pulsing Black against white
Never seen these balloon things
Certainly not in the Philippines
Carabaos, they had
You know what that is

(Silence, during which we presume ARTIE shakes No)

LEONCILLO'S VOICE: A Filipino water buffalo
It appears on the flipside of the five
centavo piece in the currency

ARTIE'S VOICE:Of the Philippines

LEONCILLO'S VOICE: In the currency* of the Philippines

(*At this word, KIRTANA's phone starts to ring. She looks at it, impassive. Lets it ring once, twice, thrice, four times, five. It dies. All the while the voice-over continues.)

LEONCILLO'S VOICE: The five-cent piece

ARTIE'S VOICE:And it's called a what

LEONCILLO'S VOICE: *Carabao*

ARTIE'S VOICE:Could you spell that please

LEONCILLO'S VOICE: You want me to spell that

ARTIE'S VOICE:Could you please

LEONCILLO'S VOICE: You want me to SPELL that

ARTIE'S VOICE:*(More authoritative)* Yes I want you to spell it

LEONCILLO'S VOICE: You want me to spell *carabao*

ARTIE'S VOICE:Is there anything wrong

LEONCILLO'S VOICE: You don't know how to spell carabao

ARTIE'S VOICE:Would I ask you if I did

LEONCILLO'S VOICE: You want to hear it spelled

ARTIE'S VOICE:Forget it

LEONCILLO'S VOICE: Maybe you should go back

ARTIE'S VOICE:Just because I don't know how to spell carabao

LEONCILLO'S VOICE: It's C-A-R-A-B-A

(Before he can say O, an amplified moo-toy sound, or a real cow mooing is heard. As soon as it starts, the lights quickly die on KIRTANA and LEONCILLO. The moo-toy sound fades soon after.)

23. *The ATTENDANT, Upstage Center, visible in the dimness because of his white male nurse's uniform, and who has been there all throughout, silent, smoking, is now better seen.*

ATTENDANT: *(Sings)*
The first half dies
with no proof or trace
no memory of dinner talk
any remnant of grace
no azure stroll
never a leisurely pace
instead a bolt a run
perpetual longing for Place.
(Speaks)
Don't be afraid Billy
of blue skin
and veins
Everything must end

(He picks up a phone, dials. Rings. JESSICA revealed. She picks up.)

JESSICA: Hello

ATTENDANT: Hello?
May I speak to
Artie Leoncillo please

JESSICA: Who is this

ATTENDANT: Who am I speaking to

JESSICA: I'm his mother
Who is this

ATTENDANT: Oh

JESSICA: He's not here

ATTENDANT: Ma'am

JESSICA: Has something happened to him

ATTENDANT: No ma'am
I was calling

to let Mr Leoncillo know
His father

JESSICA: Yes

ATTENDANT: His father has

JESSICA: Oh my God

ATTENDANT: You have my condolences
Are you his wife mam

JESSICA: No
How
How did he

ATTENDANT: In his sleep mam

JESSICA: So it was

ATTENDANT: It was very peaceful

JESSICA: Thank you

ATTENDANT: He was at peace

JESSICA: Thank you

(*JESSICA remains. Light fades.*)

END OF PLAY

FLIPZOIDS

By Ralph B. Peña

The first draft had twelve characters. Boiling it down to three was a sometimes gleeful, most times excruciating, experiment I undertook with Loy Arcenas, who directed the play's premiere in New York. Later, we were joined by Mervyn Antonio from the Public Theater, who helped steer the play into its quasi-final version.

The character of Aying is a reasonable facsimile of my great grandmother, a woman who took public buses, drew a chalk line around her seat, and promptly stuck a safety pin into anyone who violated her space. Vangie is a patchwork of observances, mostly from having attended a number of Filipino gatherings in Irvine, California, where a rosary group met every Friday night to pay homage to the Virgin and where, in between a litany of Hail Mary's, the members extolled the merits of Jazzercise. Redford is my sister and brother, and a legion of second and third generation kids who questioned their hyphenated tags and who launched into heated arguments over what was more politically correct: Filipino or Pilipino. All these characters are refracted self-images. When I decided to write, I reached for what was then closest.

But I would not have written at all if not for Damien, who makes all things possible.

RALPH B. PEÑA

FLIPZOIDS was first produced in New York City by Ma-Yi Theatre Company. It had its first performance on October 4, 1996 at the Theatre For The New City with the following cast and crew:

AYING: Ching Valdes-Aran *
VANGIE: Mia Katigbak
REDFORD: Ken Leung

*Obie Award for Outstanding Performance

Written by Ralph B. Peña
Directed and Designed by Loy Arcenas

Original music and sound design: Fabian Obispo
Dramaturg: Mervyn P. Antonio
Lighting Design: Blake Burba
Stage Manager: Sue Jane Stoker

To the New Pilgrims who roughed the fickle seas in search of mooring and moss.

Characters:
AYING
VANGIE
REDFORD

Setting:
A beach in Southern California.

A rectangular sandbox dominates the stage. Half buried in the sand, down center, is a large earthen bowl of water. Stage Left, there is a half-sided toilet cubicle, the stained bowl clearly visible. The entire back wall of the playing area is white, on which the names of Filipino-American immigrants are written in black. The walls to the left and right are negative images of the back wall. That is, black walls with white letters.

FLIPZOIDS

Sound of crashing waves.

A beam of white light pierces the dark and illuminates the bowl of water, partially revealing the shadowy figure of AYING standing over it. She is dressed in fin de siecle clothing, and evokes a likeness to a daguerreotype. As she kneels down to touch the gleaming liquid, we hear the sound of a large metal bolt unfastening.

Lights up.

VANGIE and REDFORD enter on either side of AYING. VANGIE has on earphones, listening to a recorded lesson. She wears an immaculately white nurse's uniform.

VANGIE: Excercise One Fifty-Five. The letter D. Dainty. Dandelion. Dandruff. Decapitate. *(She takes out a clothes pin and clips it onto her nose.)* Today's road to the promised land is brought to you by the letter D. Debonair, Desecrate, Donut. Doo-be...doo-be...Do bee-doo.

(VANGIE crosses upstage.)

(Lights cross fade. REDFORD is in the toilet cubicle. He sports the casually hip garb of a Gen-X renegade, and has platinum bleached hair. He carries a shoe string that he ties into knots, before undoing each one and repeating the process.)

REDFORD: *(Peeking at the occupant to his left)*

Hello? Hello...? Nice shoes. I had a pair just like that. *(Pause)* Well, no, not really. Okay, the truth. I wouldn't be caught dead in them. No, no. no. But they look like great sensible shoes. I REALLY mean that. Hello? Hi. Are you reading? Yeah? I thought I heard paper rustling. Hello? Well, you must be busy, so I'll do the talking. You listen. If at any time you want me to stop...just...grunt... or something. What a co-wink-a-dink. I like to read myself. James Joyce is a particular favorite. I just, well...am so drawn to...drunken Irishmen. They're so...manly. Oh yes. I like to read, as you do. Especially the classics. They sweep me off to someplace more sanguine. I often think I was born in the wrong century. Don't you? I imagine myself, living...say...in 18th century England. Oh...all that lace. *(Pause)* Hello? Hello? Are you breathing?

I want to live in Budapest. Or Paris. Maybe join the Black Panthers. Someplace where I can blend in. Oh but Paris. Paris would be nice, huh? I want to change my name. What do you think of... Michel Signoret, or Daniel Piaf? I can be a tour guide at Pere Lachaise. "Let me show you to your favorite dead derelict." *J'suis. J'y reste.*

Hello? I feel very close to you. Do you feel close to me? It's always easier with this metal plate between us. Don't you think? Wouldn't it be great if we all walked around in our own little cubicles? There'd be so much reaching out. Everybody would be so desperate to connect. It might be a less cynical world. Hello? Oh no...don't go. Are you mad? I was just kidding. Don't go. Can I make a suggestion? We don't have to talk. We can just sit here...quietly...just sit here...and be. Hello? *(Pause)* We'll always have Paris. *(He peeks under the cubicle to his right.)* Hello?

(Sound of crashing wave. Lights change. Music. VANGIE crosses down stage. She is carrying a pocket dictionary.)

VANGIE: Domestic. Domicile. Dominatrix. D. Noun. A woman who physically and psychologically dominates. Dominatrix. Hmmm. You see that? I'm putting Webster to memory. So far, I know every word from A to G. That's something, right? Not every nurse can say that. *(Pause)* I can.

Now I'm taking Art classes. Imagine that. Me. The nurses at the hospital say, "Vangie Dacuycuy, art classes?" What do they know? Van Gogh. Van Eyck. Van-Gie. Ha! Today's art is brought to you by the letter V. Everything with a Van. Next week, I'm starting therapy.

Eulogy. Eunuch. Eupeptic. E. Noun. Cheerful. Optimistic. Eupeptic.

Where I come from, you see, there are many flies. Bigger than your thumb. From the boarding house I stayed in with four other student nurses, you had to walk along a narrow plank to get to the main road. If you fell to the right, you landed on a pile of maggots. If you fell to the left, you went through the roof of Mang Dencio's shack and landed next to him in bed. All the girls always chose the maggots. Now I know every word from A to G, so far. And from my Art Classes, I've learned that Rubenesque is the gentler, kinder, classier way to say: Fat. Oh, yes. That's something.

Faith. Fajita. Fallible. F. Adjective. Capable of making a mistake. Fallible. *(Pause)* Oh. (Pause) Erase, erase, erase.

(Sound of crashing wave. Lights cross fade to AYING. Once again, she claws at the sand, searching.)

AYING: Do you like crabs? *Ha?* Plenty here. Sometimes you see them. Then they go away. Hiding. When you see one you tell me. I will try to catch.

(She stares out at the ocean.)

Very very blue the water. You like the water, *ha?* Me, I like. You know why, *ha?* I will tell you. *(She dips one foot in the basin of water.)* It brings me closer to my home.

AYING: *(Pause)* Yes. You do not believe? I tell you. Over there, out there, that is where I come from. When I touch the water, ha, it is almost like touching my home. That is why I like to come here. *(Pause)* You, why do you like?
Trans: J'suis, J'y reste = Here I am, here I remain.

Ay, I will tell you a story. Short only. *Ha?* You like? About the *Milagrosa*. Very nice. Short only.

[Trans: *Milagrosa* = Miraculous]

(Lights change. VANGIE walks over to AYING.)

VANGIE: Stop it Aying. No one is interested in your stories.

AYING: They like. They like.

VANGIE: No they don't. It's not allowed. You scare people. It's illegal in California.

AYING: I do not tell them anything bad.

VANGIE: You don't tell them anything good, Aying. Your stories give people the impression that we're barbarians.

AYING: What is wrong with cutting hair?

VANGIE: Barbarian. Adjective. Without culture. Without refinement. Without Art Classes. Why do you insist on sticking out? Why can't you just blend in?

AYING: I do not know how to do like that.

VANGIE: Melt Aying. Melt. Become part of the Pot, part of the soup. That is what it's all about. Everything we worked for. All of that, so we can become part of the soup.

AYING: Evangelina? Do not be angry, *ha?* But you are becoming crazy already. I tell you something. You listen to me. Do not forget. Always remember. You are the first one in our family to wear a white uniform. Me, I only finished grade four. My grandfather, he sell dried fish. His son, your *Lolo*, he carry sacks of rice all day from the market to Don Mariano's warehouse. Your *Lola*, she wash the mayor's clothes. Me, I learned how to use a Singer Sewing Machine. *(Pause)* Now you wear a white uniform. Do not forget why you are better.

VANGIE: C. Compunction. Noun. Anxiety arising from guilt. Stop it Aying. The white uniform means nothing if you act like you come from a cave. White means nothing if you can't say, emphatically, "I have never eaten a pet." If you can't say that, if you haven't MELTED, Aying, the uniform means nothing.

AYING: You have to go to church some more.

VANGIE: Aying. You know why you're like that? Why you feel sad and alone? Dejected.

Despondent, and…and oh so very…very…BLUE! You know why? Because you won't get out of the grave. You insist on spending your days with the dead. And what? Are they Eupeptic? Euphoric? No. There you go. There you are. Look around you Aying. What do you see?

AYING: I see everything. All color blue.

VANGIE: That's because of your cataracts.

AYING: But I see everything. I smell everything.

VANGIE: And what do you smell? Hmm? Tell me. Do you remember when we used to receive packages from the States? The first time you opened the box, there was this…smell. It was nothing like anything we had back home. The only way to describe it is…better. That smell that came from a box from America was better. And every time I smelled it, it gave me goose bumps, and I wanted to hold it in forever. And I did, until I started turning blue. Now, we don't have to wait for any boxes Aying. Now, we smell like the boxes from America.

AYING: I tell you something. When I first arrived here. I smelled it also. Like leather shoes. Before you step outside. Like that. I made me feel peaceful, that smell. Then it changed.

AYING: After a few months it changed. Now it smells like bad pork. You know what that is like, *ha*? You will not like to have it near you.

VANGIE: Because you choose keep rotting memories.

AYING: You like me not to remember. But I am old already. That is all I have.

VANGIE: Then you'll always be looking in – an outsider. You want that? Every time you're at a department store, people will always ask you: "Do you work here?" We've come this far…

(AYING cuts her off in mid-sentence with a dismissing gesture. VANGIE exits.)

AYING: My daughter. She is changing. She is becoming *Amerikana*. Now I think she will go to hell.

[Trans: *Amerikana* = American]

(Lights change.)

AYING: You see that. Plenty of crabs. You never know where they will come from. *(She looks around.)* Ay, I tell you story now. Short only. *Empezar Ya*! You listen *ha*? There is a fisherman who ride his boat to the sea, very early in the morning. You know this story, ha? No. This one is different. I will tell you. You listen and you remember. Do not forget. He ride his boat to very deep water…

we call that *laot*. That is where you catch the biggest fish. He put his net in the blue water, and he wait… and he pray. When he pull the net back into the boat… nothing. Empty. Not even one *dilis*. You know *dilis*? You call it… I do not know what you call it. *Dilis*. Very small fish like that. Could not catch. Not even one.

Poor fisherman. Cannot catch even one *dilis*. *Kawawa*. He stayed there, in the *laot* for three days, never surrendering. After four days, when he could not even open his eyes because of the salt, he see her. Standing inside his small boat. He see her. Dressed in blue and with long gold *belo*. She talk to the fisherman. "You do what I tell you," this one said, and you will catch your *dilis*. "What do you like me to do?," the fisherman ask, and he kneel down because he knows this is not ordinary.

[Trans: *Empezar Ya* = It begins now ; *laot* = deep sea; *dilis* = anchovies ; *belo* = veil.]

AYING: "You take me to every shore, every year, on June sixteen, and wash your spirit with water. Begin again. *Empezar Ya*." She said. And she melt with the waves. The fisherman followed her order, and the fish come back. That is the story of he *Milagrosa*. Do not forget. *Empezar Ya*. It begins now.

(Lights change. REDFORD enters down stage right, carrying a can of spray paint. He begins to write graffiti on the walls.)

REFDORD: There is a small stretch of deserted beach along the Pacific Coast Highway, just north of Laguna called the Red Cove. Nobody goes there. It's too rocky, and the cliffs that overhang the beach block out most of the morning sun. So it's no surprise why it's my favorite spot, along with a handful of other social outcasts who find solace in the company of hermit crabs and the bundles of slimy kelp that litter the shore. From my high perch, which sits atop a sandy dune about a hundred or so yards from the water, I can observe most of the goings on. Why it's called the Red Cove is anybody's guess. There's nothing in the area remotely near the shade of red. *(He crosses to the cubicle area.)* There, just to the left, is a rest area, ostensibly built to provide the public with a place to change and a shower to wash off the sand. Nobody goes in there to change. Or to shower. And it's very definitely not a rest area. People around here call it the Barracks. Once initiated, you are called a cadet. You get the picture.

(REDFORD sits on the toilet.)

I go in here, not to have sex, but to connect. I am most at ease in these fetid fuck chambers. Sitting here, in one of the stalls, I can strip my soul naked to the occupant next door. I can let go. I don't know him. He doesn't know me. Neither has to prove anything to the other. Let's face it. Nobody goes in there with very high expectations. Nobody goes in there looking for a young Kennedy.

(Pause. He peeks at the occupant next door.)

What I'm trying to say is, there is an unwritten sign on the entrance to the Barracks that says:

CHECK YOUR SELF ESTEEM HERE. *(Pause)* I like that.

This is my prison. And my sanctuary. I find a comforting sense of safety in enclosed spaces.

It was early afternoon. I was sitting on my perch at the Cove, quietly running a myriad combination of names in my head. Something exotic. Ivan Sveltskaya. Olaf Pearlstein. Jeremiah Bernhardt. When, suddenly, I was interrupted by this figure walking into my visual periphery. Hold everything. Who is that?

(AYING is heard singing softly to herself, and performing some kind of ritual.)

AYING:

Empezar Ya. Empezar Ya.	[Trans: It begins now. It begins now.
Dampian ng munting awa	Give a little mercy
Ereng araw na banal.	on this Holy Day.
Hugasan ang kasalanan	Wash our sins
sa Inyong Kapangyarihan	with your Blessed Power,
Panibagong kasaysayan	and help us start
Tulungang Simulan.	a new history.
Empezar Ya. Empezar Ya.	It begins now. It begins now.]

REDFORD: She cut a stark figure on the beach like nothing I've seen before. She wore an ensemble that can only be described as... GOTHIC. Whoa! *(Pause)* I liked her immediately.

AYING:

Empezar Ya. Empezar Ya.	[Trans: It begins now. It begins now.
Ereng araw, simulan na.	Start on this very day.
Panibagong kasaysayan.	A new history.
Empezar Ya. Empezar Ya.	It begins now. It begins now.]

REDFORD: Suddenly I find myself smack in the middle of a Val Lewton film. *(Pause)* Look it up. I am drawn to her. An enigma. Like me. And though, as a general rule, I don't talk to people outside of cubicles, I sensed this one was different.

(He crosses to the edge of the sand box.)

You there. Yes. You in the period costume. Hi. Hello. I saw you from up there. Hi. What were you doing? Just then, when I saw you?

(AYING does not respond.)

REDFORD: See, from up there, it looked like some kind of ritual. It was very fascinating and seemed fraught with symbols. *(Pause)* It's uh... very... you know... very... earthy. *(Pause)* Delightful stuff...*(There is an awkward silence.)* Angel overhead. The Angel of silence... .it... flies...

(AYING looks at the sky.)

Figuratively, really. It's uh, very hard to actually see.

(AYING looks at REDFORD.)

Just an expression. Chekov I think. *(Pause)* I know, I can be really pretentious. I'll... just uh... walk back to... uh.. where I uh... nice meeting you.

(REDFORD extends his hand. AYING does not respond and continues touching the water.)

REDFORD: You keep doing that.

(REDFORD exits.)

AYING: Howdy.

(REDFORD returns immediately.)

REDFORD: Hi. Hello. What's that you're doing there?

AYING: I am touching my home.

REDFORD: Now, see? That is so charming. I never think to come up with things like that myself. *(Pause)* You were touching what again?

AYING: This water, here, this is the same water on the shore of Pagudpud. That is where I come from. When I feel the water... when I touch it... it is like I am also touching my home.

REDFORD: Right. And home is where?

AYING: Here. Give me your hand.

(REDFORD does not move.)

AYING: I will show you Pagudpud. That is where I come from.

REDFORD: Nah. No. I don't know...are you sure? Really? It seems so personal, and I've never really gotten in touch with my *chakra*.

AYING: Okee dokee.

REDFORD: If you insist. Fine. Okay. What do I do?

(AYING takes REDFORD'S hand and lowers it into the basin of water.)

AYING: *(Pause)* You close your eyes. Please. You close.

REDFORD: Someone told me once I was psychic. I am very sensitive. This is exciting, really.

AYING: You see with eyes closed. *(Pause)* Feel that? There is small town close to the water. Pagudpud. We call it that. Very early, in the morning, you see the smoke from the house of Ka Berting. He is making pan de sal... bread. In the streets, you hear the carabao pulling big carts of rice to the market. That is next to the bus station. Do you see? Where I live, there is a big acacia tree. The biggest in Pagudpud. Nong Peping, my grandfather, he plant it in front of the house.

(She has closed her eyes, and speaks as if in a trance. REDFORD has opened his and watches her, seduced.

(Music: Strains of a Kundiman. (A traditional Filipino love song))

All around, my mother, Nang Senciang, she put Sampaguita flowers. At night, you smell how sweet they are when you go to sleep. At the back of the house, there is a mango tree. Very low... the branches... very low you can pick the fruit even when you kneel down. We sit under the branches and eat mango until our stomachs hurt. We also have small river. Very small only. When it rains, the water comes out of the river and covers the ground. You can see the fish swimming all around the house. Can you see? It begins now. The rains have started. See?

REDFORD: Yes. *(Pause)* It takes your breath away.

AYING: Yes. Never forget. *(Pause)*   I have to go to the bathroom.

REDFORD: *(To the audience)* As depraved and morally bankrupt as I am, I cannot bring myself to point her to the Barracks. *(to AYING)* The closest one is on the main beach.

AYING: What is that? *(Pointing to the Barracks)*

REDFORD: That? It's nothing. It's a...a prison...for...a...very bad surfers. You don't want to go there.

AYING: Okee dokee.

REDFORD: *(To the audience)* I am reeling from this encounter. There is a rush of... of energy... of emotions... it's like... nothing I've ever encountered in the toilet. There is a connection here that I've never sensed with anyone's shoe before. I'm good about things like that. I am a well-honed sensor of connections. This. This is a good connection and, oh my god, the woman is pissing on the beach.

(AYING has lifted her skirt and is peeing on the beach, standing up. REDFORD turns his back and tries to provide some cover.)

I can't help but notice that you can do that standing up. Here. Kleenex?

(AYING takes the Kleenex and wipes her face.)

Not what most people would do either. But like I always say, the face comes first.

AYING: What is the time already?

REDFORD: I don't have a watch. My guess is around three. I'm Redford by the way.

AYING: Howdy. Have a nice day. *(She hands REDFORD the used Kleenex.)*

REDFORD: And you are?

AYING: Rosario.

REDFORD: Like rosary?

AYING: Oh. You go to church?

REDFORD: No.

AYING: You should go to church.

REDFORD: It's not my scene.

AYING: You will go to hell.

REDFORD: I'm there already. *(He starts sniffing)* What's that? You...uh.. *(sniff)* that's... uh... *(sniff)* you smell like.... uh...

AYING: *Naptalina*. Mothballs. That is what old people smell like. When you meet people who smell like that, you better respect them. They smell dead, but they know life.

Who are your parents? ·

REDFORD: Why do you ask?

AYING: Do they go to church?

REDFORD: No. No they don't.

AYING: You have a very brave family.

REDFORD: I'm an only child. After I was born, my parents channeled all their energies into turning me from a tropical banana into a perfect Macintosh. You know what that is?

AYING: No. But my daughter, she will know.

REDFORD: It's a kind of apple.

AYING: I do not like apple. In Pagudpud, we have *macopa*. Also like apple, but more cheaper.

[Trans: *Macopa* = a tropical fruit, indigenous to the Philippines, usually pink in color and fleshy like an apple.]

REDFORD: Anyway, my mother bought a copy of the Official Preppy Handbook. "This," she said, "this will be our blue print to happiness." It became the spiritual center of our family life, more revered than the Holy Bible.

AYING: You are Jehovah Witness?

REDFORD: No.

AYING: Okee dokee.

REDFORD: Where are you from?

AYING: Anaheim.

REDFORD: No. What country.

AYING: You know Japan?

REDFORD: Yes. *(Pause)* You can't be Japanese.

AYING: No, no, no. Near Japan. The Philippines.

REDFORD: I knew it.

AYING: You know someone who is from there also?

REDFORD: You may find this hard to believe but... well, me. We came here when I was seven.

AYING: You? So you are Pilipino also? *(Pause)* What happened?

REDFORD: *(To the audience)* She can be harsh can't she? *(To Aying)* Here, they call us Flips.

AYING: That is good?

REDFORD: I don't know. *(To the audience)* I've never really thought of it as a pejorative, at least, not in the same vein as say, Catholic.

AYING: You don't look Pilipino.

REDFORD: I've been told that.

AYING: Your parents? They look like you?

REDFORD: *(To the audience)* She says that with just enough contempt in her tone. Any more and I would have been insulted. As it is, I only feel embarrassed. *(To Aying)* Yes. We have similar features.

AYING: Then they do not look Pilipino also.

REDFORD: I'll be sure to let them know that. How long have you been here?

AYING: I came after breakfast.

REDFORD: In America I mean. Have you been in America long?

AYING: Oh yes. Very long, already. And you?

REDFORD: Very long too.

AYING: What is the time now?

REDFORD: I don't have a watch.

AYING: Did I ask you that already?

REDFORD: Once. You asked me once.

AYING: I'm becoming stupid, *ha*?

REDFORD: That's okay. I'm going to hell.

AYING: You like to leave? You can leave if you like.

REDFORD: No. I don't have any plans.

AYING: I like you to stay. Little bit. *Ha*?

REDFORD: Okay. *(Pause)* Do you miss it?

AYING: What?

REDFORD: Your home. Pagudpud?

AYING: No.

REDFORD: Why not?

AYING: I took it with me.

REDFORD: Is there...I mean...I feel really close to you Rosario...

AYING: *(She screams.)* You are a rapist?

REDFORD: *(to the audience)* This is a concern? *(to Aying)* No. Of course not. Do I look like a rapist?

AYING: Why are you asking me? I do not know.

REDFORD: Can I... you know... I want to reciprocate. Can I tell you anything about America? Our land? Our People? This Realm... Orange County?

AYING: *(Pause)* No. *(Pause)* You like it here? America?

REDFORD: Sometimes.

AYING: How come only sometimes?

REDFORD: Sometimes it gets tiring. You know that 3-D game where you stare at a bunch of dots and squiggles and hope something comes of it? Well, America is like that. Sometimes, you have to be a little cross-eyed to see the good stuff. And that gets tiring.

AYING: You have plenty to say.

REDFORD: Do you? Like it here, in America?

AYING: Sometimes also.

REDFORD: Rosario?

AYING: You call me Aying.

REDFORD: A...ying?

AYING: Aying. That is my name also.

REDFORD: Aying. What can I... you know... how do I... can you tell me... what I am? I mean, I know what I am, but how do I... say... get rid of this itch? Can you recommend a book? How do I reconcile myself to... And that's not to say I'm a worthless blob of nothing, because I do have a center of power. I am. *(Pause)* But should I be? Should I even care? Is there, what I'm trying to say is, can I find redemption in public places?

AYING: Okay, you leave now.

(REDFORD looks around uneasily, then exits. Lights change.)

AYING: Evangelina should meet that boy. She will not like to change so much.

(MUSIC: Strains of a Kundiman (Traditional Filipino Love Song))

AYING: I tell you this. Before I ride the airplane, I walk around our house three times. Very slowly, very slowly three times. I stop at the *acacia* tree and stand under her branches, very long time also, so I can count her leaves. I stop by the fence, and I listen to the neighbor's pig. I stop in the middle of my kitchen and I touch the black bottom of my favorite *kaldero*. I stand there, very long time also, and I smell my mother's cooking, I will take this, I say. I will take that. Stop here, for a while. Stop there, a little longer.

This is important. Because I know, someday, you will come to me and say, "I do not remember. I do not smell. I do not feel." And I will give you my heart. "There," I will say, "you look in there. *(Pause)* I keep it all for you." Someday maybe she will look.

[Trans: *kaldero* = cooking pot, usually made from cast iron]
(VANGIE enters. She walks around the perimeter of the sandbox. AYING steps out of the box to follow her.)

Ay, good you are here. I ask you something.

VANGIE: I have advanced. Now H. Homogenous. Homo Sapiens. Hooker. Hoopla. Ha! Today H.

AYING: Where will you bury me?

VANGIE: What kind of question is that?

AYING: I think, in Orange Country they do not let you throw your dead mother in the river.

VANGIE: Do we have to talk about this now?

AYING: You please send my body back to Pagudpud.

VANGIE: Not now. *(Pause)* Why do you want to go back?

AYING: There is nothing for me here. Anaheim is not for old people.

VANGIE: Aying... I'm tired of this. What is it you want to go back to? Ha? Tell me.

(AYING remains silent.)

VANGIE: Tell me. Don't do this again. I want to understand. What do you want that I haven't given you?

AYING: *(She walks back to her place in the sandbox.)* I go back and I work with my Singer Sewing machine. You do not have to send money. *(Pause)* If you like, you can send for Christmas and my birthday, but only if you like.

VANGIE: How do you think this makes me feel? *(Pause)* I don't know what to say anymore.

AYING: *(She takes out a worn letter from her pocket.)* Evangelina, when I receive your letter that you are bringing me here, I show it to all the neighbors. Look, I say, my daughter, she is taking me to America. I was very happy.

VANGIE: It didn't last long, did it?

AYING: *(Takes a long look at VANGIE)* I have different picture in my head.

VANGIE: Do you remember what I used to say. I was what? *Ha?* No more than what? I was no taller than this. And what did I use to say? Do you remember?

AYING: I remember.

VANGIE: I was nine. At night, every night, before we slept...

AYING: I remember.

VANGIE: I used to say... someday... Aying... I will give you better than this.

AYING: You wanted to live in a cement house.

VANGIE: With long, wide stairs and screened windows... and water that came out of a faucet.

AYING: It was the only way you would go to sleep.

VANGIE: I was forcing myself to dream about it. And I didn't just want it for myself. I wanted you there with me, in the big cement house, walking up and down the wide staircase, you and me Aying... all the way up... and then down again... up... and down... and we would never get tired because outside, the neighbors were watching us through the screened windows, their eyes bulging with envy. And they were saying, "Look. Look at them. They are blessed. They have TWO floors and windows that keep out the flies."

AYING: Now we live in Anaheim.

VANGIE: And, it's better. Aying, look at me. It's better.

AYING: Yes. *(Pause)* But I do not belong to your house. I should be outside, with the others and the flies. I think... I feel... in here *(She touches her chest.)*... that is where I am happy.

VANGIE: How do you know that when you've never tried, Aying? You've never made any attempt to appreciate our good fortune. You've never once made me feel like I've done good. Instead, every time I look at you, I'm reminded of my own failure. Why is that? Sometimes, in the morning when I'm brushing my teeth, I would stare at the bathroom mirror and scream, but with no sound so you wouldn't hear me. Is it my fault she's unhappy, have I given her what she wants... am I a bad daughter... sometimes... sometimes... I wish...

AYING: Me also. *(Pause)* Evangelina... you are my daughter... come here. You come.

(VANGIE walks towards Aying, hesitantly. AYING touches VANGIE'S face gently.)

AYING: You have very sad eyes.

VANGIE: What? Where? Me?

AYING: Here, you give me your hands.

VANGIE: Why?

AYING: I show you something.

(VANGIE doesn't move, suspicious.)

You give me. Let me see you hands.

VANGIE: What are you going to do?

AYING: I show you something. You will like.

(VANGIE offers both hands. AYING takes VANGIE'S hands and drapes them around her shoulder. She sings an old Filipino nursery tune.)

AYING: *Buwabo-buwabo*   {Trans: A traditional Ilokano nursery rhyme.
napanan ni inayo   Exact translation not available.
napan tin maki   Loosely translated: A young lad went
idjay adayo manu't pinag- ilo na   to a far off town to take a crap, and washed
sa nga burnay nga suka   his ass with a jug of vinegar.}

VANGIE: What does this have to do with my hands?

AYING: Here. You look.

VANGIE: What?

AYING: We have the same. Same fingers. You see. You have my hands from many years ago.

Strong hands. *(Pause)* Someday, they will be ugly and crooked like mine.

VANGIE: Why do you say these things?

AYING: Here you put your hands here.

(AYING puts VANGIE's hands around her neck.)

VANGIE: What are you doing?

AYING: Here. Now you press hard. Squeeze it.

(VANGIE recoils in horror. She looks at AYING with contempt and runs out.)

AYING: Evangelina. You come back. *(Pause)* Joke only. I thought she was going to laugh. *(Pause)* I tell you something. My daughter, she is good. You do not always see that. This place, it does not let her show that all the time. But I know she is good. In here. *(She touches her chest.)* I know… because she is mine.

(Lights change. REDFORD sits inside the toilet cubicle. He is playing with a rock from the beach.)

REDFORD: Hello? Hello…? Don't get up. I can see your shoes. That's enough. Nice leather. Studs too? Yesiree Bob. Can I call you Bob? Hello? Do this for me, will you? Bob? Close your eyes a minute and imagine a huge… big… oak tree. *(Pause)* You with me? Just to the right, a singing brook… with water like… I don't know… Evian… and… gold fish. Can you see, Bob? In the… spring… when it rains… the water spills all around the house and you can see the darn things swimming around. And… well… that's all I have to say about that.

Do you like apples? Bob? I can never eat the skin. Mama always peeled them for us, as far as I can remember. She peeled grapes too, and peaches. No fuzz for us. Mama peeled them all. Get to the good stuff, she would say. She even took the little seeds off strawberries with a tweezer. *(Pause)* Okay, I'm lying. She didn't do that. But she peeled everything else. Hello? No. No. Don't get up.

Just peel the skin, and reveal the truth. Now isn't that an aphorism to live by? You know it's the largest organ of the body, right up there with the liver. They say you can stretch

Your skin for miles. Is that right? That may be a little overstated. Enough to cover a room anyway. Or upholster a couch. It could happen. Just peel the skin, and reveal the truth. I had this classmate in prep school, Mark Towers, he had acne so bad he couldn't breathe out of his nostrils because they had swollen shut with zits. Everybody said he ate a lot of chocolates and jerked off too much. Fatal combination for a teenager. But Mark was the nicest, most unassuming person in school. Problem is, he looked like raw meat. Just peel the skin, and reveal the truth. This world might be better for it. *(He starts cutting into his skin of his palm with the sharp edge of the rock.)* Something is under there. Something more. We have to believe that. There, you see. *(He holds up his bleeding palm.)* No. No. Don't get up.

(We hear sound of door slamming, and the distant sound of sea gulls.)

Don't get up. This is what you've gotta you do. Expose your true self to the world. None of this superficial bull crud... that just gives them ammunition they'll use against you anyway... Strip. Strip. Strip it all away. This is going to scar. Ooops. Do I frighten you? Hmmm? I don't fit the mold do I? You know what else? This is beginning to hurt. Owwwww. Hello? Hello? Bob? I see you failed to recognize my clear cry for help there. Owwww. Hello? *(Pause)* This is so gauche, I could spit. Hello? *(Pause)* Don't let's ask for the moon.

(REDFORD crosses to the edge of the sandbox, and washes his wound in the bowl of water. Lights change. Sounds of waves and sea gulls. AYING is sitting inside the sandbox, smoking a cigar. She is studying an old photograph. AYING spots REDFORD tending to his hand.)

AYING: What did you do to your hand?

REDFORD: Nothing. *(He notices the picture.)* What's that?

AYING: This is my father.

REDFORD: Can I see?

AYING: *(Hands him the picture)* He used to call me my little *kampupot*. My little *kampupot*. Flower. Yes. I learned many things from him, many stories. You?

[Trans: *Kapupot* = a fragrant flower with dainty petals.]

REDFORD: What?

AYING: You father. He tells you stories also?

REDFORD: My family shares information on a "need-to-know" basis only. You don't know my father. He's... different. *(Pause)* I never once heard him talk about the past. It was always what he was going to be in the future... And there was never any residue, you know... I mean... he never left a trail behind. My father just kept moving forward. Behind him, there was nothing. He is what he is now, and nothing of him is what he was. Does that make any sense?

AYING: No. *(Pause)* I understand a little bit and maybe my daughter will be the same.

REDFORD: Sometimes I'd be standing on a street corner, or be reading a book, or taking a shower, and my skin would begin to itch. Like I'm going to explode. And you know what keeps repeating in my head? Over and over. "I want to go home." I want to go home. Over and over. I want to go home.

AYING: This is your home.

(Silence. AYING senses REDFORD's uncomfortable reaction.)

AYING: I tell you something. I do not know where my daughter will bury me. Okay if she throw me with the garbage on Wednesdays. But I do not think they do that here. Where I come from, if you die poor, they put you in a sack and throw you into the river. I do not mind dying anymore. It does not scare me. You know what I like? Maybe she can send me home to Pagudpud. My mother is buried there. Yes. I would like to be buried next to my mother. We will have plenty to talk about. Nang Senciang, I have been to Disneyland.

Where is that she will say. In Anaheim, Nang Senciang. She will not understand at first, but we have plenty of time. Nang Senciang, in Anaheim, they can cook food faster than you can say Hail Mary. *Dios Mio*, she will say. Yes. But they do not wash their *puwet* with water after going to the toilet. They only wipe it with paper. She will say, Rosario, where is this Anaheim where people cook food faster than they pray but do not wash their *puwet*? And I will say, a place they call Orange Country. *(Pause)* And we will laugh together for a very very long time.

Nang Senciang, I do not think they have too much time for the dead here. What if I do not see you again? I do not know if the soul can ride the airplane. Maybe we can write. *(Pause)* I am not so scared of dying anymore, Nang Senciang. Not anymore. But what will happen to Evangelina?

(AYING looks at REDFORD, as if waiting for an answer. He tries to form silent words with his mouth, but remains silent. There is a long moment of uneasiness, as REDFORD squirms under AYING's gaze. AYING takes out a sandwich from her pocket and offers half of it to REDFORD, who begins to relax. They eat, content with the unspoken, as they stare out into the ocean.)

(Music. Sounds of crashing waves and seagulls.)

AYING: I will die soon. You listen to my stories. They will live with you.

REDFORD: I don't take responsibility well. Besides, I wouldn't know what to do with them.

AYING: You will know.

REDFORD: They could end up on the walls of public toilets.

AYING: You like to help me?

REDFORD: Help you how?

AYING: You help me make my daughter happy.

REDFORD: I can barely keep myself sane.

AYING: You cut my heart and you take it to her.

REDFORD: Say what?

AYING: Take my heart to my daughter and you say, here, Evangelina... now you are free.

REDFORD: Whoa. That is really bizarre.

AYING: Joke only. What? You think I am crazy I will let you cut my heart? *(Pause)* You like to play game?

REDFORD: Like what?

AYING: You know *patintero*?

[Trans: *Patintero* – A game of 'tag' usually played in the streets, along lines drawn on the ground.]

REDFORD: I can't even pronounce the damn thing.

AYING: How about *pitik-bulag*?

[Trans: *Pitik-Bulag* – Literally, "tap the blind," a guessing game.]

REDFORD: What is that?

AYING: You cover your eyes, like this with your hand. I make like this with my hand, then I tap your hand like that, and you make you other hand the same like mine.

(REDFORD just stares at her.)

AYING: You did not understand?

REDFORD: I'm still working on it.

AYING: *Ay, gago.* It's very easy only. You cover your eyes, like this with your hand. I make like this with my hand, then I tap your hand like that, and you make your other hand the same like mine.

[Trans: *Gago* = Stupid]

REDFORD: You want me to guess what you've done to your hand with my eyes closed?

AYING: Yes. Very easy. You cover your eyes now. Go ahead. All the kids play this in Pagudpud.

REDFORD: *(He covers his eyes reluctantly.)* Didn't you have any Barbie dolls?

AYING: *(She forms a fist with one hand, and slaps Redford with the other, hard.)* Pitik-bulag!

REDFORD: Oww! What was that for?

AYING: You try to guess now.

REDFORD: My head is spinning, I could have a mild concussion, how the hell am I supposed to guess?

AYING: You should eat more vegetables. Never mind. We'll play another one. You know hide and seek?

REDFORD: I don't want any more games.

AYING: One more. This one, Evangelina used to play in the back of the church. You know this also?

REDFORD: Yes, yes... I know hide and go seek.

AYING: Good. You hide. I will seek.

REDFORD: You want ME to hide?

AYING: Yes. You go. I will find you.

REDFORD: YOU will find ME? Maybe YOU should hide and I'LL be the seeker.

AYING: No, no. You go. You hide. You.

REDFORD: Alright. If you insist.

AYING: I will stand here and cover my eyes. You hide.

REDFORD: Count to twenty.

AYING: *(She covers her eyes with her hand.) Isa, dalawa, tatlo, apat...*

REDFORD: What are you doing?

AYING: *lima*, six, seven, eight, nine, *sampu...*

REDFORD: Great. Just what I need. A fugitive from *Sesame Street*.

(REDFORD exits.)

AYING: *labing-isa, labing-dalawa, labing-tatlo... apat... lima... (Pause) nauuhaw ako.*

*(Lights change. AYING stands frozen. VANGIE enters with a small shopping bag.
Cheesy Mall Music. VANGIE'S neck is craned, staring at the ceiling.)*

VANGIE: That's what she said. I am thirsty. That's all. *(Pause)* At the mall. The new pavilion... where you can get cappuccino and croissant and watch your reflection on the glass ceiling... oh my goodness, halfway...halfway... not there, but in between... by the drinking fountain.. this is so... I don't know anymore... this is so... THERE... halfway between Eddie Bauer and Baccarat... by a drinking fountain.... in front... IN FRONT AYING... WHY IN FRONT? There were so many people. HUNDREDS AYING... WHY THERE? WHY NOW?

AYING: Why not?

VANGIE: We were just looking... browsing... maybe for a Cuisinart... BUT JUST LOOKING, AYING.

AYING: *Nauuhaw ako.*

[Trans: *Nauuhaw ako* = I am thirsty]

VANGIE: I'm thirsty, she said. Very innocent, like that. Very naive, just like that. And I, what do I know...? You like a glass of milk? How about a coke?

AYING: Tubig lang.

[Trans: *Tubig lang* = Water only.]

VANGIE: I pointed...THERE... conveniently located in between Bauer and Baccarat... in between a lumberjack and a chandelier, AHA! First World accessibility. THERE, AYING, RIGHT THERE.. A WATER FOUNTAIN.

(AYING enters a pool of light. Sound of rushing water.)

VANGIE: STOP. NOW. That's what I should have said. Looking back... that's what I should have said. Instead, I allowed it... I said: RIGHT THERE. GO AHEAD. DRINK. *(Pause)* Well? What? *(pause)* I should have said STOP. But I was distracted. I was absorbed by the pictures in ceiling... lost in the reflection of a perfect world below... the cappuccino and croissant world... and the mirror was saying to me... you're part of it.

AYING: The *Milgrosa*, she say to the fisherman, "You begin again." *(To Vangie)* What is today?

VANGIE: Tuesday Madness. Everything Half-Off. Hurry Aying. Drink already.

AYING: Tuesday what? What is the date today?

VANGIE: RIGHT THERE. RIGHT THEN... But I was distracted, looking at my reflection in the glass ceiling. There I was, standing in the middle of the very classy and the very fortunate... and I was thinking in my head... if you looked up quickly... like that... just a passing glance... like that... very quick... quicker... you could not tell me apart. You could not say... she does not belong... No you could not... I was distracted. *(To Aying)* What difference does it make? There's a sale at Sears. It's Tuesday. JUNE SIXTEENTH.

AYING: Yes. Tuesday. Wash your spirit. June sixteen. *Empezar Ya.*

(*AYING bends over to take a drink from the water fountain. Sound of rushing water. She straightens up slowly, and looks around. AYING begins her ritual dance, and singing. She speaks in almost inaudible tones.*)

AYING: *Empezar Ya. Empezar Ya.*
           Dampian ng munting awa
           Ereng araw na banal.
           Hugasan ang kasalanan
           sa Inyong Kapangyarihan
           Panibagong kasaysayan
           Tulungang simulan.
           Empezar Ya. Empezar Ya.

VANGIE: Oh my goodness. Look at that. HURRY UP, AYING. DRINK.
I Was distracted again. BY THAT. Look at her. Is that confidence? Ha? AYING, HURRY. I was distracted. THERE. See? Her. Her. That one. That dress. The walk. Miss Gucci, or Mrs. Ralph Lauren? Oh my goodness. How much is that?

AYING: Not even one *dilis.*

VANGIE: AYING. And then… and then…I noticed. THERE. Her reflection.

AYING: I see everything. All color blue.

VANGIE: Standing. THERE. By the stainless steel water fountain. I noticed but denied. Who is that? She doesn't belong in my mirror.

AYING: You begin again. That is what she said.

VANGIE: WHO IS THAT? I denied. Again. I should have said, STOP. STOP
NOW. And suddenly, this stranger, this intruder… all of a sudden…HER… the pictures in the ceiling…it was like a dream.

(*Suddenly AYING spits a stream of water at the imaginary shopper.*)

AYING: *Empazar Ya.* I wash your sins away.

VANGIE: From its mouth…the intruder's mouth…shot the venom. Like a stepped-on snake. It burst from the corner of its wrinkled lips…from the flared nostrils…from the small slit of its yellow eyes. I stood there. I could not move. All I could do was trace the stream as it flew across the air…past me…past the potted yellow tulips…and onto the very classy, very confident shoulder of Miss Gucci. STOP. STOP. STOP. STOP. My mother's saliva. Her venom. It was intended for me. She wanted to bite. Me.

AYING: I wash your sins away.

VANGIE: AY! AY! AYING! AYING! DO NOT NOT NOT DO THIS NOT NOT THIS
NOT HERE NOT NOW NOT NOT NOT HER. AYING!

(Lights change. Suddenly speaking with a heavy Tagalog accent, VANGIE drops to her knees.)

VANGIE: Ma'am...ma'am...I am sorry...ma'am. Miss Gucci. *Naku*...ma'am. I...please...ma'am...
you forgive ha? Please...you are so pretty ma'am...so fortunate...and blessed...let me touch your being,
may I? Me. *Pangit ako. Pangit.* I am ugly. Yes. Can I clean you ma'am? I am humble...humble...for-
give...ma'am...forgive. We are worthless...You like, I will clean your house? *Kasi...Kasi...Misis...* Where
I come from...*Doon...* There is so many flies...so many flies...*Kaya...* That is why...you must forgive
ma'am...ma'am?

AYING: Evangelina? What are you doing? There is nothing to forgive. It is June sixteen. Water
will wash her sins away. She has plenty. Begin again. *Empazar Ya.*

Help me remember, Evangelina. Come. We will remember together. *Empezar Ya. Empezar* Ya. The
fish will come back.

*(A waltz. AYING is seen doing a dance and throwing water around her. We also hear the distorted screams of
people running away.)*

AYING: Evangelina! It is like Pagudpud. *Ano?*

(VANGIE looks up at the ceiling.)

AYING: I wash you. And You. And you. And you also. You are clean now. The fish will come
back. Evangelina...it is like Pagudpud.

(Lights change. Sound of voices rising to an excited roar.)

VANGIE: STOP. STOP. STOP. Why here? Now, in front of them? Somebody stop HER. I cannot
anymore. Somebody...anybody...please...please. YOU. YOU. THAT ONE. Mamang Pulis. Mr.
Officer. YOU WITH THE GUN. STOP HER. MAKE HER STOP. SHOOT HER AND MAKE
HER STOP.

(Voices stop suddenly. Lights change.)

AYING: Evangelina...why? Why do you not see? Why do you not want to remember?

AYING: It's water only. June sixteen. *El Viaje de La Milagrosa.*

VANGIE: Take her away. *(Pause)* I do not know her.

(VANGIE exits. AYING stands isolated in the center. She is dazed from the previous encounter, unsure of where she is. She fixes her stare at the direction of VANGIE's exit. REDFORD enters and sneaks up to AYING.)

REDFORD: Boo. *(Lights change)* You're IT.

AYING: You again.

REDFORD: Couldn't find me?

AYING: No. *(Still focused on VANGIE direction)* You are very good. You win.

REDFORD: *(Pause)* You never even looked, did you?

AYING: Did you really want me to find you?

(REDFORD doesn't answer. He sits next to her.)

AYING: I ask you something.

REDFORD: Lay it on me.

AYING: No. I like to stand up.

REDFORD: I meant… never mind… ask me the question.

AYING: Why are we here?

REDFORD: "Why are you here?" *(To AYING)* What the heck kind of question is that?

AYING: Then you do not know also.

REDFORD: I love the way you can be so… concise. It's so… endearing… in a twisted sort of way.

AYING: I ask you something else.

REDFORD: Alright. But start with something simpler.

AYING: No. No. This one is not a question. This one, I ask for your help.

REDFORD: Oh. Okay. What do you want me to do?

AYING: You tell me how I will understand better. Ha? You teach me how to see like you, and Evangelina. Sige na. You teach. Please.

REDFORD: Look at me. I look like a teacher? *(Pause)* I thought you were going to start with something simple.

AYING: When I look at my daughter...my Evangelina...here *(She touches her chest.)*...it does not feel so good. I am like a big heavy stone in her shoes. She likes to walk very fast, my daughter...she likes to run after new things...but she has me inside her shoes...so she cannot. *(Pause)* I think, maybe...she should run very fast is she likes...she can fly if she likes.

REDFORD: I dream that, you know. Flying. Except I never get more that a few feet off the ground.

AYING: You have stones in your shoes also. *(Pause)* Teach me.

REDFORD: I'm not qualified. *(Pause)* Do you like enclosed spaces? *(To the audience)* What am I saying? *(He takes out his shoe string.)* Here.

AYING: What is that?

REDFORD: Take it. Go ahead.

(AYING takes the shoe string. She examines it. Unsure of what to do, she smells it.)

AYING: It does not help.

REDFORD: It helps me. When I'm all knotted inside… when I don't.. as you put it… understand… I use that. I tie it up in knots… you know… like this *(He demonstrates.)* Like that. See? That's what my insides feel like, in here. Then I untie the knots, one by one. It helps me relax. It's a visualization thing, and yes, a nod to triteness. *(Pause)* You can have it.

AYING: Ah…*(Still confused)* Very nice. Thank you.

REDFORD: Try it sometime. It can't do any harm.

AYING: Ah… Yes. Very nice. I keep it. *(She puts the shoe string around her neck.)* What is the time already?

REDFORD: By now, my guess it almost six.

AYING: It is very bright still.

REDFORD: Longer days.

AYING: In Pagudpud, you will hear the church bell ring at six o'clock. We call that *orasyon*. It is time to pray.

(Lights change. VANGIE enters.)

M. Maladroit. Adjective. Awkward. *(Pause)* Tactless.

She should be in a home, with people her own age, where… there's less pressure, I think… to be… I don't know… to be normal. It would be hard, yes in the beginning. Not just for her. But it will be for the best. I'm certain of that. As it is, the way things are… don't look at me like that. Not like that. I can see you think I'm a monster. I'm not. I'm melting. I'm following the rules of the game. *(Pause)* Last night, I dreamt, for the first time, in English. I could see the letters coming out of my mouth, coalescing into perfect words in the air, and everyone around me was saying, "Who is that? Who is that who speaks perfection?"

Don't look at me like that. She spit at Miss Gucci. What do you want me to do? You, what would you have done? Besides, nothing happened. The security man took her to the office, that's all. She was given a lesson, that's all. They asked her to sit in a corner for two hours to think about her sins. Is that so bad? Considering? We're lucky to get away with a only dry cleaning bill. Sometimes, we need to be reminded… that when in Rome, do not do as you would do in Pagudpud.

She can't go back. There's nothing to go back to. I know you probably think, listening to her stories, that where she comes from is a magical place, well it's not. She says to me all the time, "Evangelina, do not forget." *(Pause)* That's exactly what I've done.

(Lights change. VANGIE exits.)

REDFORD: I better go.

AYING: Where?

REDFORD: Away.

AYING: You do not like what I tell you?

REDFORD: It's not that.

AYING: You do not understand?

REDFORD: Not really. I want to.

AYING: I tell you some more.

REDFORD: You should go home. Your daughter will be worried.

AYING: No. No. Short only. One more story. This one you will like. *Sige na*. Short only.

REDFORD: Maybe next week.

AYING: You do not like anymore?

REDFORD: I like. I like. I told you. *(Pause)* It's just that I don't know what to do with your stories. I'm the wrong person....I can't... I don't know how to process these parables...your
allegories...whatever...into anything that will make a difference. They're wasted on me.

AYING: You said you like to know about Pagudpud.

REDFORD: I was curious...it all sounded so...exotic. But it's... a can of worms, you know? You... it
brings up more uncertainty than answers, and... it's my fault, really.

AYING: I do not understand.

REDFORD: I was convinced that I was deprived of all that. I was sure there was this entire mysterious world...that I felt...I thought...I was somehow tied to...like an umbilical connection. That I was
somehow entitled to say, I belong to this...I am part of this. But it's not. It's rings hollow in me.
(Pause) It's getting late. You should head home. *(He looks at his watch.)* Six o'clock.

*(REDFORD suddenly falls to his knees and takes AYING's hand. He touches the back of her palm to his fore-
head.)*

REDFORD: *(Stands)* I don't know why I did that.

AYING: I know. You want to know what it means?

REDFORD: No, I don't *(Pause)* Sorry. I better go.

(REDFORD starts to leave. He stops, and turns back to AYING.)

REDFORD: Teach me a Philippine word?

AYING: Tagalog?

REDFORD: Yeah, yeah. Will you? Teach me one?

AYING: What do you want to say?

REDFORD: I don't know.

AYING: You say that a lot.

REDFORD: I feel it a lot. It's a crutch.

AYING: What do you want to say?

REDFORD: I don't know. Something. Anything, simple. *(Pause)* How about "I love you."

AYING: *(She studies Redford a moment.)* Like this. *"Pangit ako."*

REDFORD: *Pangit ako.*

AYING: *Pa-ngit ako.*

REDFORD: *Pangit ako.* That's "I love you?"

AYING: Yes. *(To the audience)* It means I am ugly. *(Pause)* You are not pretending only? You really do not know how to say "I love you" in Tagalog?

REDFORD: *Pangit ako.*

AYING: *(She smiles, then touches his cheek.)* Me also.

REDFORD: *Pangit ako. (Pause) (He stands up.)*   It was nice meeting you.

AYING: Where are you going?

REDFORD: Around. Here. There. *(Pause)* I'll see you again.

AYING: Yes. Howdy.

REDFORD: Howdy. *(He runs away.)* Au revoir! *(He yells at Aying.)*   *Pangit ako*!

(AYING suddenly remembering, takes out a small camera from her pocket.)

AYING: Wait. *Sandali.* Wait...Red... Red... Redwood!

(She is not able to take his picture. AYING is on the beach, alone.)

AYING: I can see things, all blue. But maybe I should be blind. Where I come from, stories grow from trees. This is what I know.

I will tell you a story. Short only.

There is a very pretty girl who lives in a town far away. Esmeralda. Every boy in this town, they like Esmeralda to be their wife. But she was very choosy, this young Esmeralda. One boy, Santiago, he wanted her more than anything in the world. So one day, he went to her house and said, "What will make you love me, Esmeralda?" And the girl said to Santiago, "You bring me your mother's heart, and I will love you." So, Santiago ran back home and found his mother sleeping, very peaceful, on the floor. He took a very sharp *bolo* knife from the kitchen, and he kneeled down by his mother's sleeping body. He was about to cut her breast, but suddenly, she was awake. "Santiago," she said, very soft...not afraid. "What are you doing, my son?" Santiago said to his mother, "I want Esmeralda to marry me, I need to take your heart." That is what he said. Santiago's mother touched her son's head and said, "Take my heart, and be happy my son." And Santiago plunged the *bolo* knife into his mother's chest and cut out her heart. He wrapped it, still beating in banana leaves and ran back to Esmeralda's house. "Esmeralda, Esmeralda," he said, running, "I have what you want." Santiago opened the banana leaves and showed her his mother's beating heart. Esmeralda screamed. "What have you done?!" "But...but..." Santiago said, he did not understand. "You asked for my mother's heart," he said. "I was only kidding," said Esmeralda. "I cannot marry a man who would cut out his own mother's heart. You get away," she said. And Santiago, very sad, not understanding, walked away with his banana leaves and beating heart. He was crying and could not see very well. This made him trip on a rock. The banana leaves dropped from his hand, and his mother's beating heart rolled out, there, in the dirt. *Sayang.*

Then the heart, it started talking. "Santiago, my son," the heart said, "do not be sad. You took something that was always yours."   The heart said this. And then the lightning hit Santiago and turned him into a lizard. That is my story. That is all I know.

[Trans: *Sandali* = Wait ; *bolo* – a machete; *sayang* – wasted]

(We hear the discordant cacophony of voices, murmuring the words to some prayer.)

(AYING looks around her. Very deliberately, she begins to smooth out the sand around her—erasing every evidence of herself—building in urgency as she kicks up a cloud of dust. AYING walks to the edge of the bowl of water. She takes VANGIE's letter and gently drops it into the bowl, as if sending it away with the waves. She does the same with her father's photograph.)

(The cacophony of voices grow louder. Suddenly, AYING plunges her face into the basin of water.)

(The voices peak into a garish scream that lingers as the lights change to reveal VANGIE's silhouette against the back wall, standing next to a chair, and holding a tray with a glass of milk. She waits as AYING makes her

way up to her to sit on the chair.)

(REDFORD has entered and is seated on the edge of the sandbox, down left. AYING is on her chair, tying knots on a piece of string.)

VANGIE: I'm thinking of getting a dog. Not too big, you know. Maybe a small German Shepherd. Something like that...for peace of mind.

(VANGIE tries to give AYING her milk.)

Here's your milk. Aying?

(AYING doesn't respond, but continues tying knots.)

You don't like? *(Pause)* Ha? *(Pause)* Here. *(Pause)* So you can sleep.

(AYING remains silent. REDFORD enters, down Left.)

REDFORD: I have nightmares. I dream I'm some super hero.
I can fly. In this dream, I run. You gotta have to reach speed before lift off.
Back arched...disengage from terra firma...two feet, three feet, and climbing...
I'm a bird.
Then, a great weight pulls me down... Down. Down.
Here comes the crash.
But no impact. It's a soft landing.
I am safe–and–I am pregnant.

VANGIE: *(She kneels in front of AYING, trying to catch her mother's eyes.)* Maybe we'll get a dog. Nice to have around the house. Ha? *(Pause)* We can take it to the beach. You like that? *(Pause)* And we. have to name it. *(Pause)* What? *(Pause)* You like to sleep? *(Pause)* OK. *(Pause)* Good night.

(VANGIE walks down right.)

She just stopped. Just like that. One day...just like that. This is what, ha? Punishment? Say something. Go ahead, I said. Yell at me at me if you like. Tell me you wish you had put a pillow over my face when I was in the crib. Tell me anything. *(Pause)* But she just stopped. Completely. Just like that. She never said another word. Not one more word.

And that knotting business. What is that? That's all she does now. And not just on that stupid shoestring. Everything. All around the house. All in knots. The fringes on the table cloth. The tassels on the curtains. My dental floss. I would wake up in the morning to find everything in knots. By the time I get back from work, they would all be untied. What do you do with someone like that? What? And she won't talk.

REDFORD: I contract. Dilate. Whoosh! It's a fuckin' pink baby. We're sitting in a pasture. I know because I can sense a cow nearby. I AM CONTENT. Until it cries, and cries so implacably, I....(*He covers its mouth with his hand.*) SHUT UP. Pink baby turns to Red baby. Red to blue, baby...Blue to purple. OH BABY (*He takes his hand off in horror.*) Good god...what am I...? You hungry? That all? Here. (*He offers his breast.*) Holy shit. I have nothing. IS THIS SOME CRUEL JOKE?

REDFORD: The cow? The cow...Cow, cow, cow...Yes. There, chewing cud under the apple tree. Baby, Bessie. Bessie, baby. SUCK GODDAMIT!

By instinct, it grabs a hold of two udders and drinks. I watch.
Purple progeny turns, first blue, now red, now pink again.
Beautiful pink thing-a-ma-baby.
But it didn't stop there.
Pink to yellow. Come in Yellow.
But paler, and paler and paler still.
Yellow invited White. Come in White. As white as the milk it devoured.
Now black spots form on its tiny hands and feet.

MY POOR BABY IS BECOMING A BARN ANIMAL. Help. (*He tries to pull the baby away from the cow.*) Let go. Let go. But it would not, and I could not. And my child, which has now fully metamorphosed into a black and white spotted calf, turned to me, as if to say:

VANGIE: All of them say...three different doctors...all of them you're fine. They can't find anything wrong. You choose not to talk. Choose? What are they saying? You choose? You can talk but you choose? What is this, ha? What are you doing to me? Ha? (*Pause*) *Punyeta kayo*!

[Trans: *Punyeta Kayo* – Damn you.]

REDFORD: I turned and I knew it wanted to say:
Don't be sad, Initial Life Giver.
But I CHOOSE to be part of what sustains me.
Only none of these tender words come out.
Instead. Instead of a blessing,
Instead of Daddy,
a long and disgusting MOOOOO.
I wake up with a spoiled taste in my mouth.

I've been coming here, week after week, to the same spot. She never came back. (*Pause*) The three hours we spent together now seem much longer than it was...and each day since seems to stretch those hours into...something more.

VANGIE: My mother died three months ago. *(Pause)* When her heart stopped, I felt her fingers squeeze my hand...not hard...just a little...almost unnoticeable. At that moment, I took a mouthful and air and I didn't breathe for a long time. I just kept it in. I was trying to decide how to feel...

(VANGIE becomes aware, as if for the first time, of her own words. She is unable to talk. She exits.)

(REDFORD has gone back to his toilet cubicle.)

REDFORD: *(He peeks below at the occupant next door.)* Hello....? Hello? I know those shoes. Haven't spoken to you in a while...How've you been? See if this rings a bell. *To be born again, first you have to die. To land upon the bosomy earth, first you need to fly.* Sound familiar? Salman Rushdie. You with me buddy? Hello?

REDFORD: What's there to say? Did I tell you, where I come from. You know, where I've been...stories grow from trees. No, you heard right. Trees. *(He closes his eyes and takes a deep breath.)*

(REDFORD walks out of the cubicle. This time he begins a slow run around the sandbox, building in speed as he jumps into air, hands outstretched as if reaching for a cloud. He steps into the sandbox, falls to his knees, and then lets out a piercing scream.)

REDFORD: *PANGIT AKO.*

[Trans: *Pangit ako*—I am ugly]

(Kneeling down, he makes his way to the edge of the bowl, which is now lit by a single beam of bright white light. Slowly, REDFORD takes his hand and dips it into the water.)

(MUSIC: Broken strains of AYING's kundiman.)

(He closes his eyes, forcing his memory to yield.)

REDFORD: The only thing I remember...from the other side...maybe I was six...maybe seven... the only thing that survives...is a fuzzy picture...a small blue window over a bed. Maybe...over my bed. Lying down, I recall catching a slice of the sky outside and the rusted roof with its peeling blue paint. When it rains, it sounds like...it makes the same sound as when you drop pennies into a tin can. The first few clinks...are like the opening notes...tentative...just before the sky lets loose its change, and you're swallowed by a wave...of...music. There is comfort. There.

(SOUND of metal bolt refastening. Lights off on REDFORD, as the names on the wall are washed in blinding white light. REDFORD remains silhouetted against the names, briefly, before the lights dim into blackness.)

END OF PLAY

PEELING THE BANANA

excerpts from the "PEELING THE BANANA" Troupe

About four and a half years ago, I embarked on an amazing journey that first began on the "other" coast, the West Coast, in my hometown, the City of Angels. Ten Asian men in a writing/performance workshop led by fellow performance artist Dan Kwong called, "Everything You Ever Wanted to Know about Asian Men-But Didn't Give Enough of a Shit to Ask…" changed my life forever. It was the first time our community saw Asian Men with bravery, respect and vulnerability. This was the real shit. The real stories. The harsh realities. The triumphs and victories. For the first time, I saw something I could be proud of and there was no turning back.

When I left Los Angeles bound for the Big Apple, I was fucking scared as hell leaving everything behind for a chance at being on my own and an opportunity to create a new home called, "Peeling the Banana." The stories developed by "peeling" over these last three and a half years are stories that need to be heard and have never been heard. They are stories that move us and challenge us. Make us feel pride and shame. But above all, they show truth and honesty.

These "peeling" selections showcase the evolution of this group from an Asian Men's workshop in 1995 to becoming the first truly collective and cohesive pan-Asian American performance troupe in New York City.

I have chosen to arrange the work as an evening of "classic" peeling pieces. They are in no chronological order to the PEELING THE BANANA timeline but counter point each other to show that we have distinct and varied life experiences that make us who we are as Asian Americans. And it is only through our individual stories that we can truly claim our community as Asians in America.

Warning: The selections you are about to read provide a direct contradiction to any notion of tokenism.

FABA.

-Gary San Angel
 Artistic Director, PEELING THE BANANA

Excerpts from the PEELING THE BANANA troupe 1995-98

"To My Sisters and Brothers on the West Coast" –Ed Lin

"Wild Turkey" –Aileen Cho & Calvin Lom

"Too! Too! Too!" –Ching-Ching Ni

"P.E." –Michel Ng

"The First (2)" –Ngo Thanh Nhan

"Margarita's Kicking Racist Ass Workshop" –Margarita Alcantara-Tan

"One Cheap Chinaman" –Ed Lin

"Tough Love" –Hugo Mahabhir

"A Waiter Tomorrow" –Bertrand Wang

"Secret M.U.T.A.N.T." –Gita Reddy

"Asia Files" –Ed Lin & Ching-Ching Ni

"The Right Stuff" –Gary San Angel

"Sex 2" –Ed Lin

"The Voice Behind the Jazz" –Dave Lin

To My Sisters and Brothers on the West Coast
Written and Performed by Ed Lin

Spotlight comes up on a man wearing glasses carrying a large red book.

Hi, my name is Ed Lin and I never memorize anything.

(Thumbs through the pages of red book)

I recently traveled to the West Coast and I felt a special kind of kinship to the other Asians out there. I'll be going there in the next couple weeks and I look forward to being in the warm embrace of my sisters and brothers on the West Coast…

(Screaming at the top of his lungs)

FUCK YOU! YOU SUCK!
STUPID THREE HOURS BEHIND, PACIFIC-TIME DUMBASSES. I HEARD YOU EAT RICE-A-RONI INSTEAD OF WHITE OR BROWN, YOU FUCKING SAN FRANCISCO FREAKS.
YOU WANT TO LIVE IN 90210 BECAUSE BRENDA LOOKS KINDA ASIAN, BUT YOU CAN PROPOSE ONE-EIGHTY-SEVEN REASONS TO KEEP THE REAL ONES AWAY FROM YOU.
I DON'T EXPECT MUCH FROM YOU SURF-WASHED AND SUN-DRIED BRAINS, BUT YOUR MOMMAS AND POPPAS-SANS BEEN CALIFORNIA DREAMIN' TOO.
RONALD TAKAKI IS JUST TOO COCKY.
I'LL SHOW YOU WHO'S REALLY FAKE, FRANK CHIN. COME OUT TO MY NEIGHBOR-HOOD, YOU'LL BE A DEAD FUCKING DUK.
I WILL NEVER CELEBRATE ACETATE, KRISTI YAMAGUCHI, AND I LOVE MY BEAUTI-FUL BROWN EYES.
YOU SEE, OUT ON THIS COAST, I DON'T HAVE TO MAKE FUN OF MY MOTHER'S ACCENT TO BE ALL AMERICAN, GIRL.
YOU EVER WONDER WHY YOU GOT EARTHQUAKES, MUDSLIDES AND OTHER NAT-URAL DISASTERS AND SHIT?

(Clutches the book like a bible)

BECAUSE GOD HATES YOU, TOO!

(Blackout)

WILD TURKEY

Written and performed by Aileen Cho and Calvin Lom

WOMAN enters a bar stage left and orders a drink from an invisible bartender.

WOMAN: Bartender! Give me a wild turkey please, on the rocks. *(Takes a gulp, addresses audience)* Oh great! Another lonely night on Long Island. I'm going INSANE! There are no decent guys around here, let alone decent Asian guys! They're all dorky engineers! Nobody who relates to me! Where's the perfect guy when you need him?

(MAN enters stage right. WOMAN does a double take.)

WOMAN: Oh my god! He's gorgeous! *(MAN looks at her staring, looks away nervously.)* He's not looking at me! Why isn't he looking at me!

MAN: *(To audience)* Is she looking at me?

WOMAN: He doesn't like me. Maybe he doesn't date Asian women. Maybe he isn't attracted to me!

MAN: *(To audience)* She is so hot! Did she look at me? *(Looks at WOMAN)* She's looking at me! I'm so excited! But why am I so... scared? And intimidated? Bartender...a Wild Turkey please!

WOMAN: Hey...Wild Turkey? Hey! I drinkWild Turkey!

MAN: *(To audience)* Was she talking to me? *(To WOMAN)* Did you say something?

WOMAN: *(Embarrassed)* Ummm...sorry, I didn't mean to bother you. Forget it.

MAN: Did you say you liked Wild Turkey?

WOMAN: *(Hopeful)* Yeah...yeah I did.

MAN: Bartender! A Wild Turkey for the lady!

WOMAN: Thanks?...

MAN: Cal. And your name?

WOMAN: Aileen. Nice to meet you!

MAN: Nice to meet you! Cheers!

WOMAN: Thanks. Here's to...to Wild Turkeys!

(They gulp shots simultaneously and eye each other. They start to move center stage toward each other.)

MAN: So, Aileen, what are you doing out here on Long Island?

WOMAN: *(Grimly)* I ask myself that question every day. No really, I work as a journalist. And you? Are you a...an engineer?

MAN: Yes, I'm afraid I'm the Asian stereotype...but I'm really an artist and a writer.

WOMAN: Really?! I'm a writer...and an artist! There aren't too many Asians out here, let alone ones who are writers...or artists!

MAN: Wow! How about another Wild Turkey! So...are you Chinese?

(They get more drinks.)

WOMAN: Yeah!

MAN: ME too!

(They are visibly excited.)

WOMAN: Well! Here's to being Chinese...

MAN: And artists...

WOMAN: And writers!

(MAN and WOMAN turn to audience simultaneously.)

MAN AND WOMAN: This is too good to be true!

MAN: This is so different.

WOMAN: I feel as if I know this guy already!

MAN: Usually Asian women confuse me!

WOMAN: He looks like me...

MAN: They send me mixed messages...

WOMAN: He's cute! And...

MAN: But this time...

MAN AND WOMAN: (S)He's...interested!

(They face each other, start to move closer with each phrase.)

WOMAN: You know...you have nice hair. It's like mine.

MAN: It's long...and thick...

WOMAN: And our eyes...

MAN: ...Brown...and almond-shaped...

WOMAN: With high cheekbones...

MAN: And smooth...skin...and...

MAN AND WOMAN: ...not white!

(They grab each other fervently.)

WOMAN: I've never dated someone who looks like me!

MAN: You've never gone out with another Asian either?

WOMAN: There aren't too many of us out here to choose from...it gets...lonely...

MAN: ...and isolated...

WOMAN: ...and dysfunctional...

(WOMAN tries to regain control of herself, pushes Man a little bit away.)

So...do you have any brothers or sisters?

MAN: No...I was adopted.

WOMAN: Really? Me too! My grandfather was a famous assassin!

(The two become even more intimate.)

MAN: Me too!

WOMAN: His name was Some Lom Gai.

MAN: Me too!

(They stop suddenly.)

MAN AND WOMAN: Some Lom Gai?

(Beat)

SOME LOM GAI???? BARTENDER! Another Wild Turkey! NOW!

(Beat. They look at each other.)

WOMAN: Brother...

MAN: Sister...

(They take each others hands and leave the bar together.)

(Lights fade out)

TOO! TOO! TOO!
Written and Performed by Ching-Ching Ni

Music rolls: Cui Jian's "Lang Zi Gui: Vagabond Returns." A woman dressed in a red overcoat carries a suitcase on stage, as pillow, baby and airplane. Music fades out. The woman slowly rests her suitcase on floor.

I see my father at the airport. Behind the plexiglass, he looks exactly like he did 18 years ago when my mother flew us out of his life, only a lot shorter and squatter than I remembered. Ba! Ba! Ba! The first thing he says to me is...

(Acting like him, lugging the heavy suitcase back home, and dropping it off on a stool.)

Ayiiiiia! Dai zhema duo dongxi gan shenma? aiya, Zou zou zou! My father loves to remind me that I never learned how to pack light. He even gave me his favorite suitcase, the one he used to travel between military bases playing his clarinet for the People's Liberation Army. Everyday he would stay home and rearrange my things, everyday I would wonder if he thought the lost years of our lives together were some how hidden in the chaos of my suitcase.

(She opens suitcase, starts throwing things out piece by piece and becomes her father again, agitated, waving, pointing, pressing a T-shirt against the body, trying to make it flat and smooth before folding it back into the suitcase carefully.)

Buxing Buxing! aiyha! zhe me da de hai ze lian yifu do bu hui die...The more he fussed over my things, the more junk I brought. It's as if I needed him to touch my things, I needed him to leave his fingerprints on my life.

(Picks up a yellow Chinese toy tiger and pets it close to her face)

What I really want, is to put my father inside my suitcase. Like my Chairman Mao charm.

(Opens jacket to reveal charm)

These cheap souvenirs are luckier than my dad. They get to go all the way to America with me.

(Spins the charm like a plane through the air)

But my father has never been to America. I would look for him, wherever I go. I would find him, every morning in the mirror when I notice my eyes are exactly like his. Why don't they look more like my mom?

(Stretches her big eyes)

I would find him, when I am driving to work, listening to his favorite Peking Opera tape, pretending I am the daughter of a communist martyr, murdered by the imperialist running dogs,

(Shrieks like a Peking opera star)

You killed my father, I will kill you!! I would find him, in every man I've ever loved, searching for the one person who really knows how to pack a suitcase. I would find him, in the old black and white picture of my parents, long before the big divorce turned my life into a frequent flyer program. My father was a poor boy from the countryside, but he was a man in uniform and he was so handsome, he set the standard for all Asian men.

(Proudly displays father's military portrait)

The first time my sister and I went back to China to visit him, we had forgotten how to talk to him in Chinese. So we forced English on him the way we forced potato chips on him. My poor father was gagging on the words, allergic to English. But we kept telling him, Ba, English is good for you. English will make you big and strong. English will help you conquer the world! But wou baba said he's already yo gao yo da and he has no desire to zhanling shijie. The only English he ever cared to remember was something he learned on his own.

(In Ba's voice:)   "Easta, westa, home is da besta."

All we really wanted to do was hear him say, I love you too. But instead we got...

(In Ba's voice:) "ayiieee-la-ayiiee-tu...ayiieee-la-ayiiee-tu...lale-yo-tu...tule-yo-la...ayie-la-ai-tu...tu...tu...tu...tootootoo...."

"too! too! too!"

My sister and I couldn't believe it! Our father has created our own secret love code! "too too too!" We used it everywhere we went. But all these Chinese people were laughing at us because in Chinese, we were saying the words for "rabbit! rabbit! rabbit!" and "vomit! vomit! vomit!"

There's only three people in the whole world who know what it means.

We depend on it, every time we say goodbye.

(Tape 2 rolls : Cui Jian's "Lang Zi Gui: Vagabond Returns.")

(The woman goes back to pack the suitcase, picks it up and walks to center for the departure.)

Too! too! too!

(She starts walking away, waving into distance to Ba.)

Too! too! too!

(She walks away more.)

Too! too! too!

(Pauses in a final goodbye. Music and lights fade out.)

PE 101
Written and Performed by Michel Ng

Lights come up on a row of high school boys who are standing on the school playing field. A whistle is blown. The voice of a gym teacher offstage yells out the order, "Give me fifty!" The Village People's "YMCA" starts up and the boys do a series of exercises—jumping jacks, push-ups, etc.

MICHEL: Of all the classes in grade school, the one I hated most was P.E.—Phys Ed. You know, that dreaded class where boys were supposed to be able to do boy things like dribbling basketballs while running into each other, wrestle with the strength of Hulk Hogan (and those other homos whom we would later discover)...

(The BOYS bond by bumping chests and grunting. When they get to MICHEL, they bump him back and forth like a ping pong ball between them.)

MICHEL: ...and ram into each other with our puny bodies on the field and absolutely love every glorious moment of it...and finally, when it was all over, smell our armpits in the locker room as if the molding smells of decaying lockers weren't enough.

(The scenery changes to the wrestling room. A match begins between MICHEL and the biggest APE of a boy in the class. The APE picks up MICHEL and twirls him helplessly over his shoulders as the other BOYS around cheer. "Kick his ass!" "Get him!" etc.)

MICHEL: P.E. was the litmus test of butchness...the be-all end-all class where you could prove yourself as a man once and for all, or be cursed for the rest of eternity as a flaming mahu. I hated it.

(The BOYS exit to hit the lockers. The sound of water runs as a shadow play of the BOYS in the shower is projected on a scrim behind MICHEL. The BOYS joke around, snapping towels at one another's bare asses.)

MICHEL: I remember having to do sit-ups, push-ups, dribble balls against boys who were two times my size, and wrestling with guys who were ten times my weight. I'll admit, being pinned down can be fun—but not in front of a bunch of closet case high school jocks.

(The scenery changes to the locker room. The BOYS re-enter in towels led by JOCK 1 and JOCK 2. MICHEL stands in the corner silent. MIKE, also in a towel, enters a little behind the rest, drying his hair.)

JOCK 1:   Hey, man. Good game!

JOCK 2:   Yeah, boy! Kicked some ass today.

JOCK 1:   Yo, man, you see that bitch Larry trying to throw the ball? He was like, "Ughhhnn!"

JOCK 2:   You know, they should have separate gym classes. One for real guys who wanna play for real, and one for guys like Larry. It's bad enough we gotta get undressed in front of those queers.

JOCK 1:   No, shit. Yo, I saw Larry checking you out. He almost grabbed your ass on that one play.

JOCK 2:   Shut up. If I ever caught that piece of shit Larry looking at me, I'd have to crack his head open.

JOCK 1:   Yeah, I don't give a shit what fucked up shit faggots do on their own time, but they better not try any shit on me.

JOCK 2:   Don't worry.

(They exit, followed by the rest of the BOYS. Only MIKE and MICHEL are left. Mike is half-naked. They make eye-contact and smile.)

MIKE: Those guys are idiots.

MICHEL: Yeah.

MIKE: I don't even think Larry is, you know.

MICHEL: Yeah, me neither.

MIKE: I mean, even if he was, who cares? Right?

MICHEL: Yeah, I guess. It's no big deal.

MIKE: Yeah.

(MIKE jumps up onto the bench. He flexes his muscles in the mirror.)

MIKE: Hey, man, I've been working out. You think it's starting to show?

(MICHEL giggles.)

MIKE: Oh, c'mon. It's not that bad.

MICHEL: Yeah, it's not bad.

(Pause)

MIKE: Hey, can I ask you something?

MICHEL: What?

MIKE: Never mind.

MICHEL: What?

MIKE: No. Forget it.

MICHEL: C'mon.

MIKE: Well…

(He scans the room for anyone.)

Uh, do you ever…I mean, do you…uh, you know.

MICHEL: Do I what?

MIKE: You know. I mean, you know what I'm trying to say right?

(MIKE begins to move closer to MICHEL, they are more intimate.)

MICHEL: Ummmm. I'm not sure. I mean, maybe. I don't know.

MIKE: C'mon. You know. You know what I'm talking about, right?

MICHEL: Uhhh. I should really get to class—

(They stare at one another. Beat.)

MIKE: I know that you check the other guys out. I do it too. I've seen you check me out. It's
OK. Really. Just say it.

(Uncomfortable silence)

MIKE: Say it. C'mon. Don't do this to me. You know what I'm talking about. I'm talking to
you because you understand. You know? Just say it.

MICHEL: (Long pause) Maybe. Yeah, sometimes.

(They stare at one another. MIKE has his face a breath away from MICHEL's. MIKE leans in.)

MIKE: Faggot.

(MIKE exits. MICHEL stands alone in the tiny pool of light.)

(Lights fade out)

THE FIRST (2)

Written and Performed by Ngo Thanh Nhan

Dedicated to the killed Paris Commune workers, France.

A spotlight comes up on a man sitting on a wooden stool. He is dressed in black and begins to play his guitar. The music is from "Le Temps des Cierises" (poem by Jan-Baptiste Clément, music by A. Renard, 1866), Music starts for 2 phrases...meticulously.

1. I was twelve when I called his name
from the roster in my class
I vaguely remember him
when my friends called him sissy
and he chased them around the schoolyard
I got to know him the following year
when he sat next to me in the first row...
we became close
when I crossed the railroad tracks
up the hill to his house
his older sister treated me with fried *bánh-chu'ng*...
I remember she giggled
when my eyes never left her face
he smiled and told me she was sixteen
that was our first secret.

(Music continues for 2 phrases.)

2. We rode bicycles
every day next to each other
we held hands in line
walking to class side by side...
I began to draw flowers and girls
and drew his face with his sister's hair and chest
I began to get bad grades for talking in class
I spent a lot of money playing billiard
during the siestas
anyone calling him sissy
also got a revenge from me
we rode bicycles to p.e.
next to each other
he did not like soccer

my friends told me he ran funny
he did not like high jumping
he did not like javelin throwing
he only like to run with me
so I ran with him slowly...
I watched him in the shower
and discovered he grew a few hairs
and I was delighted...
and kept looking...
but knew not why

(Music continues for 2 phrases.)

3. We went to camps together
for many years
I could not bear his absence
even for just one moment
we were together
and we were together
even at night I saw his smile...
we touched each other many times
we played each other's penises
and giggled until both were hard...
we took out a ruler to measure...
and argued as to where they should begin
his was straight and pointed downward
mine curved leftward
and I sighed every time he pulled the skin...

(Music continues for 2 phrases. Tempo a little faster.)

4. We were in bed one night
the summer was hot
and our chests were bare
sweat-soaked underpant shorts
during my sleep I dreamt
kissing him in his cheeks
then on his eyes
then gently on his lips
like lovers on movie screens
he hugged me
and I wrapped my arms around his waist
hearing his heart beats

not wanting to let go
I did not remember how it happened
both our underpants disappeared
our penises were in full blown
I felt excited
and he was trembling as
he pulled down the skin
I immediately came
And...as I was drowned...gasping
I grabbed his penis
like a safety post in a furious tempest
I felt his soft hair soaking wet
and I felt it jumping
and felt the warm juice spurting on my belly
he shook and yelling "ôi!"
and held me tight
I was surprised
I could not shake him off
until much later

(Music continues for 2 phrases relaxing to finale.)

5. We agreed that night
it would be another secret until we die
I learned he went out on a boat
and drown somewhere in the Malaysian Gulf...

(Music continues for 2 phrases, phasing out, clean break.)

(Blackout)

MARGARITA'S KICKING RACIST ASS WORKSHOP

Written and Performed by Margarita Alcantara-Tan

Lights come up on the "Margarita" show sign as the theme music plays and the voice of an announcer introduces the host.

ANNOUNCER: You know her as the best selling author of *"How to Kill 2 Asiaphiles With One Stone,"* and as consultant to the stars. She needs no further introduction.....Please welcome...MARGARITA!

(MARGARITA enters from back of audience with mic in hand. Lights come up on the whole studio audience as music fades.)

MARGARITA: Hello! Welcome to my *"Kicking Racist Ass Workshop!"*

I'll be guiding you through some fun-filled exercises that'll get your heart pumpin' and your Asian self in check! As women, we've all have had some experience with being harassed on the streets. But, as ASIAN women, we get a special kind of harassment, based on our *(Sarcastically)* EXOTIC features, and the overblown fantasies Asiaphile men have because of them.

Who here has been harassed?

(A woman in audience raises her hand. MARGARITA approaches her with mic.)

What's your name?

TAMINA: Tamina.

MARGARITA: Tamina, tell me—what kind of racist and sexist things have guys said to you?

TAMINA: *(With difficulty)* "Do you girls have slanted vaginas too?"

MARGARITA: *(Nodding with sympathy)* Yes. I've heard that all before myself.

(Switch to upbeat)

But today, I'm going to teach you how to defend yourself using *(Pause)* Pananandata—the Filipino Martial Art of Weapon Fighting.

(She demonstrates.)

You can use sticks, whips, balisongs, or just your pretty little hands!

But first, I'm gonna teach you how to verbalize. Yes. You can defend yourself without lifting a finger. That's the best way to go as a first tactic.

So tell me, girls! What do you say if someone calls you "his cute little china doll with a slanted pek pek?"

(CHING-CHING, stage L, and AILEEN, stage R, jump out.)

CHING-CHING & AILEEN: FUCK YOU!

(They retreat.)

MARGARITA: I can't hear you!

(CHING-CHING and AILEEN jump out.)

CHING-CHING & AILEEN: FUCK YOU!!!!!!!!!!!

(They retreat.)

MARGARITA: Much better!*(To Tamina)* Tell me, what would you do if someone grabbed you physically, let's say, on the thigh or ass?

TAMINA: *(Pause)* Cry and run in humiliation?

MARGARITA: No!

(She goes to side of front stage to prepare video.)

MARGARITA: Let's see what happened to Stephanie Park of Greenwich, CT. This is a re-enactment of what actually happened...Harry! Roll the tape!

(Spotlight focuses on Stephanie Park a.k.a. NORIKO. "The Mission Impossible" theme song plays. NORIKO walks from stage L to bus stop. While NORIKO walks out, AILEEN passes stage L holding "Re-enactment" sign then retreats. White guy cardboard cut-out held behind curtain, looms out and grabs NORIKO. She freaks out.)

NORIKO: Margarita, help!

(Jumping back into limelight, horrified)

MARGARITA: Help is on the way Stephanie! *(To side)* Thanks, Harry.
(Spotlight off. NORIKO, stage L, and AILEEN, stage R, come out, holding up white guy cardboard cut-outs)

MARGARITA: Here's what you should do if you ever find yourself in Stephanie's unwelcome predicament. Aileen, grab my thigh.

(Demonstrate on cut-outs.)

MARGARITA: Nudge your elbow into their floating ribs, punch the face with the back of your fist, and rake your fingernails down their face to draw blood, get some of that DNA under there!

(To NORIKO, poking eyes of cut-out)

MARGARITA: If ever in doubt, go for the eyes. No matter how big the guy is, the eyes are always vulnerable. Thanks girls, for helping me illustrate those points!

(NORIKO and AILEEN exit.)

TAMINA: Have you always been this fearless?

MARGARITA: Of course not! I too have been the fragile Pacific flower, a product of an Asian household...When I was younger, I grew up in a house where there was a lot of physical violence. But that was then.

TAMINA: You have tattoos and you look tough, so why do you get harassed?

MARGARITA: I know, you can't tell that my mom ever sent me to the Lea Salonga School of Charm, can you? But that's OK, that never stops any of those sexist jerkoffs from harassing a chick of color, especially if they're Asian.

(Sound of a bell)

MARGARITA: I can't believe it, our time is up! This is the end of yet another successful workshop. Let's do our Healing Affirmations—Tamina, I'd like for you to join us!

(TAMINA and the GIRLS join MARGARITA on stage.)

MARGARITA: "I am a wonderful Asian woman!"

GIRLS: I AM A WONDERFUL ASIAN WOMAN!

MARGARITA: "I am strong!"

GIRLS: I AM STRONG!

MARGARITA: "I can kick ass!"

GIRLS: I CAN KICK ASS!

MARGARITA: That's just a little taste of what you can do to defend yourself using the martial arts that's in OUR blood. Our powerful, Asian, female blood.

(Closing theme music plays.)

Margarita: Until the next workshop, entitled, "How to Flay Off Those Pesky Neo-Nazis," this is Margarita signing off! And remember: DNA under the fingernails!

(The girls get weapons and pose. Spotlight on MARGARITA, who gets balisongs and plays. MARGARITA freezes on her last move as music fades.)

MARGARITA: Yeah, I'LL show you "china doll."

(Blackout)

ONE CHEAP CHINAMAN
Written and Performed by Ed Lin

Spotlight on man with glasses. He returns once again with large red book.

GODDAMN, HE WAS CHEAP.

He wore size extra large, irregular everything.
He kept a drawer full of dead batteries in case they found a way to recharge 'em, even though they were leaking what looked like a small pool of fried Coca-Cola on his stockpiled pennies.

GODDAMN, HE WAS CHEAP.

He ate low-fat Twinkies and drank diet chocolate-chip soda. He wasn't watching his weight, but they were four for a dollar at Wholesale Liquidators.
He lined his birdcage with subway maps.
He couldn't make plans for the first two weeks of the year because he wouldn't buy a new calendar until the middle of January, 40% off and he got to read "The Far Side" comics he missed when he couldn't find a newspaper for free.

Goddamn, he was cheap, although he fancied himself to be "an educated shopper," like the Syms ads.
He did get ripped off once, though.
He bought a 50-cent used tape which he thought was a Chinese opera star. Instead, he got two white boys telling him and everyone else to "Wang Chung tonight."

He was so cheap, he would take the bus to Atlantic City, watch other people play and ride on the free drinks instead of going to a bar because with the casino bonus plan, the bus ride was cheaper than the subway.

And once and only once, when he was very, very drunk, he played out half his life's savings at the $5 craps table and tipped the waitress with what he could have used as his last bet.

Because, although he was one cheap Chinaman, he never cheated anybody.

(Blackout)

TOUGH LOVE
Written and Performed by Hugo Mulchand Mahabir

Lights come up on a living room with a couch and TV flickering; large group enters dancing to the beating of a bottle and spoon rhythm, all singing a calypso.

GROUP: "Ah goin' down San Fernando
          Down deh ha plenty tempo
          Pan and steel orchestras jammin' sweet
          Ah want to dance up Coffee Street
          So leh me go...tempo..."

(They repeat the verse in a soft whisper as HUGO moves center stage. He sings the song as if to himself now, while the rest of the ensemble behind him beats the rhythm softly. He begins to speak his memories.)

HUGO: "Child, where yuh went last night?"
"To a Carnival party, Grandma."
"Deh place was fulla negroes, nah?"
"No grandma...not really."
"Carnival jump ups is full ah dem...dat is their culture...you didn't meet any girls, ah hope!"
"No grandma...not really."
"Leh me tell you something...don't you ever bring any ah dem kaffers home, you know!"
"Yes, Grandma."

FAMILY MEMBER: *(Screams)* Hey, y'all it's Peyton Place...

(The group comes back to life. Everyone shouts and cheers. They rush to the couch, everyone jumps down and sits together excitedly to watch TV. HUGO makes his way to his usual spot on the coach and squeezes in.)

HUGO: We sit on the old couch next to my grandma and cousins and aunties eating the peanuts she has just finished roasting for us, watching TV, it's Peyton Place, her favorite show...Ryan O'Neal and Mia Farrow in a small, snowy town somewhere in America making their drugstore and diner intrigues from Main Street, U.S.A...and us, a bunch of cousins and aunties all squeezed together with grandma on the old couch, brown peas in a Trinidad pod, eating roasted peanuts together.

(He stands up and leaves the others who are still watching TV...faint calypso music can be heard in the background.)

HUGO: But I never could tell Grandma that I had danced with a black girl somewhere at a party in Arima, that she had her hands around me our hips gyrating to the reggae and calypso beats pulling me close to her on the slow songs. That we went out behind the garage, and fooled around all night, kissing and kissing. That I came in my pants, my head lost in the sweet perfume of her neck.

(The calypso music fades out as HUGO walks around his family still entranced by the TV.)

HUGO: But Grandma hated Carnival and Calypso, still I loved her and she loved me...And she cared more about skin color than anyone I know, who was lighter, and who was darker whose hair was straight, and whose hair was kinky separating Indians from Negroes in her Peyton Place world...I had to keep secrets from Grandma if I still wanted to sit on the couch with her. Love and racism, we're all prisoners there.

(He sits back on the couch with his family.)

HUGO: So find your place above the niggers...my brown-skinned grandma forgetting that we were the servants of the empire, then and now in this Peyton Place world...

(As he says the following lines, each person in the group stands up from the couch and moves forward, one at a time, miming the action named, as the group creates a tableau.)

HUGO: Serving tea...
washing clothes...cleaning bathrooms...
cutting cane...dying cotton...picking coffee...
sweeping lobbies...driving taxis...selling newspapers...
Then and now...in this new world...

(From their positions in the tableau, each person mimes a new action, as he says the following lines.)

HUGO: Laboratory experimenting...
computer programming...heart operating...
particle accelerating...AIDS researching...gene splicing...
plastics testing...mathematical modeling...post-colonial theorizing...

(Everyone freezes.)

HUGO: Asians in America...
looking for some place to call home.
Now I walk the streets of this city.

(The group breaks and starts walking around the stage as though they're on a busy city street.)

HUGO: A border child, in between worlds
black, white, yellow, and brown
inside and out,

outcast and castaway...*(Pause)* Am I a ghost?

(Everyone vanishes from the stage. HUGO is left alone, frantically looking around to see only an empty stage. HUGO slowly moves back to the couch and sits down, looking out into space as if for his grandmother.)

HUGO: But I did everything right,
Grandma learned the proper way to dress
and cut my hair
the right way to speak
and look at things.
But I am still afraid
like a teenage boy
coming home from a party
afraid to speak the unspeakable,
afraid to say the truth.

Isn't the first duty of love to listen,
listen to your child...listen to your lover...listen to your friend,
that we all have secrets to tell,
that love comes in many forms.

Sometimes...sometimes...I just want you to listen
and hear the whole story.

(Lights fade out)

A WAITER TOMORROW

by Bertrand Wang

An East Village Japanese restaurant. Two Asian waiters, BERT *and* MIKE*, are working hard for the money...and some dignity!*

ANNOYING HAKUJIN: Excuse me, I asked for extra wasabi.

WHITE GIRL: Waiter, could I have some more water with a slice of lemon?

MR. REGULAR SILVERWARE: (*Snotty*) Can I have some regular silverware please?

ANNOYING HAKUJIN: Excuse me, is all Japanese food raw? I want cooked food. I want some chicken.

MR. REGULAR SILVERWARE: Do you have tea?

MIKE: We have green tea.

MR. REGULAR SILVERWARE: No like regular tea, like Lipton tea.

(*Backlit stage* BERT *and* MIKE *on break, probably smoking cigarettes—even though they're not good for you— while the restaurant rages on.*)

MIKE: Busy night huh?

BERT: Hell, yeah. But at least we'll make money tonight.

MIKE: No shit.

BERT: I really hate being nice to all these...people.

MIKE: I totally know what you mean. We get so many racist and sexist assholes in this place. Did you hear the guy at table 3, asking me for 'regular' silverware? I was like chopsticks are pretty regular to me ASSHOLE!

BERT: Usually, I'm good at shutting off the thinking part of my brain when I come to work. But it still gets to me. Like that sugar in the tea shit. That's just not right, I don't go to their houses and pour fuckin' soy sauce into their Frosted Flakes.

MIKE: I just wish we didn't get treated like, like hired help.

BERT: But we are hired help.

MIKE: I know, but just because people tip us a few bucks doesn't mean they own us.

BERT   :Yup, there is no dignity for the waiting proletariat. We'll be fine as long as you know who doesn't show up.

MIKE: Oh you mean that sushi bar guy? The one that usually comes by himself?

BERT and MIKE: *(Together)*   Mr. Asshole.

MIKE: He is the worst.

(People start calling for the waiters.)

BERT: Case in point.

ANNOYING HAKUJIN: Excuse me, do you have eggrolls?

BERT: No.

WHITE GIRL: Excuse me...Do you have that omelet that they have in Japan. I've been to Japan and they had it, do you have it? Isn't this an authentic Japanese restaurant?

MR. REGULAR SILVERWARE: Are you Japanese? I've been taking Japanese classes and I want to practice.

MIKE: *(Annoyed)*   Actually, I'm Korean.

MR. REGULAR SILVERWARE: Oops, sorry.

(He and his friends laugh off the mistake. Enter MR. ASSHOLE.)
(Music cue: John Woo's "Hard Boiled" score plays underneath scene.)
(MIKE and BERT look at MR. ASSHOLE and then exchange Woo-esque operatic looks.)

MR. ASSHOLE: Two for the sushi bar.

DICKHEAD BUDDY: Did they hear you? Better yet did they understand you?

MR. ASSHOLE: *(Pointing towards BERT)*   Oh yeah, this guy's cool....He speaks English real good. Hey buddy.

BERT: I'll be right with you.

(MR. ASSHOLE and DICKHEAD BUDDY get sick of waiting and seat themselves. Other customers flee to the other side of the restaurant.)

BERT: Do you have any questions?

DICKHEAD BUDDY: What's the difference between a tuna roll and a spicy tuna roll?

BERT: *(Slowly)*   Well, one is spicy...and one isn't.

DICKHEAD BUDDY: I'll have chicken teriyaki.

MR. ASSHOLE: I'll have a Village Jumbo Sushi with a spicy tuna roll and a large sake.

BERT: As long as you know that spicy tuna costs extra?

MR. ASSHOLE: What?! I never have to pay for spicy tuna!

BERT: It's a new policy.

(DICKHEAD BUDDY gets up and MR. ASSHOLE waves his hand to sit him down.)

MR. ASSHOLE: *(Gets up)* I happen to be a close personal friend of Tony...the manager.

BERT: I know who he is.

MR. ASSHOLE: *(Slaps BERT in the face)* Then you won't have any problem finding him. Make sure the spicy tuna is fresh. The last time I was here it was old and no good.

(MR. ASSHOLE and DICKHEAD BUDDY leave and brush past BERT and MIKE. The rest of the customers start to mutiny and demand to see the manager.)

EVERYONE: Waiter! Waiter! I want to see Tony!

BERT and Mike: Let's go get Tony!

(The two waiters leave the chaotic restaurant floor and return wearing dark shades and a new attitude.)

MIKE: You want to see the manager! Here's the manager!

(The Fight: BERT and MIKE reveal guns from their aprons and start killing everyone in the restaurant some in regular speed and some in operatic slow-mo. BERT shoots MR. REGULAR SILVERWARE. WHITE GIRL ducks behind a chair, unveils a gun and tries to shoot BERT. MIKE jumps over the chairs and shoots WHITE GIRL. BERT shoots the cowering customers on stage left. MIKE shoots ANNOYING GWAI LO.

BERT and MIKE back into each other and almost shoot one another but then realize its another 'good guy.')

CANNONFODDER: TABLE for TWO!

(BERT shoots CANNONFODDER. The over the top violence crescendos as customers, flower delivery people, (anyone but restaurant workers) and would be patrons all die in a fiery blaze of bullets. After everyone is dead, MR. ASSHOLE and DICKHEAD BUDDY return from the can. After entering the stage, they all draw guns and assume the classic stand off position. Guns are all up in each other's faces.)

MR. ASSHOLE: *(Unfazed by the situation)* You're one Hard Boiled waiter. Is my sushi ready?

BERT: Oh it's ready!

MR. ASSHOLE: I even told my friend that you were a cool Japanese guy!

BERT: Well, you were half right. I'm Chinese, you stupid fuck!

(At that instant, DICKHEAD BUDDY clicks his gun and shoots MIKE. MIKE shoots DICKHEAD BUDDY. MR. ASSHOLE shoots MIKE. BERT shoots MR. ASSHOLE. MR. ASSHOLE and BERT are wounded.)

MR. ASSHOLE: What do you have against me anyway? I always leave a good tip!

BERT: Shut up and eat this sushi!

MR. ASSHOLE: Wha..?

BERT: *(Force feeds sushi to MR. ASSHOLE.)*   EAT IT!! To you, sushi is part of a bad Japanese joke. But to us, it's a lo-fat, high protein gift from the sea. And you NEVER turn down a gift. EAT!!

(Just as he is about to eat, MR. ASSHOLE spits it in BERT'S FACE. MR. ASSHOLE tries to draw another gun or knife. BERT shoots MR. ASSHOLE.)

BERT: Sayonara asshole...*(Going to MIKE's aid)* Mike, you're gonna be all right.

MIKE: *(Coughing blood)* I don't think I'm gonna make it. I think...I think...I think I'm gonna call in sick tomorrow.

BERT: Don't talk crazy man. You're gonna be fine.

MR. ASSHOLE: *(Comes to life and lunges at the two waiters)* AAAHHHH!

(BERT and MIKE shoot MR. ASSHOLE.)

BERT: C'mon, we gotta bus these tables and set up for lunch.

(Blackout)

SECRET M.U.T.A.N.T.
Written and Performed by Gita Reddy

Lights come up on a small, brightly colored karaoke tape player with attached mic ("Minus One") located down-stage center. Ponytailed and wearing a "Velveeta" T-shirt, a woman enters and exits the stage first in leaps, and then hesitantly. She finally circles the tape player and quickly picks it up. She addresses the audiences via Minus One mic.

Hi. My name is Gita Reddy....Hi. My name is Gita...Josephina Teresita Imeldacita Pinky Bong-Bong Pilar Del Rosario Santos Banaag Arce...Reddy.

(She puts the Minus One down.)

OK, that's not true. My name is just Gita Reddy. Gita...Reddy. Very Indian, my name, just like my dad. Bhaskara Reddy. Unlike...Aida Catalina Florenda Arce Reddy Fusilero. My mom. Very unlike my mom, my name. When I was little, it didn't matter.

(Lights dim as the sweet opening strings of ABBA's "Chiquitita" plays. GITA kneels and walks around as if she is a little kid again. Two women enter and hold her hands, giggling and pretending to chat with others as if at a party. One of them coos "Chiqui-Gita!")

After the divorce, I would dance with all my Titas, all my mom's fellow Filipino nurses, and they would laugh at me because at age nine, I could fit into their dressy shoes.

(She tries on one of her Tita's shoes on her right knee. They laugh. GITA stands and pulls down her long hair.)

But when I got older, they wouldn't dance with me anymore.

(She towers over them. The women look up at GITA in suspicion and whisper to each other. With fake smiles, they quickly take the Minus One and exit as "Chiquitita" fades out.)

So I would dance all by myself.

(She hums the ABBA tune and dances melancholically.)

I mean, I understand. Now my Titas had children of their own, and when they all went on camping trips together to Yellowstone National Park, or balikbayan to the Philippines, they would ask me to...house sit for them.

(People enter and freeze, they pose in joyous family and friend portraits: Christmas morning; high school buddies; singing karaoke at a party. In the final portrait, someone is "singing" into the Minus One's mic. She steps for-

ward, confiding.)

And with no one around, I could pick up and touch all their family photos.

(Excited, she sneaks right up to the first portrait. As GITA speaks, she points to what the girl's holding, then surreptitiously caresses the girl's cheek. GITA touches her own face in reflection.)

Look! Clarissa and her brother Norbert at Christmas! Maligayang Pasko! Look what Clarissa got for Christmas—Clinique loose powder, shade #01...

The lightest shade. That's the shade my mother wears. I wear shade #04....

(She jumps over to the next portrait group and points to everyone, absent mindedly hunching over and covering her skin.)

Oh, they got one of those mall portraits! Clarissa...that's her cousin Jaime, he's on the basketball team, and that's his girlfriend, oh...her name is...Joybelle! Everybody loves her!

(She poses deliriously next to Joybelle, trying to become part of the portrait.)

Look, she's so happy...and so petite! Look at her shoes, they're so tiny! My feet were never that tiny! Never!

(Now also limping, she gathers her last vestiges of excitement to approach the final portrait, drawn by the sight of the Minus One.)

Minus One! Home karoake! Minus One! Minus One! They never let me sing on the Minus One!

(GITA pries the mic out of the person's hand, and sings desperately "I Can't Smile Without You", leaning so near to the Minus One that feedback drowns her out. She grabs the Minus One, clutching it to her defiantly, occasionally caressing it, even talking to it. Hunched over, limping and now sniffling, she makes her way in front of all the portraits.)

I'll never be like them, because they're perfect...perfect Filipinas! Me, I'm just a mutant...a mutant Filipina! Mutant, I'm a mutant! Mutant! You understand, Minus One, don't you! Mutant...

(She accidentally presses "play" on the Minus One and Tito Puente's rousing "Kiss of Fire" begins, which sends her body into uncontrollable shakes. Looking around confused, GITA "transmutates" and feels herself straightening up and standing tall and proud, in response to the beats of the music. She "hears" instructions coming from the Minus One and nervously responds into the mic. Nodding my acceptance, I lift my head and tango with the mic, taking long leaps up to the portraits, dismissing each of them from the stage. They exit. GITA continues the Secret Agent dance to the music, then suddenly stops the tape and addresses the audience via the mic.)

Do you know who I am? They did not know who I am. But I know you know who I am....I am...

(She spins around and looks back over her shoulder.)

...Secret Agent...

(She jumps around and salutes first with the Minus One then quickly extends her mic hand in the air.)

...Filipina!

(GITA plays "Kiss of Fire" and dances Secret Agent dance. She stops and peers into the audience.)

Filipinas? Filipinas anyone?

(House lights come up. This section varies, and may be completely improvised, according to audience response. GITA walks into the audience, continuing to address them via the mic. She offers them the mic briefly to answer, and then lifts the Minus One deck to her ear as if "hearing" instructions on how she should respond.)

Are you Filipino? Prove it! What do you have in your pantry right now...do you have SPAM? VELVEETA? Hmmm....I'll have to get a full dossier from headquarters on your...supposed Filipinoness...!

(GITA plays "Kiss of Fire" and dances Secret Agent dance. She stops and addresses the audience again.)

Anyone else? Filipinas? Are you Filipino? Prove it! How many shoes did Imelda have when she fled Malaca–ang Palace? Are you sure that's your answer? She had...one thousand, two hundred and sixty...seven! Because she lost one...in flight!

(House lights fade as she Secret Agent dances to music. She stops to reflect.)

It is not always fun and games being Secret Agent Filipina, because I have accepted the lifelong mission of being...undercover!

(She puts down the Minus One and lowers her head, then with a whoosh of her hand lifts her head in presentation, and looks blankly ahead.)

Example! Operation: covert interaction with the Pilipino public! Location: the Philippine Independence Day Parade—a food booth! My people are...everywhere! But I am...

(She repeats the undercover gesture.)

...undercover!

(Relaxing, she excitedly addresses the food booth.)

Hi! I would like...one green mango with bagoong, please! How do I know what green mango and bagoong is?...Don't you know who I am...I am Secret Ag...

(She begins to do Secret Agent salute, but then covers it up.)

...I mean...Why are you laughing? Well, actually I...My mother is from the Philippines. Yes, really! No, I can't speak Tagalog, but...You don't have to laugh. Why are you bringing over all of your friends...? Don't you know...who I am...don't you....

(In a panic, she picks up the Minus One and tries to press play to "hear" instructions. "Chiquitita" plays. Shocked and confused, she clutches the Minus One, and then resigns to put it down. Gathering herself, she addresses the food booth again.)

You don't know who I am? Well...I know who I am! I am...the Filipina who wants her green mango with bagoong! NOW!

(As GITA extends her hand for the mango, her two Titas enter and line up behind her. She turns around and sees them, hesitates then walks back ceremoniously between them. Turning to one, GITA curtsies and takes the back of her Tita's hand to her forehead in respect, and they dance in a tango-esque circle to the music. She turns and repeats the "Mano" ritual with her other Tita, with increasing joy. Lights and music fade out.)

ASIA FILES

Written and Performed by Ed Lin and Ching-Ching Ni

(Stage dark, but not completely black. Dimly lit like the interior of a movie theater. ANONYMOUS CHINESE MAN, in T-shirt and jeans, sits in folding chair in middle of stage. ASIAN MULDER and ASIAN SCULLY, dressed like their television counterparts, run through audience with flashlights as theme from "X Files" plays. Music dies down as ASIAN MULDER and ASIAN SCULLY make way to stage. ASIAN SCULLY and ASIAN MULDER, now at Front Stage Right and Stage Left, respectively, shine flashlights onto each other's faces.)

ASIAN SCULLY: *(In a loud whisper)* Asian Mulder! Where are we?

ASIAN MULDER: *(Whispers)* Asian Scully! We're in the Music Palace, the last movie theater in Chinatown!

(Begins slowly walking to ASIAN SCULLY, behind ANONYMOUS CHINESE MAN's seat.)

ASIAN SCULLY: *(Whispers)* This place smells awful!

ASIAN MULDER: *(Whispers)* Lonely Chinese men come here to kill time.

(Reaches ASIAN SCULLY, stands next to her)

ASIAN SCULLY: *(Whispers)* What's a nice guy like you doing in a dump like this?

ASIAN MULDER: *(Whispers)* I come here to see the beautiful Hong Kong movie stars.

(ANONYMOUS CHINESE MAN slumps over onto ground at ASIAN MULDER's feet and comes to rest on his back.)

ASIAN SCULLY: *(Screams)* Freeze! Federal Asians!

(ASIAN MULDER turns off flashlight, pockets it, lights go up.)

ASIAN MULDER: He's dead.

(Takes ASIAN SCULLY's flashlight and pockets it. ASIAN SCULLY drops to knees and touches ANONYMOUS CHINESE MAN's body.)

ASIAN SCULLY: There's no visible signs of trauma.

(Pulls up ANONYMOUS CHINESE MAN's head a few inches as if to administer mouth-to-mouth. In a knowing way, ASIAN MULDER kneels down, pulls open ANONYMOUS CHINESE MAN's mouth, retrieving note.)

ASIAN MULDER: Except for this suicide note.

(Stands up, reads from note)

ASIAN MULDER: "Goodbye, cruel world. I'm not getting any."

ASIAN SCULLY: Any what?

ASIAN MULDER: Well, he wrote it on an unused condom.

(ASIAN SCULLY opens evidence bag and ASIAN MULDER puts condom into it. Movement is slow and sexually suggestive.)

ASIAN SCULLY: Why would he come to the Music Palace to die?

(Moves to chair, pulling ANONYMOUS CHINESE MAN. ASIAN SCULLY sits in chair, cradling ANONYMOUS CHINESE MAN's head. ANONYMOUS CHINESE MAN is in sitting position on floor. ASIAN MULDER moves to front stage right, looking into distance, as if looking for UFOs.)

ASIAN MULDER: Maybe he wanted to see Chinese men and women in love.

(ASIAN SCULLY pulls up ANONYMOUS CHINESE MAN's shirt, exposing chest.)

ASIAN SCULLY: Look! Look at all this writing on his chest! 'Maggie Cheung.' 'Anita Mui.' 'Ming-na Wen.' These are all women he could never have!

(In a knowing way, ASIAN MULDER walks up to ANONYMOUS CHINESE MAN, back to audience and apparently unzips ANONYMOUS CHINESE MAN's fly.)

ASIAN MULDER: And what do we have here! "Asian Scully"!

(Zips fly back up. ASIAN SCULLY jumps up, runs to front stage right. ASIAN MULDER walks to front stage left. Both face audience, not looking at each other.)

ASIAN SCULLY: Asian Mulder! I have a confession to make! I know this man.

(Sounds a little embarrassed)

We went out a few times...

ASIAN MULDER: *(Faces ASIAN SCULLY)* He must have been pretty desperate.

ASIAN SCULLY: *(Faces ASIAN MULDER)* I told him I had a boyfriend.

ASIAN MULDER: You just don't go for Asians.

ASIAN SCULLY: My boyfriend's Filipino!

ASIAN MULDER: Filipinos aren't Asian! Not like you or me. *(Softer)* Or this dead guy down here.

(Gestures to ANONYMOUS CHINESE MAN)

ASIAN SCULLY: Filipinos are Asian enough because they like me!
And Filipinos would never let themselves get so lonely they get stuck at the Music Palace on a Saturday night!

ASIAN MULDER: Sometimes I come here on Fridays.

(Arms raised in pleading gesture, walks slowly toward ASIAN MULDER)

ASIAN SCULLY: Asian Mulder, you know I've been looking my whole life for that perfect...Chinese man.

(Drops to knees at ANONYMOUS CHINESE MAN's body. Pulls ANONYMOUS CHINESE MAN into upright position.)

ASIAN SCULLY: Someone who can slow dance with me to Chairman Mao love songs!

(Pulls ANONYMOUS CHINESE MAN's arms and embraces ANONYMOUS CHINESE MAN's upper body in a dance partner position. Cheek to cheek with ANONYMOUS CHINESE MAN.)

ASIAN SCULLY: Someone who's not afraid of passion! Someone who understands that small is beautiful!

(Pulls up ANONYMOUS CHINESE MAN's shirt and caresses exposed breasts and then pulls him up on his feet as they stand face to face.)

ASIAN SCULLY: Someone who will let me look for my father in his Chinese eyes!

(Turns ANONYMOUS CHINESE MAN's head to point to ASIAN MULDER)

ASIAN MULDER: You see your father in all Chinese men?

ASIAN SCULLY: Yes!

(*Throws ANONYMOUS CHINESE MAN at ASIAN MULDER. ASIAN MULDER catches ANONY-MOUS CHINESE MAN, stumbles then supports ANONYMOUS CHINESE MAN at shoulder. The two look like a study for a war memorial.*)

ASIAN SCULLY: That's why I go for Filipinos.

ASIAN MULDER: Asian Scully, I have evidence that suggests direct government intervention in preventing Chinese men from dating Chinese women!

ASIAN SCULLY: Asian Mulder, you're letting your personal feelings get in the way, again! Where's your proof?

ASIAN MULDER: Asian Scully, I also have a confession to make. I know this man, too.

(*Drops ANONYMOUS CHINESE MAN into kneeling position. Walks in semicircle behind ANONYMOUS CHINESE MAN, facing ANONYMOUS CHINESE MAN entire time.*)

ASIAN MULDER: We both wanted to be writers, but our parents forced us to go to engineering school. It was like living in a single-sex society. You take classes like "Sexuality in Crime Fiction" just to meet women. But the only thing they teach you is what good writers white guys are. And all the Asian women hooked up with white guys. (*Softly*) And I was the best writer in that class. I was the best FUCKING writer in that class!

(*Lets ANONYMOUS CHINESE MAN gently onto back, closes ANONYMOUS CHINESE MAN's eyes.*)

ASIAN MULDER: Sometimes people don't appreciate what you've written until you're dead. Even if all you ever wrote was a suicide note.

(*Walks back to stage left, faces audience*)

ASIAN MULDER: So, Asian Scully, do you still believe the perfect Chinese man really exists?

ASIAN SCULLY: I know he's out there...I can feel him.

(*Looks above as if looking for UFOs*)

ASIAN MULDER: What does he look like?

ASIAN SCULLY: I don't know...I've never been close enough to find out.

(*Walks to ASIAN SCULLY*)

ASIAN MULDER: He might be standing right next to you.

ASIAN SCULLY: How would I know he's real?

ASIAN MULDER: *(Softly)* Asian Scully...

(ASIAN SCULLY turns and seems shocked to see ASIAN MULDER so close, so obviously emotional, as if recognizing him as the perfect Chinese man.)

ASIAN SCULLY: Asian Mulder?

(ASIAN MULDER takes ASIAN SCULLY's hands and holds them to his face.)

ASIAN MULDER: Touch me.

(Lights fade out)

THE RIGHT STUFF
Written and Performed by Gary San Angel

A confessional booth glides across the stage. There are no panels. The interior is completely visible. Inside, a priest-like figure dressed in white lights Roman Catholic candles. An Alleluia Spiritual sung by monks can be heard in the distance.

I like…
I like…
To touch…
Myself…
I try to do it at least two times a day.
I don't know why I do it.
I just do.
It makes me feel so good inside.
I remember the first time I touched it.
It was like I was on fire.

I was twelve and I had just finished watching the movie *The Right Stuff*. And all I could think about was this one scene where the nurse asked the astronaut played by Dennis Quaid for a sperm sample. He didn't know how to do it so the nurse threw him some dirty magazines and shut him in a room all by himself. And I began to wonder what it was like and how it…

Felt like…
And that night I could not stop thinking about it. The feeling inside me started to grow and I could not squish it back.

(The confessional begins to creak as it slowly rocks back and forth.)

It began to ask me. Beckon me. And I could not resist.
So I just let myself…
I let myself feeel…
It…
Ohh… Ahhh…

My whole body became stiff and hot. My legs were sweating and I just kept going. I just could not let go. I wanted to show my right stuff. But then every time I felt it I saw the Virgin Mary and God standing right there with me and they were not very happy. This was not good behavior for someone who is preparing to be an altar boy.

Oh, God. GOD. Ohhhh. GAWWD. Noo. Noooo.

sorreee..

(Begins praying)

HAIL MARY! FULL OF GRACE! THE LORD IS WITH YOU! BLESSED!! ARE YOU
AMONGST WOMEN!! AND BLESSSES!!! BLESSSEED IS THE FRUIT... OF THY WOMB!!
JESUS...
JEESUS!!

(Rocking grows even more frenetic.)

PLEASE!! STOP!!
OOHHHH! GOD! NOOOO... NOOOOO...
YOUR NOT SUPPOSED TO DO THIS!!!
NOOOO! NOOOOOO! NOOOOOOO!
AHHHHHHHHHHHHH!

(Climaxes)

Something started to spill out and it wasn't pee.
It was gooey and it smelled real awful like the stench of Clorox bleach.
Oh God. My mom must have heard me. She was sleeping in the other room. What would she think?
Oh God...
OH!! NO!!
OH, GOD!!
I SPILLED IT ON THE BED!!!
Sh!! Shhhh!!
Be quiet. Don't tell anyone.
Please. Please.

(The confessional turns and becomes the inside of a bathroom. He rubs his hands in front of an imaginary sink
and mirror.)

I just went to the bathroom and I scrubbed my hands with soap and hot water and I threw my
underwear at the bottom of the hamper because I didn't want my mom to smell my sex.

(It now becomes the bed. He lies down.)

Before I got to bed I stared at that bed stain.
I laid beside it.
And I began to wonder...
When would be the next time...
I will...

Touch myself.

(Blows out candles. Blackout)

SEX 2
Written and Performed by Ed Lin

A man is seen in the dimly lit shadows of a spotlight. He is speaking gently into a mic. He has no glasses and no red book.

You say I've got a one-track mind But it's only because I've been working on the railroads for so long

Darling, bring your eyebrows to mine
And I will kiss you soft as butterfly nets
And hold you closer than memories
Of a misspent youth

With my—in your—
I promise
It'll be so good
I promise

Think of an island spelled like the letter O
With too many colors to fit in the circumference of the eye
You say I'm just a computer geek
But like a PC
I will go down on you when you need me the most

With your—in my—
I promise
It'll be so good
I promise

Then we'll lie together
And I will kiss you soft as butterfly wings
And hold you closer than Incan blocks
Forever
Or at least until you fall asleep

(Lights fade out)

THE VOICE BEHIND THE JAZZ

By Dave Lin

Fade in. "Blue in Green" by Miles Davis plays in background. Lights come up and we see the silhouette of DAVE, a radio announcer.

DAVE: You're listening to WUSB, Jazz 90.3 on your FM dial. I'm Dave Lin, bringing you the best of the old and the new, from now until 5 AM. Thanks for tuning in. My phone number here is 632-5500. For you cats across the water, that's a 516 area code. Call in your requests, or call just to say, "Hi!" Right now, I'm gonna kick it off with some Miles, from his *Kind of Blue* album. I'll play it first, and tell you what it is later.

(The announcer's face is revealed.)

DAVE: Freshman year was an awkward time for me. In the first few months, I shied away from people. Immersed myself in school and in my college work-study job at the campus radio station as the night-time jazz DJ. I played the music I liked, and people liked what I played. Miles. Mingus. Coltrane. Dizzy. Sonny. Toshiko. I played them all. I had regular listeners. I had   regular callers. Drugged-out jazz hippies...

DRUGGED-OUT JAZZ HIPPIE: *(Sound of inhalation/exhalation)* Dave! Big Dave! What's up, Dave? Here! Yo! My man, settle a bet for me and my buddies... Was Duke's big comeback performance at Newport in 1956 or 1957?

DAVE: Paranoid angry loners...

PARANOID ANGRY LONER: Those microwaves you're beamin' into my head are sendin' me a message. They're tellin' me to come over there and hit you over the head with a lacrosse stick and trash your studio! Whaddaya think of that, Jazz boy? You hip to that, you friggin' be-bop playin' bastard?

DAVE: Sleepless alcoholics.

SLEEPLESS ALCOHOLIC: Hey, Dave. Can you play some Kenny G? I fuckin' love Kenny G!

DAVE: Jilted lovers.

JILTED LOVER: Can you play the next song for my ex-girlfriend Serena? She won't return my calls! Could you say that I won't turn off the gas until she calls me?

DAVE: And occasionally...

SEXY FEMALE VOICE: Hey, Dave. I can't sleep. Can I come over to the studio and hang out?

DAVE: I never took any of those offers. Because I knew from past experiences what would happen if those women met me. But then, one night, she called. USB.

MARIA: Hey, can I speak to Dave?

DAVE: You got me. How's it going?

MARIA: Pretty good. I just wanted to call and say I love your show. I don't usually like jazz, but I've been tuning in for the last few weeks.

DAVE: Let me guess. I'm the only station that comes in on your stereo.

MARIA: (Laughs) Well, that is true. But I do enjoy the music you play. And I really like your voice. I'm really glad you quit smoking.

DAVE: How'd you know I quit smoking?

MARIA: Because I used to always hear you blowing smoke and lighting your cigarettes. I haven't heard that for the last couple of shows.

DAVE: 17 days since my last cigarette.

MARIA: Congratulations! I'm glad you quit. You sound too cute to be a smoker.

DAVE: (Pause) Are you hitting on me?

MARIA: It all depends. Are you single?

DAVE: Yes, but I don't date my listeners.

MARIA: The station won't let you date listeners? Even me?

(Pause)

DAVE: No. It's a personal rule I keep. Hold on for a sec...

That was Miles doing "Blue in Green." This next one's for my man Chris, who's studying late into the night for his organic chemistry midterm. This is a song called "Misterioso" by the great Thelonius Monk. Just remember, Chris, when in doubt, you can always use the Grignard reaction to link anything together. Keep the faith, brother...USB.

MARIA: Dave?

DAVE: Hello?

MARIA: You hung up on me!

DAVE: I'm sorry about that. I'm still learning how to use the phones around here.

MARIA: That's OK. Can I ask you a question?

DAVE: Sure.

MARIA: Is the reason you won't go out with me something to do with my voice?

DAVE: Excuse me?

MARIA: My accent?

DAVE: You don't have an accent. You have a beautiful voice.

MARIA: Thanks! But I moved here when I was six. I learned English as a second language, and it took me a while to speak it. I still have a little bit of an accent.

DAVE: I can't hear it. Where are you from?

MARIA: *(Slight pause)* I'm Chinese. My parents are from Hong Kong.

DAVE: Really?

MARIA: Uh huh. Have you ever been with a Chinese girl?

DAVE: Actually, I haven't. I've never been with a Chinese girl. A strange thing for a Chinese guy to say, huh?

MARIA: *(Pause)* You're Chinese? Are you half black or something?

DAVE: No. I'm all Chinese.

MARIA: Wow. You don't sound like, uh…

DAVE: Like I'm Chinese?

MARIA: You must get that a lot?

DAVE: Not really. I think you're the first listener I've ever told. It's never come up before. I've never had any reason to…hello?

MARIA: I'm still here.

DAVE: Are you?

MARIA: Yeah…listen, this is really going to sound bad…but I thought you were…well, not Chinese. I thought you were probably black, and I really like black men.

DAVE: Well, I'm sorry I'm not.

MARIA: I hope you're not upset with me.

DAVE: Not at all. In fact, I'm gonna play a song for you. What's your name?

MARIA: Maria.

DAVE: Well, Maria, you have a good night. And keep listening…This next song's for my friend Maria, who I sincerely hope finds what she's looking for. This is "Fair Weather" by Chet Baker. I'm Dave Lin. 90.3 WUSB.

(*DAVE searches for, finds, and lights a cigarette.*)

END OF PLAY EXCERPTS

SILENT MOVIE

By Jessica Hagedorn

SILENT MOVIE is a ten-minute play which was originally commissioned by Chay Yew and the Asian American Theatre Project at the Mark Taper Forum in 1996, as part of a larger piece called THE SQUARE. THE SQUARE involved the contributions of many other playwrights, all commissioned to create their own ten-minute pieces. Han Ong, Maria Irene Fornes, Constance Congdon, David Henry Hwang and Tony Kushner were among the playwrights included. Aside from the ten-minute length, one of the main stipulations was that the plays were to be set in New York City's Chinatown. Each writer was also assigned a specific year and a specific number of characters. Everything else (race, gender, class, conflict, etc.) was left up to the play-wright. I was assigned four characters and the year 1920.

JESSICA HAGEDORN

SILENT MOVIE was originally developed in the Center Theatre Group/Mark Taper Forum Asian Theatre Workshop Gordon Davidson, Artistic Director/Producer. It was first presented at the Mark Taper Forum in Los Angeles on December 17 & 18, 1997 as part of the "New Work Festival # 10." with the following cast and crew:

EMMA HANLON: Liann Pattison
LUCY BURROWS: Jodi Thelen
MAN: David Warshofsky

Directed by Lisa Peterson

Dramaturg: Chay Yew
Stage Manager: David S. Franklin
Set Consultant: Rachel Hauck
Lighting Consultant: Geoff Korf
Costume Consultant: Joyce Kim Lee
Sound Consultant: Nathan Wang
Directing Assistant: Wendy McClellan
Literary Assistant: Padraic Duffy
Production Assistants: Anna Louise Paul, Stephanie Schaefer

SILENT MOVIE

A dark, unfurnished room above the curio shop. The only window is covered by a makeshift curtain of flimsy transparent fabric. Lights fade up on EMMA HANLON, a politician's wife, naked and barefoot under her long, black velvet cloak. She is a fading beauty in her late forties—make-up smeared, hair disheveled. EMMA cautiously peers out the window. She obviously does not want to be seen. By the door a couple of expensive suitcases and a worn carpetbag have been set down. Scattered about are Emma's dress, stockings, high-heeled slippers, and an evening purse with its contents spilled—cigarette case, money, gloves, keys, and a silver flask, which EMMA grabs. As she paces tensely around the shadowy room, EMMA sips greedily from the flask. A freak storm rages outside. Sounds of rain pouring down. Distant thunder. Lightning brightens the room, making EMMA jump.

LUCY BURROWS, Emma's personal maid, is sprawled on a pallet downstage. She is in her slip. LUCY is twenty, Emma's physical opposite. Her unpainted face is an inscrutable mask, all angles and planes—her body lean and strong. LUCY seems totally at ease in the dark, sucking contentedly on an opium pipe. Next to her is another pallet, another pipe—possibly Emma's—and drug paraphernalia arranged on a tray. Tiny spoons, a bowl, matches. A short black rubber straw. A razor. The residue of cocaine and gummy opium on a saucer.

EMMA: I told you. We should've waited.

LUCY: No way. Tonight's our only chance.

EMMA: We're in deep shit now. Dear God. Why'd I listen to you? You're just a—

LUCY: What? Yer l'il dumb maid? *(Pause)* Oh, Emma. Stop.

EMMA: Stop? The rain won't stop. And then what?

LUCY: Then nothing. We ain't goin' back.

EMMA: That's right. It's flooding pigshit out there and I'm stuck in this Chinatown shithole with you and can't go home—

LUCY: —because you're high. Face it Emma. You're too high, and it's OK, and you're never goin' back.

EMMA: He'll find us.

LUCY: Shut up. You said he'd be away till tomorrow. *(Pause)* He ain't found us yet, has he? Hasn't figured any of it out, and it's been a whole year. *(Laughing softly)*

EMMA: Don't tell me to shut up. You're getting just a wee bit too cocky, dear. *(Pause)* I know he knows. He's known all along—

LUCY: You're high.

(Silence. EMMA glares furiously at LUCY, who ignores her. A series of low, urgent knocks at the door startles them both.)

LUCY: *(Mutters to herself)* What the fuck.

EMMA: *(Frantic)* Oh Jesus shit. Mother of Mary. I knew it. *(Backs up against the wall, terrified)* What shall we do, Lucy?

LUCY: Will you calm down? *(Struggles off the pallet, then crawls slowly to the door and speaks in a hoarse whisper)* Uncle Wong? Is that you? *(Pause)* Everything OK! We're getting ready to go, promise! Soon as...soon as the weather changes...soon as the sky goes from gray to black...*(Pause)* There. He's gone. Emma.

EMMA: It's not the Chink I'm worried about.

LUCY: *(Offers her the pipe)* Here. Better than your damn whiskey.

EMMA: *(Hysterical, knocking the pipe out of Lucy's hand)* Are you listening to me? It's not that harmless old man I'm worried about. It's my husband! Don't you understand he wants to kill me? And you! *You!*

LUCY: *(Stonefaced)* Don't ever do that again.

EMMA: I'm sorry, Lucy. *(Gets on her knees and crawls around in the dark to find the pipe, which she cautiously hands back to Lucy.)* I'm sorry—

LUCY: Don't ever. *(Refills the pipe, offers it to EMMA. Her tone softens.)* I think you need to slow down and refresh yourself, Mrs. Hanlon.

(EMMA lays on the pallet next to LUCY and reluctantly takes a deep toke. She watches while LUCY snorts cocaine.)

EMMA: That powder's evil. I hate when you get so damn arrogant.

LUCY: *(Amused)* Yeah? And I hate yer damn whiskey breath. And whiskey sweat.

EMMA: *(Agitated again)* Oh, Lucy, sweet Jesus. Let's get out of here. We'll find another way out of town. We will—

LUCY: You just jumpy, that's all. Rain'll let up soon. It's early—nothin' to fret about. We'll get away soon enough. We're halfway there, ain't we? We'll be outta this shithole, soon as the sky... *(EMMA nods off into sleep.)* Dream a while. Yeah. That's it. *(Pause)* I hate you sometimes. Hate havin' to make it all better for you, the way I always do, like I'm expected to. You pay me enough. I s'pose. And you trust me. *(Pause)* I love you too, Mrs. Hanlon. I know how to make you cry, don't I? Stupid pitiful Emma. Beautiful Emma. And you love me back in your own way. Lookit you. Old enough to be my mother. Cow. Beautiful cow. Moo. I love makin' you moo. *(Pause)* But we can't stay here forever, darlin'. Too dangerous. Uncle Wong will most definitely be back. We make him nervous, don't we? I hate the way he scurries around after takin' our...*your* money. Can't wait for us to leave! He's worse than a girl. *(Shouts at the door, waking EMMA briefly. EMMA drifts back into sleep.)* I KNOW YOU'RE THERE. YA OLD GEEZER! EAVESDROPPIN' AND PEEPIN AT US! *(Grabs rubber straw and pokes it through keyhole)* ARE YA PLAYIN' WITH YOURSELF AGAIN? I CAN HEAR YA GASPING AND WHEEZIN' IN CHINESE! *(to audience)* "The Chink's scared shitless of my husband," Emma says. *(Pause)* That's milady's favorite word: SHIT. *(Mocking and mimicking)* "Hurry, hurry, missee. Don't want no trouble. Why you no get stuff from Uncle Wong and just take home? Go home, misses! No safe here! No safe here!" *(Laughing)* Can you imagine? Emma Hanlon, smokin' goo in the privacy of her bedroom? Makin' hoochie-coochie with me, her little servant, while Mr. Bigshot's at the office? Yeah, sure, Uncle Wong. *(To audience)* She likes goin' to the pictures. That's how it all started. The bigshot husband had no time, but she had all the time in the world.

(EMMA sits up, disoriented.)

EMMA: Come with me to the pictures.

(EMMA gazes out at the audience as if she is watching a movie. As she and LUCY speak, flickering, unfocused images from the 1919 D.W. Griffith film, Broken Blossoms, are projected on the wall behind them)

LUCY: *(To audience)* I felt sorry for her. Sure, I said. Anything to get outta cleanin' that mansion of hers. Every damn day the same old grind. *(Image of Lillian Gish as the movie version of LUCY BURROWS, in the squalid hovel she shares with her father. She is on her knees, tearfully wiping her angry father's shoes as he stands there glowering at her.)* Dustin' where there ain't no dust, moppin' them already shiny floors, scrubbin' spotless toilets. Fixin' food she don't eat. She don't like food. You wouldn't know it, lookin' at her... Would ya? *(Touching Emma's hip tenderly)* All that *flesh*. *(Pause)* They got a son somewhere I've never seen, sent away to school in another country. She don't like him, either. *(Pause)* I made my eyes real big and round, like this *(Demonstrates)*—"Swell, Mrs. Hanlon. I've never been to the pictures"—

EMMA: Poor thing.

LUCY: Guess she felt sorry for me, too. I acted all meek and grateful. Like my Pa didn't teach me to be. Like my Ma, well—she's dead, so it don't matter. Folks say I take after Pa, anyway. *(Pause)* Anyway. Off we went to the Bijou. *(Pause)* What a dumb picture. *(Movie projection stops.)* I couldn't wait to get outta there. *(To EMMA)* Please, Mrs. Hanlon.

EMMA: It's beautiful. Let's sit through it, again. Please, Lucy. Think of it like a beautiful, scary dream.

LUCY: No thanks. I come from a family of lunatics, and I think you're just like them, Mrs. Hanlon.

EMMA: *(Bursts out laughing)* You're a funny dear. Why don't you call me Emma? *(Stares at her, then kisses her impulsively)* Forgive me. I must truly be out of my mind. Please, dear. Don't tell anyone. I promise I'll never do it again.

LUCY: *(Kisses EMMA)* Then I'll do it. *(Pause)* Emma.

EMMA: I know this place where we can be alone. You ever been to Chinatown?

LUCY: Sure. Once or twice.

EMMA: I grew up there, before the Chinks moved in.

LUCY: I thought you were rich.

EMMA: My husband's rich. *(Pause)* I know this place on Baxter Street, right by where I was born. We'll have fun.

LUCY: Fun. *(Dryly)* I don't know the meaning of the word.

EMMA: I'll show you.

(A thunderclap explosion. Terrified, EMMA makes a move to bolt and run, but LUCY stops her. They struggle until EMMA finally gives up, exhausted and resigned. The two women stare at each other for a moment, the sound of rain pouring down.)

EMMA: *(Sheds her cloak)* Dance with me again.

LUCY: Sure.

(As LUCY and EMMA make love in the dark, specific clips from Broken Blossoms *are projected on the walls, but clearly this time. The entire room is bathed in these black and white images; the images are not shown*

in order, and can be repeated. Richard Barthelmess in obsequious, effeminate pose as "The Chink," his taped eye-lids perpetually downcast. Lillian Gish as the abused Irish girl, LUCY BURROWS, cowering in terror from her brutal, drunken father, played by Donald Crisp. The Chink attempting to kiss the terrified White Girl, then suddenly pulling away from her in shame. The White Girl's immense look of relief. Her subtitles which read: "What makes you so good to me, Chinky?" The enraged Drunken Father killing his daughter. The Chink shooting the Father, then carrying the White Girl's limp body back to his curio shop. The grief-stricken Chink kneeling on the floor by the bed on which the White Girl's corpse lies, then stabbing himself to death in glorious slow-motion.)

EMMA: *(Disengaging herself from LUCY)* Good. The rain's stopped. We can go.

LUCY: What's the hurry? *(Teasing)* You're hurtin' my feelings, Mrs. Hanlon.

(The naked EMMA starts putting on her clothes. For a brief moment, the room is eerily lit by lightening. A sound outside the door.)

LUCY: Not again.

EMMA: *(Nervous)* Is that you, Uncle Wong?

LUCY: *(Taking another hit of cocaine)* He don't understand English.

(The door is kicked open by a brawny, fiftyish white man dressed in an elegant suit, overcoat and hat. He points a gun at EMMA.)

EMMA: *(To man)* I knew you'd find us.

(The man shoots EMMA. She collapses. He shoots her a second time, then a third. Meanwhile, LUCY has pulled her own revolver from under the pallet. She points it at the man. The man, aiming his gun at her, hesi-tates.)

LUCY: Go ahead. You'll either die with me—or die first.

(LUCY shoots. The man drops to the floor, near EMMA. LUCY stares down at them for a moment. She runs to the window and tries to climb out to escape, but realizes how high up she is and loses her nerve. She goes to the door and peeks out into the dimly-lit hallway.)

LUCY: *(Soft and tentative)* Uncle Wong? Where are ya, old man? *(Pause)* Ah, Mother of God, he got you too.

(LUCY gets dressed quickly. She rummages through the dead man's pockets and takes his wallet. She starts to take his gun, then changes her mind. Kneeling down next to EMMA's body, she runs a hand gently over

EMMA's open eyes, to close them. LUCY snatches her gun, EMMA's spilled money, and, after snorting the last of the precious cocaine, takes what's left of the opium. She stuffs everything into the carpetbag and starts to leave, then turns back once more to survey the room. EMMA's luxurious cloak lies on the floor. LUCY scoops it up and wraps herself in it. She slowly backs out the door. Lights fade down.)

END OF PLAY

JAMAICA AVENUE

By Chiori Miyagawa

In JAMAICA AVENUE, a woman says, "When the lightning strikes a tree in California, monarch butterflies die in Mexico. We are all part of the same web." It is a play about something profound that connects all of us, perhaps not only in this life time and dimension, but beyond, with our ancestors and ghosts and guardian spirits. Everything we do has relevance; we are responsible for each other, for what we have become and for what we will be.

"Seven" punctures the story of JAMAICA AVENUE: the first part spans over seven years; there is a seven-year gap between the two parts; and the second part takes place in seven days. In Buddhism, the number seven has a significant meaning. After death, a soul is supposed to stay in Bardo for seven days. If it does not find a place of reincarnation, it will remain there for seven more days. It can repeat this for seven cycles, up to 49 days. I did not know this as a child growing up in Japan, but I remember whenever there was a death, families officially mourned for 49 days. They seemed to feel a little better after all the rituals that happen during the 49 days following a death were completed. Although in Buddhism coming back to life means suffering, I still view this cycle as a symbol of healing and renewal, a hope in doing it right this time.

My deepest inspiration lives in His Holiness The Fourteenth Dalai Lama of Tibet. I write to keep the promise I made to him: to make small attempts in changing people's mind about hate.

CHIORI MIYAGAWA

JAMAICA AVENUE was first presented at the New York International Fringe Festival in August 1998 at The Soho Repertory Theatre

Directed by Sonoko Kawahara
Dramturg: Judythe Cohen
Lights: Lap-Chi Chu
Costume: Anne Lommel
Set: David Martin
Associate Producer: Michael Yawney

Cast:
CARLOS: Clark Jackson
LAUREN: Anna Wilson
WOMAN/YUMI: Sophia Skiles
INTRUDER: David Altman

JAMAICA AVENUE is scheduled for a workshop at The Women's Project and Productions in the 1999-2000 season. This new version of the play will have songs, lyrics written by Mark Campbell, music composed by Fabian Obispo.

For Kevin

Time:
The play spans over fourteen years of love,
disappointments, and hope.

Place:
New York City

Characters:
CARLOS: African American or Latino Man
LAUREN: Caucasian Woman
WOMAN/YUMI: Asian Woman
INTRUDER: voice over when necessary

CARLOS and LAUREN age seven years in Part I. Their physical deterioration is paralleled by that of
an emotional one.

Part I spans over seven years, Part II seven days. Seven years pass between Part I and II. LAUREN
stops aging at the end of Part I. CARLOS is seven years older at the beginning of Part II, but much
healthier.

WOMAN/YUMI remains the same age throughout the play.
In Part I Scene 1 and in Part II, YUMI's speech pattern should be somewhat different from
WOMAN's.

Jamaica Avenue

Part 1

Scene 1

Two young women stand facing each other. LAUREN is dressed in a ragged fur coat. WOMAN is in summer clothes. Woman holds a large shopping bag.

LAUREN: Excuse me, can I see your bag? Oh, I've heard of that store. They got nice things?

WOMAN: Yes.

LAUREN: What did you get?

WOMAN: Candles.

LAUREN: My father used to tell me about it. He's dead now. He was gonna take me shopping to the store someday. For a fur coat. Do you know what it's like to feel you deserve the best, but fate fucked you up just enough so your father ends up dead?

WOMAN: You'll be alright.

LAUREN: It's funny, you think it's a small thing, but it isn't. It'll never be all right. The empty space gets deeper and deeper in you, and you just can't get out. There are bigger problems. People are starving. Still, your personal tragedy, whatever it is, will ruin you in the end. It won't be alright.

WOMAN: I have to go.

LAUREN: Don't go. What day is it today?

WOMAN: It's Wednesday.

LAUREN: How long have I been crying?

WOMAN: Seven years.

(WOMAN takes a candle out of her bag and hands it to LAUREN. She exits, leaving LAUREN looking at the candle.)

Scene 2

Seven years earlier. A dingy, desolate bar. The TV is playing. CARLOS has been looking at LAUREN who is at the juke box. LAUREN is in her early 20s, dressed "sexy." She occasionally looks over to him. After a while, she approaches him. Woman is sitting next to CARLOS at the bar, listening.

LAUREN: Hi.

CARLOS: Hi.

LAUREN: I'm Lauren.

CARLOS: Carlos.

LAUREN: You live around here?

CARLOS: Flatbush.

LAUREN: You wanna come get some pizza with me?

CARLOS: OK.

WOMAN: Seven years.

CARLOS: What?

WOMAN: Seven years of descent into the deep, dark pit until you find the pink spider.

CARLOS: Do I know you? *(To LAUREN)* Let's go.

WOMAN: Where are you going?

CARLOS: I'm going to the theater. It's the opening night. I gotta get dressed up and pick up some flowers. Does that meet your approval?

WOMAN: I'll see you at the theater.

LAUREN: Is she your girlfriend or something?

CARLOS: I've never seen her before in my life. She must be nuts.

(They exit. WOMAN sits alone and watches TV and drinks.)

Scene 3

The pizzeria.

CARLOS: Do you like pepperoni on your pizza?

LAUREN: It's OK. I really like white pizza. They don't have it here.

CARLOS: What's that?

LAUREN: You don't know? It's pizza with ricotta cheese. No tomato sauce.

CARLOS: That's strange.

LAUREN: It's the new thing. I like it because it looks soft. And nothing drips. Like a perfectly made bed. When I have a house of my own, I'm gonna have all white sheets and comforters and pillows and curtains with wall to wall soft white carpet.

CARLOS: Nice. Where do you live now?

LAUREN: Oh, with my mother. I'm moving out soon. She wants me to get a job at the donut factory or something and pay her rent. She doesn't understand who I am.

CARLOS: My father wanted me to learn refrigerator repair. But I didn't want to be anything like him.

LAUREN: What did you want?

CARLOS: I don't know. My father always said if I didn't get my act together, I'd be fucked up for life. When I didn't make it to the senior year, I thought, shit, I fucked up. There is no way to make it right anyway, so I dropped outta school. After that I stayed home a while. I watched my parents go to work, come home, eat dinner watching TV, and go to bed everyday. I don't spend the evenings there anymore. My father doesn't talk to my mother. I feel bad for her.

LAUREN: Most married people don't talk. My daddy is dead. But when he was alive, he never talked to my mother. He drove the bread truck, you know, the Sunbeam bread. He would leave the house real early to make deliveries. He worked hard. But the bitch slept like a pig and didn't clean the house. My mother is ignorant. If daddy was alive, he'd understand what I'm about.

CARLOS: What do you mean?

LAUREN: I mean I'm nothing like my mother. I'm a freelance artist. Fashion designer. I design celebrities' clothes.

CARLOS: Wow. Who?

LAUREN: Oh, TV and movie stars. But I'm not working right now. Things are slow.

CARLOS: The pizza is on me.

LAUREN: Thanks. Next time, we'll go to Manhattan for white pizza. My treat.

CARLOS: Sounds good.

LAUREN: When I have my white house, you can come live with me if you want.

CARLOS: Sounds good.

Scene 4

Another day. A restaurant.

LAUREN: Try a piece of mine.

CARLOS: What is it?

LAUREN: Raw fish and rice.

CARLOS: Noooo, thank you. I'll stick to my cooked food. Chicken something. Chicken Terayaku.

LAUREN: I can't believe you don't eat sushi. Everyone I know eats sushi. I've eaten sushi with Al Pacino.

CARLOS: Yeah?

LAUREN: Yeah, I used to design his girlfriend's clothes, you know.

CARLOS: Maybe I'll try a little piece.

(LAUREN takes out some pills and takes them. Then she hands CARLOS some.)

LAUREN: Here, take this first.

CARLOS: What's this?

LAUREN: The food will taste better.

CARLOS: Sure. I need something to make raw fish taste better.

(CARLOS takes the pills.)

LAUREN: They are magic pills, Carlos. You'll wake up tomorrow morning and recite Shakespeare.

CARLOS: I've never even read Shakespeare. When I was in school, I couldn't keep focused on math or English. I loved history, though. And I loved my grandmother. I guess once your grandmother dies, there isn't nothing you can do to keep yourself from dying slowly inside.

LAUREN: I know. Having nobody can kill you. That's why you need a white house where you can live forever. This house has everything; and there is a puppy in every room that matches the color of the room. A golden retriever in the gold room, a dalmatian in the polka dot room.

CARLOS: I thought the house was all white.

LAUREN: It's a big house.

CARLOS: A big house can get lonely.

LAUREN: Carlos, I'm all alone in the world. My brother is in jail and my mother hates me. So you are the only person I can live with in my white house.

(The waitress, the same WOMAN from the bar, approaches them.)

WOMAN: Would you like something else?

LAUREN: You know, the sushi wasn't fresh. I'm gonna get sick. I'm not paying for this.

WOMAN: But you ate it all.

LAUREN: So? I feel sick, OK? I'm not paying for this. I'll sue your ass.

WOMAN: And how about you?

CARLOS: Huh?

WOMAN: How did you like your sushi?

LAUREN: Listen, bitch,

WOMAN: The dinner is on the house. *(To CARLOS)* Well? Did you enjoy your sushi?

CARLOS: What happens if I ate a bad piece?

WOMAN: You suffer for seven years.

(WOMAN exits.)

CARLOS: You were mean to her.

LAUREN: Carlos, you gotta take care of yourself in this world. Nobody is gonna help you. We have to protect each other.

Scene 5

WOMAN stands behind LAUREN, but LAUREN does not sense her presence.

LAUREN: I long for things beautiful. I search my memories for a beautiful moment in my life. A song, a dream, an unforgettable feeling of warmth, a smile that fulfilled a small expectation of being alive. But my mother's red eyes block everything else on the other side of my memory. Red from booze, from my father's death, from my brother's stealing. I can't see past the red. It isn't possible that I've had no beauty in my life, is it? I've just misplaced my history. That makes me a child of nothing.

(Pause)

Life should be beautiful, don't you think?

(WOMAN places her hand on LAUREN's shoulder from behind. LAUREN does not feel this.)

Scene 6

One year later. A tenement apartment. There is a knock on the door. CARLOS goes and opens the door. The same WOMAN from the restaurant stands at the door.

WOMAN: Hi. Did you just move in? I'm your neighbor. This package came for you today.

(She gives him a package, invisible to the audience.)

CARLOS: For me? No one knows we are here. We don't even have a phone yet. Hey, haven't I seen you before?

WOMAN: I don't think so.

CARLOS: I used to live in Flatbush. There was a Korean deli around the corner from my parents house...

WOMAN: It wasn't me.

CARLOS: Huh? I was just... Oh, oh, you thought I was gonna say...noooo, I'm not that ignorant. I was just... I guess I was imagining. We've never met before.

WOMAN: Welcome to East Jesus.

(WOMAN exits. LAUREN enters.)

LAUREN: Who was it, Carlos?

CARLOS: A package. It's from my grandmother.

LAUREN: You gave her our address already?

CARLOS: She is dead.

LAUREN: ...Open it.

(He opens the package. WOMAN comes in and dances around CARLOS and LAUREN. CARLOS and LAUREN look in the box. He looks up and sees WOMAN. LAUREN does not see her.)

Scene 7

One year later. LAUREN watches TV in the apartment. CARLOS enters with groceries.

CARLOS: I got food for the week.

LAUREN: Any money left?

CARLOS: A little. Let's go to Coney Island this weekend. I haven't been there for years. They have the best hot dogs.

LAUREN: You're not serious. I wanna feel well this weekend. I'm sick. I gotta get high.

CARLOS: Sure. Whatever you want.

LAUREN: The guy next door got a puppy today. Labrador. He's really cute. I saw him in the hall way. The guy is strange though.

CARLOS: What do you mean strange?

LAUREN: He looks at me all weird. He didn't want me to touch his dog.

CARLOS: Why not?

LAUREN: How do I know? He's just an asshole.

CARLOS: He was probably worried about messing up your white shirt.

(He hugs LAUREN.)

CARLOS: You look nice in white.

LAUREN: It's my color. Not everyone can wear white, you know.

CARLOS: I know. Don't you wanna go outside tomorrow? It's supposed to be real nice this week-end. Maybe we'll see some dogs with friendly owners at Coney Island.

LAUREN: Maybe.

CARLOS: Let's eat now.

(CARLOS takes out a loaf of white bread, jars of peanut butter and jelly, a box of spaghetti, and a jar of tomato sauce.)

CARLOS: The food has to last a week, OK? Monday and Wednesday we eat spaghetti. The rest of the week is peanut butter and jelly sandwiches. Was there any hot water today?

LAUREN: You ask me that everyday. We've lived here for a year now. There has never been any hot water.

CARLOS: What did you do today?

LAUREN: You ask me that everyday. I watched Oprah. Carlos, let's get a dog of our own.

CARLOS: It's expensive to have a dog, you know. I can't even take the bus to work, how can we afford a dog?

LAUREN: But I need company. You don't understand how lonely it gets around here.

CARLOS: Maybe in the future, OK?

(LAUREN cries softly.)

CARLOS: Did you see something sad on Oprah today?

Scene 8

The apartment. Another day.

LAUREN: Did you make sure the ice cream wasn't refrozen?

CARLOS: I'm sure it's OK.

(She opens the ice cream and examines it.)

LAUREN: I can't eat this. It's refrozen. Take it back.

CARLOS: The store was closing already.

LAUREN: Take it back. I'm too good to be eating refrozen ice cream. Who the hell do they think they are? Take it back to them.

CARLOS: Don't start, Lauren. I'll eat it.

LAUREN: What about me? I want some ice cream.

CARLOS: Here. I'll eat the top. It's OK in the middle.

LAUREN: No, it's not. It's not OK. This isn't fair. Do something.

CARLOS: It's OK.

LAUREN: *(Suddenly very sad)* Are you gonna fix it? Are you gonna fix everything?

CARLOS: Jesus. Yes.

(LAUREN sobs silently. The door opens and WOMAN enters. LAUREN doesn't see her.)

WOMAN: Delivery.

CARLOS: What?

WOMAN: One absolutely not ever refrozen strawberry ice cream.

CARLOS: Thanks. I don't know why such a little thing is so traumatic for her.

WOMAN: Why isn't it for you?

CARLOS: Because I'm OK. I had a good childhood or something, I guess.

WOMAN: Didn't you grow up in the house where your parents didn't speak to each other for years?

CARLOS: What do you know about it? It was no big deal, anyway. I didn't take it to heart.

WOMAN: I'm sorry she is so sad.

CARLOS: Yeah.

WOMAN: I know how she feels. A tiny seed from an unknown tree drops in your heart. You try to ignore it, but you can't. It grows to the size of a watermelon in one minute. It crushes your heart. You can't stop it.

CARLOS: Why are you here?

WOMAN: To give you ice cream.

CARLOS: Am I gonna survive this?

WOMAN: I'm not a fortune teller.

CARLOS: Aren't you my guardian angel?

WOMAN: Don't be silly. I have to go now.

CARLOS: Thanks for the ice cream.

(WOMAN exits. LAUREN stops sobbing.)

LAUREN: I guess the middle is OK. I can eat some.

CARLOS: *(Tired)* That's good, baby.

LAUREN: *(As she eats)* It isn't possible that I've had no beauty in my life, is it?

CARLOS: How's the ice cream?

LAUREN: The ice cream is OK. I can still have good strawberry ice cream. That's not nothing. Thank you, Carlos.

Scene 9

The bar. CARLOS is drinking beer. WOMAN comes in and sits next to him.

WOMAN: How are you?

CARLOS: Have I seen you somewhere before?

WOMAN: I'm sure.

CARLOS: I can't remember. Sorry.

WOMAN: You look tired.

CARLOS: I mix concrete all day. But I'm glad I have a job. I gotta pay the rent. Sixty dollars a week.

WOMAN: I think this belongs to you.

(WOMAN hands him an object invisible to the audience.)

CARLOS: *(Surprised)* Where did you get this?

WOMAN: Have you been looking for it?

CARLOS: No, not really. I've forgotten about it. I must've lost it months ago. It belonged to my grandmother.

WOMAN: It's possible to find it again, isn't it.

CARLOS: I guess so. Thanks.

WOMAN: Shouldn't you go home?

CARLOS: I don't know. Tomorrow is Christmas, right?

WOMAN: What are your plans?

CARLOS: Are you kidding? For people like us, everyday is the same. No heat, no hot water, the tub is coated black with I don't know what, so I gotta take a drip drip ice cold shower wearing my sneakers.

WOMAN: But you are in love.

CARLOS: Lauren and me, at least we got each other. What do you have?

WOMAN: I don't know. Nothing yet. Years later I may end up dead on a roof of a suspicious hotel in Times Square. Death by suicide or racial hate. Or I may pass by a theater on Broadway one day and be mesmerized by the signs. I'll get a job at the concession stand where *Chorus Line* is so I can see the show many many times.

Scene 10

Two years later. The apartment.

CARLOS: I had a job interview today. For UPS package delivery. This guy from the construction job set me up. It's less money, but I think it's cool.

LAUREN: Less money? Are you nuts?

CARLOS: It's a better job.

LAUREN: How're we gonna get by on less money?

CARLOS: How about you getting a job for a change? You haven't worked in three years!

LAUREN: I'm a freelance artist! Anyway, I heard it's easy to get on welfare. You just have to take some humiliation at the office, that's all. Will you come with me tomorrow?

CARLOS: Forget it. We'll manage.

LAUREN: I'll pay you back everything. I promise.

CARLOS: OK.

LAUREN: So what do you wanna do tonight? We need some money for dope.

(Pause)

LAUREN: Don't worry. I'll get it.

(She goes to the telephone and dials.)

LAUREN: Hi ma? I'm coming over. I need money. I just need it. I'm coming over now. What? It's an emergency. If you don't give me money, I'm gonna kill myself. I'm killing myself for real. You bitch!

(She hangs up.)

LAUREN: Why don't you do something?

CARLOS: I don't wanna get high today. Let's watch TV, baby.

LAUREN: Fuck. I'm gonna kill that bitch.

CARLOS: Stop talking like that about your mother.

LAUREN: She owes me. She lets her boyfriend live in the house. She gives my brother money. She is jealous of me because I'm a fashion designer. I don't care. I had my revenge. Once I took thirty thousand dollars from her. All the money in her saving account. I spent it in two weeks. She didn't notice it was gone for a long time, because she just never notices me.

CARLOS: Come here. (*He holds her.*) My mother, she is always so understanding. She lets me smoke pot and everything. No trouble. I owe my mother. Maybe she will give us some money.

LAUREN: My mother went off on me when she found me smoking pot.

CARLOS: My mother is cool. I wouldn't be here if it wasn't for her. She can be your mother, too.

LAUREN: It's nice to have a mother who loves you.

Scene 11

The apartment. CARLOS and LAUREN are sitting on the floor. He opens a small bag of heroin and puts it into the spoon. LAUREN heats the spoon with a disposable lighter.

LAUREN: I copped it from the same shooting gallery where that guy ODed last week.

CARLOS: That means we are in for some good shit.

(She prepares the syringe. He wraps a belt around his arm. She taps his arm for a vein and shoots him up. She repeats the process and shoots herself. They are relaxed instantaneously. LAUREN picks a short cigarette from an ashtray full of buds and lights it. She is dosing off with a burning cigarette. CARLOS throws up in a paper bag.)

LAUREN: It feels good, doesn't it?

Scene 12

Another day. CARLOS is sleeping. LAUREN is smoking a cigarette. WOMAN is in the room with them, but visible only to CARLOS.

CARLOS: *(Startled)* What time is it?

LAUREN: It's nine-thirty.

WOMAN: It's dried roses crinkle after dream.

CARLOS: What?

LAUREN: Nine-thirty at night.

CARLOS: I had a dream. I was a heroin addict. You, too. We went to cop on Jamaica Avenue late at night. This guy pulled a knife on me because my twenty dollar bill turned into a red balloon. But you protected me from the knife.

LAUREN: It wasn't a dream.

WOMAN: The red balloon popped.

CARLOS: It wasn't?

LAUREN: Do you want some tea?

CARLOS: OK.

(LAUREN exits. CARLOS looks at WOMAN.)

CARLOS: I know you, right?

WOMAN: Didn't you call me?

CARLOS: In my dream?

WOMAN: No, on the phone.

CARLOS: I don't remember.

(LAUREN comes in with tea. CARLOS and LAUREN drink in silence.)

LAUREN: I'm gonna start designing soon. I've got ideas. I'm thinking pink. Do you like pink?

CARLOS: Yeah.

LAUREN: I'm gonna have my own boutique. In Manhattan. What do you think?

CARLOS: Sounds good.

(He looks at WOMAN. She shakes her head no.)

Scene 13

One year later. The bar.

CARLOS: Tell me. What was it that came in the mail from my dead grandmother? Then I lost it for a long time, but you gave it back to me. Remember? What was it?

WOMAN: Don't you know?

CARLOS: I can't remember. We've moved so many times in the past five years. It's lost.

WOMAN: Maybe you'll find it again someday.

CARLOS: When my grandmother died, I stopped drinking coffee. No one could make coffee that tasted like my grandma's.

WOMAN: We lose so much.

CARLOS: I guess. It's no big deal. When will I see you again?

WOMAN: When the seven years are up.

CARLOS: What comes after that? How can life be different now? Don't misunderstand me, this is a pretty good life. I have no problems when I'm doing dope. I'm all right.

Before I started doing dope, things weren't as easy. I was a scared little kid, scared shitless of everything. The nuns at school, the bus driver. Everyday I was so nervous about getting on the school bus after school. So one day I decided to walk home. It took me forty minutes to get home. I guess I was about ten then. I peed in my pants walking home. Because I was too scared to use the bathroom at school before I left. The nuns were yelling at the kids to get on the bus right now.

At home, my parents were always fighting or not talking to each other, but it was no big deal. I had grandma. That's all I needed. Without her, I just didn't think I could make it in this world.

WOMAN: I think I'm from a different place.

CARLOS: I see.

WOMAN: My story hasn't begun yet.

CARLOS: You are like, a vision?

WOMAN: Something like that.

CARLOS: Why do you visit me?

WOMAN: When you are high on heroin, there are already pink spiders crawling all over my future.

CARLOS: I don't understand.

WOMAN: If a lightning strikes a willow tree in California, monarch butterflies die in Mexico. We are all part of the same web.

CARLOS: I don't want to be part of anything. I think whatever potential I had to be something was lost on the day I peed in my pants. I'm tired.

WOMAN: What are you so tired of?

CARLOS: Keeping it up. When I go to Jamaica Avenue to get Methadone, I feel so warm and safe as soon as I have a little cup of metamusel mix in my hand. Sometimes I have to wait an hour until my regular shows up at the clinic. He is on the program, but he sells me his share. You can trust his stuff to be the real thing. He won't rip me off. He's a good guy. I hold the cup in my hand and know everything will be fine in a few minutes. I go across the street to this dive of a diner and order hot coffee. It's supposed to speed up the effect of methadone. When it's gone, I have to figure out how to get some more tomorrow. I gotta do this everyday.

WOMAN: Coffee?

CARLOS: Yeah, I started drinking coffee again a coupla years ago. Drugs helped a lot. It's a good thing I can drink coffee without grandma, right?

Scene 14

One year later. The apartment.

LAUREN: I had another bag.

CARLOS: What?

LAUREN: There. On the side table.

CARLOS: So look.

LAUREN: It's not here. Did you take it?

CARLOS: No.

LAUREN: Who else? Tell me. Why?

CARLOS: I didn't.

LAUREN: Why do you wanna do this shit to me?

CARLOS: I didn't.

LAUREN: It's my share.

CARLOS: You are crazy.

LAUREN: Give it back to me.

CARLOS: Look. I didn't take it. Don't start.

LAUREN: You stupid low life. Gimme back my stuff.

CARLOS: Shut up. I told you to quit crack. It makes you crazy and nasty.

LAUREN: I'm not doing crack. I'm talking about my dope, which you stole from me.

CARLOS: You are hopeless.

LAUREN: Oh, yeah? And there is hope for you?

CARLOS: At least I'm not a crack head.

LAUREN: You are a waste. Don't preach to me.

CARLOS: Crack is a whole different game. It's the devil. I told you to stay away from it. Look at yourself.

LAUREN: Listen you low life.

CARLOS: Call me low life one more time, bitch, you'll be paying for your own dope.

LAUREN: All right. Just gimme back my bag. It's mine. I left it right here. I saw you take it.

CARLOS: What? You didn't see nothing.

LAUREN: I did. I did. I saw you take it.

CARLOS: Liar.

LAUREN: Where did you hide it? Where? Let me check.

(She goes over to him and sticks her hand in his crouch.)

CARLOS: Get away from me, you lunatic!

LAUREN: *(Screaming)* I KNEW IT I KNEW IT I KNEW IT YOU TOOK MY STUFF YOU ARE A LIAR IF YOU DIDN'T TAKE IT PROVE IT TAKE OFF YOUR PANTS

CARLOS: Shut the hell up.

LAUREN: I'll tell your mother. I'll tell her her precious son is a liar and a thief and a junkie.

CARLOS: Yeah, right.

LAUREN: Watch me.

(She goes to the phone. CARLOS goes after her. They struggle over the phone.)

LAUREN: AHHHHHHHHH

CARLOS: SHUT UP!

LAUREN: TAKE OFF YOUR PANTS. IF YOU HAVE NOTHING TO HIDE, PROVE IT!

(Pause)

(*He takes off his pants.*)

LAUREN: Bend over.

CARLOS: What?

LAUREN: Bend over and let me check your asshole.

(*Tense silence. They stare at each other. He takes off his underwear and bends down. She looks quickly and then starts sobbing.*)

LAUREN: I'm sorry. I'm sorry. I gotta detox.

(*He puts back on his clothes.*)

LAUREN: I swear. I'm gonna detox.

CARLOS: What for?

LAUREN: I got nobody. You gotta take care of me. Hey look at these.

(*She shows him dark patches on her elbows. Pause.*)

CARLOS: Shit. What's wrong with you?

LAUREN: These patches appear and disappear all the time. You don't have them?

(*Pause*)

LAUREN: It's because I've misplaced my history.

Scene 15

Another day. LAUREN watches TV in the apartment. CARLOS enters with groceries.

CARLOS: I got food for the week.

LAUREN: I need twenty dollars, Carlos.

CARLOS: No.

LAUREN: I swear this is the last time.

CARLOS: I told you no crack. Crack fucks you up.

LAUREN: It's not that. I just need it. I promise I won't ask again.

CARLOS: Here.

(He holds out the bill. LAUREN reaches for it, but he pulls back.)

CARLOS: I want you gone for three hours. Understand? Stay out and give me some peace.

LAUREN: OK.

(She takes the money and exits. CARLOS prepares heroin and shoots up. He lights a cigarette and nods off in front of the TV.)

Scene 16

Another day. LAUREN watches TV. CARLOS enters.

CARLOS: I got food for the week.

LAUREN: I need twenty dollars, Carlos.

CARLOS: No.

LAUREN: I swear this is the last time.

(He gives her the money.)

CARLOS: Here. You know what to do, right? Three hours. Go look for crack for all I care.

(She takes the money and exits. CARLOS shoots up.)

Scene 17

Another day. LAUREN watches TV. CARLOS enters and puts down groceries.

LAUREN: Carlos,

(He gives LAUREN a bill.)

CARLOS: Here. Disappear.

(LAUREN exits. He shoots up.)

(Time passes. LAUREN enters again.)

LAUREN: Carlos, give me five. Please. I swear this is the last time.

(He stares at the wall.)

CARLOS: What's that?

LAUREN: What? What? Shit, I knew it. The cops!

CARLOS: No, on the wall. Over there.

(He attacks the wall. Tries to grab something.)

CARLOS: Did you see that? A Big Pink Spider.

LAUREN: Get the fuck outta here. Com'on, check outside. I think people are following us. Cops, probably. You know what? I think my mother's hired a hit man to kill me.

CARLOS: Why?

LAUREN: Because she is jealous. Because I'm daddy's favorite.

CARLOS: Your father is dead.

LAUREN: Because I'm a fashion designer. Because I'm pretty.

CARLOS: Look, do you see that?

LAUREN: What ta hell?

CARLOS: A big pink spider on the wall.

LAUREN: Forget it. Listen, I think the guy next door is gay. Let's ask him if he is a faggot.

CARLOS: Why?

LAUREN: Why not? It's disgusting. Besides, I think he steals stuff from us.

CARLOS: What?

LAUREN: Stuff. When we leave the apartment; he comes in here and steals. Let's get him.

(CARLOS is examining his arm with horror.)

CARLOS: I got bugs coming outta my arm. Look. What are they?

LAUREN: Carlos, you are just sick. You don't feel good, right? Let's get you a coupla bags. It'll take care of you.

CARLOS: Shit. I got worms or something.

(He scrubs his arm violently.)

LAUREN: I don't believe this. Stop that, you low life. Shit. I had a bright future in front on me. Then you came along. You were my downfall. I was a very successful designer before you messed up my life. I could've had my own boutique.

CARLOS: You never worked a day in your life.

LAUREN: You don't know.

CARLOS: I know. You haven't worked in seven years now. I doubt all of a sudden you stopped working when you met me. You never designed nothing. It's all in your head.

LAUREN: You are a liar. Liar. Liar!

(They get into a struggle. WOMAN enters. Only CARLOS sees her.)

WOMAN: Are you ready?

CARLOS: For what?

LAUREN: What?

WOMAN: Ready to go to the theater. It's the opening night. You have to dress up and buy some flowers.

CARLOS: Right. Yeah, I'm ready.

LAUREN: What's wrong with you?

CARLOS: I've never been to the theater.

LAUREN: What are you talking about?

WOMAN: It's been seven years, Carlos. You survived.

CARLOS: Why?

WOMAN: Because you wanted to take care of somebody. Because Lauren had no one to love her. Because you didn't know what to dream about except for the things you saw on TV. Who knows?

LAUREN: *(Punching CARLOS)* Don't do that!

CARLOS: Lauren, I'm going to the theater.

LAUREN: Yeah, right.

CARLOS: I've never been to the theater. I think you are supposed to dress up. Isn't it amazing?

LAUREN: What's so fucking amazing?

CARLOS: I've never been to the theater. Amazing. But I can go if I wanted to, believe that? I'll quit dope and save some money. Buy a decent shirt and new sneakers. Maybe even leather shoes. I'll go to Broadway when I have enough money. Look around. Have you ever thought anything that outrageous?

LAUREN: Bullshit. You don't know what you are talking about. I used to go to the theater all the time. People like you don't go to the theater. Because you are nobody. Nobody.

CARLOS: Do you remember what it was I got from my grandmother in the mail seven years ago?

LAUREN: Your grandmother's been dead for twenty years.

CARLOS: I think I know what it was. I thought I lost it, but I didn't. You can never lose something like that. It's yours for life.

LAUREN: Let's just smoke some pot. Just pot, that's all. Let's relax, OK Carlos?

CARLOS: Lauren, I'm going to the theater.

(WOMAN opens the door for him. He looks back once, then walks out.)

Scene 18

The same street as Scene 1.

LAUREN: I never had a candle before. I almost always had electricity in my life.

WOMAN: You are lucky.

LAUREN: I ain't lucky.

WOMAN: The candle is scented. It smells like vanilla.

LAUREN: Nice. Is it Chinese?

WOMAN: I don't think so. It's from Bloomingdale's.

LAUREN: I know. But where are you from? Are you Japanese? I used to eat sushi. It's my favorite food in fact. I stopped when I got together with Carlos. He didn't like it much, plus he could never afford it. I've had better boyfriends you know, men with money and respect. With this one boyfriend, I had a new dress every week and we went out to eat sushi all the time. But Carlos needed me. He needed my company. He came from a fucked up family, so I was all he had.

WOMAN: Where is he now?

LAUREN: I had to send him away. He was no good for me. I had to take care of myself. I'm gonna write a book about my life. I can call Al Pacino to play my father in the movie version. I have plans. Carlos was gonna hold me back. What do you think about my idea?

WOMAN: Years from now, you often think about writing this book, but it doesn't matter. You get arrested for trying to walk out of Bloomingdale's wearing a fur coat you tried on. Instead of sending you to jail, they send you to the hospital. You are clean and sober when your mother dies.

LAUREN: What are you, a fucking fortune teller?

WOMAN: You'll be alright.

LAUREN: No, I won't. Don't go. I got AIDS.

WOMAN: What will you do now?

LAUREN: I'm serious. A book about my life. A song, a dream, an unforgettable feeling of warmth, a smile that fulfilled a small expectation of being alive.

WOMAN: Sounds beautiful.

LAUREN: It's a lie. A true book about my life. How fate can fuck you up, and you have two choices. You can either live with the pain or have a little bit of pain killer, you know. To numb you just a little. And what kinda life that would be, living in the fog of high happiness. My tragedy couldn't have been just mine. Right? Right?

WOMAN: I know.

LAUREN: One day, Carlos' kids can read it. They'd have no idea who I was, but they'd be moved by it anyway. I owe Carlos some money. This is how I'll pay him. His kids will read my book.

WOMAN: I have to go. It's time.

LAUREN: Ask me who I am.

WOMAN: Who are you?

LAUREN: A child of nothing.

WOMAN: Again.

LAUREN: A child of a bread truck driver?

WOMAN: And?

LAUREN: A child of...me.

WOMAN: Good bye.

LAUREN: Yeah, take care of yourself.

(WOMAN exits. LAUREN remains.)

LAUREN: I like that. I'm a child of me. Hello, me.

Part 2

Scene 1

Seven years later. A lobby of an apartment building in Queens.

WOMAN/YUMI: Hi. I'm the new tenant in 4C.

CARLOS/DOORMAN: Your name?

YUMI: Yumi.

CARLOS: I'm Carlos. You look familiar.

YUMI: I just moved to New York.

CARLOS: My mistake then. I've never been outside New York.

YUMI: You look familiar, too.

CARLOS: Where are you from?

YUMI: Japan.

CARLOS: Far away. Are you here to go to school?

YUMI: I wish. If I was in school, I would at least have some company.

CARLOS: You'll meet people. It's a friendly town.

Scene 2

Another day. The lobby again.

CARLOS: You never came to visit New York before this time?

YUMI: No.

CARLOS: I feel like we've met.

YUMI: You haven't been to San Francisco, right? I went to school there.

CARLOS: What were you studying?

YUMI: Survival.

CARLOS: Is that like camping?

YUMI: No. English.

CARLOS: Oh. I wish I could go to school. Study history. You know there are people whose job is to restore history. Archeological objects. I saw a documentary on PBS once. People paste together broken vases and statues from ancient time. I didn't know such jobs existed when I was a kid.

YUMI: Do you like your job now?

CARLOS: It's a good job. People are friendly. I watch out for the old ladies in the building. Before I came here, I had a rough time. But life is decent now. It's been seven years. How about you? If you could go to school again, what would you study?

YUMI: Movies. In Japan, I worked in an office job for six years and saved money. I wanted to make movies. But there is no such thing as a woman film maker in Japan. So I spent most of my money studying English in California. My parents think I'm insane.

CARLOS: Why?

YUMI: They are respectable people. My father is a lawyer and my mother is married to one.

CARLOS: But you always wanted to make movies.

YUMI: No. I always loved watching movies. But didn't even know there were such people as film makers. I thought movies just appeared.

(Pause)

YUMI: Most of what's going on in the world is still a mystery to me.

CARLOS: I like it that way. I can't imagine the pain of knowing everything.

(Pause)

CARLOS: Maybe you remind me of Yoko Ono.

YUMI: I do not.

CARLOS: I guess not.

YUMI: See you later.

CARLOS: Wait. Do you ever think of making a book into a movie?

YUMI: Why?

CARLOS: Here, you can have this book. I hear it's pretty good. Take it. I'm not going to read it. Maybe there is a movie in it.

YUMI: *Living in the Abyss* by Lauren O'Neill. I don't know. It sounds like a melodrama.

CARLOS: I heard the author died of AIDS.

YUMI: That doesn't mean she wrote a good book.

CARLOS: But it's her last book. It was published after her death.

YUMI: Why don't you read it?

CARLOS: Because I know it by heart.

YUMI: What do you mean?

CARLOS: It's my gift to you. Welcome to Jamaica.

Scene 3

In her apartment. She is reading the book. Silence. She looks up to find LAUREN standing.

LAUREN: Remember me?

YUMI: ...No. This is my apartment.

LAUREN: It's nice. You need some curtains. White will look nice.

YUMI: You have to go.

LAUREN: Do you like the book?

YUMI: I just started.

LAUREN: True story.

YUMI: Do you need help?

LAUREN: No, I thought you might.

YUMI: I'm fine. I'm going to call down for the doorman, OK? He can show you the way out.

LAUREN: There is no need. I'll go. Enjoy the book.

(She exits.)

Scene 4

In the lobby.

YUMI: Someone came into my apartment unannounced.

CARLOS: Last night?

WOMAN: Around nine.

CARLOS: I'm only here til seven everyday. The door is unmanned at night. The tenants have to be careful not to let strangers in.

YUMI: She wasn't dangerous.

CARLOS: Someone you knew?

YUMI: She looked familiar, but I don't think so.

CARLOS: Maybe it was someone who lives in the building. What did she look like?

YUMI: She was in her thirties, I think. Very skinny and pale. She had a long black hair and a small scar on the corner of her mouth.

(CARLOS is surprised.)

YUMI: Carlos? Is something wrong?

CARLOS: No, it just reminded me of someone I used to know.

YUMI: Maybe it was your friend looking for you?

CARLOS: No. She is dead.

YUMI: I'm sorry.

CARLOS: Listen, be careful at night. Jamaica isn't the best neighborhood. It used be worse. They've cleaned up a lot of drug activities in the past few years. Still, you should watch out for yourself. Don't let a stranger in your apartment.

Scene 5

The apartment.

LAUREN: Remember me, Yumi?

YUMI: Of course. You know my name. Come in.

LAUREN: Did you finish the book?

YUMI: The book? Oh, *Living in the Abyss.* Yes.

LAUREN: What did you think?

YUMI: Have you read it?

LAUREN: Yes.

YUMI: I thought it was good. Sad. Honest.

LAUREN: Maybe someone will make a movie of it.

YUMI: Maybe.

LAUREN: What are you doing now?

YUMI: Nothing... I'm trying to be a film maker. But it's silly. Right now I'm trying to meet some people and get a job.

LAUREN: Years from now, you will be working at the concession stand at the Broadway theater where *Rent* is. You get to see the show as many times as you want. Then you decide to write your own work. You become a poet. Your poems are read by Carlos' children.

YUMI: What?

LAUREN: It's all part of the same web.

YUMI: Why are you here?

LAUREN: Didn't you call me?

YUMI: Maybe I did. Thank you for coming.

LAUREN: You'll be all right.

Scene 6

The lobby.

YUMI: Carlos, I forgot to tell you I finished the book you gave me.

CARLOS: How was it?

YUMI: I liked it. I'll bring it down.

CARLOS: Don't bother.

YUMI: It's no bother.

CARLOS: Maybe later. Don't worry about it now. So what was the book about?

YUMI: It's about a woman whose father dies early in her life. She is lost without him. Later she falls in love with a man who is also lost, and together they become heroin addicts in order to stop the pain.

CARLOS: What...what happens at the end?

YUMI: She dies. He recovers and writes a book about his life.

CARLOS: You mean she writes the book before she dies.

YUMI: No. The man is the one who writes the book.

CARLOS: But the author is a woman. It's a true story about her life. She wrote the book.

YUMI: I guess the ending is fictionalized. I don't know why.

CARLOS: ...I know why.

(Pause. CARLOS is pale.)

YUMI: Carlos, are you feeling OK?

CARLOS: Yeah.

YUMI: Are you sad about something?

CARLOS: No...I don't get sad about too many things. I'm lucky to be alive. I got no right to be sad. How about you? What makes you sad?

YUMI: I feel sad after a mid-day nap that I didn't intend to take. I wake up empty and closer to death. When I finish eating lunch or dinner. Right after the meal, I feel an enormous fear of the time passing.

CARLOS: Breakfast?

YUMI: It doesn't happen to me after breakfast. I think that's because I don't really like breakfast food. So when it's gone, there is no regret.

CARLOS: I like breakfast food the best.

YUMI: I guess we are different.

Scene 7

In Yumi's apartment. She is still unpacking. LAUREN stands behind her (in a reverse position from Part 1 Scene 5).

YUMI: Starting my life over from scratch. I often romanticized it. Moving. Leaving everything old behind. In the land where I know no one, and no one knows me, I can invent a whole new life.

I can dress in long skirts and wrap my head in colorful fabric. But after a certain point in your life, you are who you are. My head wrapped will never feel comfortable. It will always feel like a hundred and nine degrees and itchy and the scarf about to fall off.

The awkwardness that I have carried deep in my body for thirty years is now part of my being. I realize that leaving doesn't mean birth or death. It means negotiation.

My life is in these boxes. In New York City. In Queens. The rent is reasonable. I look at the help wanted section in the Sunday *Times* every week, but I'm not qualified for anything. Qualification means accumulation. You have to stay, not leave. My phone never rings because I don't know anyone. Sometimes I'm overcome by fear. What if I die in this apartment? It will be weeks before anyone notices. I guess that's why people don't often pick up and leave. For the fear of dying alone.

(LAUREN places her hand on Yumi's shoulder from behind. YUMI feels this.)

YUMI: I was just thinking about you.

LAUREN: Have you misplaced your history?

YUMI: No. I still have it.

LAUREN: You are lucky.

YUMI: I'm not lucky.

LAUREN: You'll be all right.

Scene 8

The lobby.

YUMI: Carlos, are there good restaurants around here? Inexpensive.

CARLOS: I don't really know. I live in Brooklyn.

YUMI: Maybe I'll just cook. I hate ending up at a wrong restaurant. It's depressing to pay money for bad food and be upset for not being smart and hip.

CARLOS: You'll get used to living here. You'll be all right.

YUMI: Maybe. The first month I was in California, I picked up some spaghetti and a jar of pasta sauce at a supermarket. Cook the spaghetti for eight minutes. OK. But there was no instruction written on the jar of sauce. I didn't know what was already understood and agreed on by everyone. You just open it and heat it as if that is your birth right. No doubt. No apprehension. I felt so lonely. I called my parents in Japan and asked them to airmail me some rice crackers.

CARLOS: Did they?

YUMI: Yes. Even though they were very angry when I left. I think they were angry with me for most of my life.

CARLOS: It's important to take care of your parents. I had a rough life before I came to this job. But I don't blame my parents for anything. My problems were my own.

YUMI: What kind of problems?

CARLOS: Nothing big. A little experiments with drugs. I started out smoking pot when I was twelve, but my mother was understanding. She didn't try to discipline me. I owe my mother.

YUMI: You came to your senses because she left you alone?

CARLOS: Not until later. She had her own problems anyway. She was young and poor. Besides, I turned out OK. I've been completely clean for five years now.

YUMI: I don't understand. How did your mother help you?

CARLOS: Look. You've got to have something to hold onto. Something good. Home. You can't give it up. You have to believe.

YUMI: I don't think it helps to be in denial.

CARLOS: In Egypt?

YUMI: What?

CARLOS: De Nile. Get it? De Nile River? It's a joke me and my mother tell each other.

YUMI: How nice.

Scene 9

YUMI walks out to the streets.
The sun is setting. She pauses, takes out a small bag of rice crackers from her pocket and eats one. After a moment, she begins walking again. She sees a pizzeria and enters. The woman employee is LAUREN.

YUMI: Is it you?

LAUREN: Can I help you?

YUMI: I don't know... What's that?

LAUREN: White pizza.

YUMI: OK. White pizza, please.

LAUREN: But you don't even know what it is.

YUMI: It looks good. I'll try it.

LAUREN: What if it's a mistake?

YUMI: How can I know that before tasting it?

LAUREN: You had plans for dinner. Pizza. Usually that means a regular slice.

YUMI: I was just passing by to go to the supermarket.

LAUREN: So this isn't even part of the plan.

YUMI: I guess I'm not very good at keeping on a track. I want to see where the side street leads to.

LAUREN: If you detour from the main route, you may die alone.

(Pause)

YUMI: What are my options, then?

LAUREN: A regular cheese slice. Or with pepperoni. Very popular.

(Pause)

YUMI: ...White.

(LAUREN *gives her a slice*.)

YUMI: It's delicious. I have been waiting to taste this all my life.

Scene 10

The lobby. YUMI gives CARLOS the book.

YUMI: Thanks.

CARLOS: I told you, you can have it.

YUMI: OK. I'll get it back from you after you read it.

CARLOS: It's OK.

YUMI: I think you should read it. It's very good.

CARLOS: I don't have to read it.

YUMI: Why?

CARLOS: Just leave it alone.

YUMI: I think you are scared of the book for some reason. It reminds you of a painful time maybe. You don't like that.

CARLOS: If you think I can't face pain, you are wrong.

(Pause)

YUMI: Carlos?

CARLOS: My parents never ate dinner together when I was a kid. Family that eats together doesn't produce drug addicts. That's just basic, stupid psychology. I know my mother should have cared whether or not I was smoking pot when I was twelve. But I lose so much if I held onto that. I have to remember the good times. Otherwise it was all for nothing.

YUMI: I think you'll like the book. You know it's her only book ever.

CARLOS: I'll think about it.

(Pause)

YUMI: Carlos, would you call me on the days you don't see me? Just to make sure.

CARLOS: Make sure?

YUMI: That everything is OK with the apartment. Just on the days you don't see me in the lobby at all.

CARLOS: Sure.

Scene 11

CARLOS is reading the book in the lobby. LAUREN enters.

LAUREN: Hi, Carlos.

CARLOS: Shit.

LAUREN: You look good.

CARLOS: Shit.

LAUREN: You are sober.

CARLOS: Shit.

LAUREN: Carlos, stop saying shit. We won't be able to repeat this. So concentrate.

CARLOS: What are you doing here?

LAUREN: I'm just visiting. You gained weight.

CARLOS: Yeah, I detoxed five years ago. I've been clean since. This is strange.

LAUREN: I just came to say good bye. We never did that.

CARLOS: Lauren, I didn't know you were in the hospital...

LAUREN: I didn't want you to visit me anyway. No one came. My mother had died already. I was clean for her death. She saw me sober... How did you feel when you heard the news?

CARLOS: Relieved. Sad. I took the test so I knew I wasn't infected. It seemed strange not to share that fate after so much.

LAUREN: Do you think we could have done better?

CARLOS: No. We were like two wounded animals. We needed each other in the process of healing, that's how I look at it. We had to do it the way we did. We both came out of it all right. I mean...your book and everything.

LAUREN: Do you go to the theater?

CARLOS: Yeah, I always take my dates to the theater. Sometimes to the opera even.

LAUREN: I'm glad.

(*Pause*)

LAUREN: I should go now.

(*Pause*)

CARLOS: Good bye.

(*LAUREN turns to go.*)

CARLOS: Hey, it's a good book. I like the ending. Thanks.

LAUREN: Carlos, what was it you had that belonged to your grandmother?

CARLOS: Your book, I think.

LAUREN: Thank you.

(*LAUREN exits.*)

CARLOS: (*Reads from the book*) It isn't possible for your history to be ruined completely. One day you are standing out on the streets crying, and a strange woman gives you a vanilla scented candle. From that day on, you will always have a candle in your life. Vanilla scented. When you light the candle, memories of songs, dreams, smiles and warmth will come back to you. You'll go on to have an ordinary life, a job, dates at the theater, and ordinary hope to stop the cycle of personal tragedies.

Scene 12

YUMI's apartment. A knock on the door

YUMI: Who is it?

MALE VOICE:Delivery.

YUMI opens the door. A man rushes in and knock her down breathless. LAUREN appears suddenly and stares at the man. He does not see her.

MAN: Don't move.

(YUMI begins to get up.)

YUMI: red hot splashes of
splintered mirage,
ice cold in three seconds.

behind my left eye,
a hole large enough
to store a cherry or
an acorn.

(MAN fires. YUMI falls backward slowly, holding her left eye. LAUREN goes through the same motion simultaneously. YUMI falls to the floor. LAUREN kneels and holds her head.)

YUMI: I was going to be a film maker. Spent all my money learning English. My parents were angry at me for chasing my dreams across the Pacific Ocean.

LAUREN: Years from now you often think about the movie you meant to make based on the book, *Living in the Abyss*. But your book of poems about seeing the world with one eye is published. Your parents read it when it is translated into Japanese.

YUMI: I was hoping you would come back. I wanted to ask you something.

LAUREN: I have to go now. Help is on its way.

YUMI: Am I supposed to be here? Is this how things should have turned out? Is this right?

LAUREN: There is no design. Only connections.

YUMI: What will happen to me?

LAUREN: *(Kidding, to encourage YUMI)* You are going to make my book into a movie. I suggest Al Pacino for the role of the father.

YUMI: It'll never heal.

LAUREN: Everything heals in seven years.

(Sound of an ambulance and a police car approaching. CARLOS rushes in. LAUREN stands, looks back once, then exits. CARLOS doesn't see her.)

YUMI: my mother calls early
Japanese are being murdered
you have to be careful
spending a dollar a minute
for an echo in the strange place
between Tokyo
and Jamaica

everyday
somewhere in the world
the phone rings
wakening a gray haired couple
hearts pounding
with visions of red

CARLOS: Yumi, Yumi, can you hear me? Just hang in there. Help is coming. You'll be all right.

(He holds YUMI's head in the exact same position that LAUREN was.)

(Blackout)

END OF PLAY

Big Dicks, Asian Men

By SLANT

While lounging in a sauna with a case of beer and talking about what the three of us had in common, we were conjuring up names for our debut show. Thus, BIG DICKS, ASIAN MEN.

What you will read in our script is the SLANT genesis, the first of five original theatrical and musical works in our repertory to date-a tapestry of amplified and acoustic music, scene and monologue text, shadowplay, puppetry and choreography that currently characterizes our performances. In BIG DICKS, ASIAN MEN we satirize pop and media images of Asian masculinity, share experiences of our American upbringing while paying homage to the guiding influences of our Asian heritage.

A big thank you to Alvin Eng for including BIG DICKS, ASIAN MEN. This is the first publication of our work.

Many, many thanks to our teachers, friends, girlfriends, wife, brothers and sisters, and the thousands of fans and supporters we've been blessed with thus far.

Special thanks to Ellen Stewart who gave SLANT a beginning and an artistic home at La Mama Experimental Theater Club.

And eternal gratitude to our parents and ancestors who showed us the way.

Peace,

Rick Ebihara, Wayland Quintero, Perry Yung - SLANT

BIG DICKS, ASIAN MEN had its World Premiere at the La Mama E.T.C. First Floor Theatre, November 30-December 10, 1995.

Written and Performed by SLANT-Rick Ebihara, Wayland Quintero, Perry Yung

Lighting Design: Howard Thies
Police Dispatcher Voice-over: Sarah Boggan
Police Sergeant Voice-over: Christopher Gomez
Sumo Stablemaster Voice-over: Brian Nishii
Dr. U's Receptionist Voice-over: Erin McDonnell
Final End Dance Music Composer: Genji Ito

SLANT is a registered trademark.

BIG DICKS, ASIAN MEN

Vietnamese Muzak of American pop songs play as the audience enters and is seated. Gradually a sound loop of a cheering arena audience takes over as SLANT *plays its opening song. Quickly lights come up from behind the performers so that they appear as a shadow band behind a white screen that is hung downstage of them. The song is a short, lively, grungy rock tune.*

SLANT

(Intro)

S-L-A-N-T, S-L-A-N-T, S-L-A-N-T, S-L-A-N-T

We're not the waiters on TV
Not the model minority
No little dicks for you and me

We're BIG DICKS ASIAN MEN

S-L-A-N-T, S-L-A-N-T, S-L-A-N-T

Turn the channel and burn the paper
Television says I'm a masturbator
Television says I'm a masturbator

We're BIG DICKS ASIAN MEN

(Instrumental break)

We are the product of TV and cable
I have my eyes and penis labeled
Now it's time to turn the tables

We're BIG DICKS ASIAN MEN

S-L-A-N-T, S-L-A-N-T, S-L-A-N-T, SLANT!

(Right after the song ends there is a blackout as police sirens and flashing red lights come up. A female police dispatcher's announcement is heard:)

POLICE SERGEANT *(Voice-over)*: All units in the vicinity of Chinatown please respond. Suspect is a young oriental male dressed in dark clothing, last seen on Canal Street selling counterfeit Gucci purses. Repeat, suspect is young Oriental male dressed in dark clothing wanted for selling counterfeit Gucci purses. All units in the vicinity of Chinatown please respond.

(Lights come up as 3 Asian males enter and take their places in front of the white line-up screen.)

POLICE SERGEANT *(Voice-over)*: Well ma'am, take your time. Identifying a suspect in a line-up ain't easy. We'll get the guy that sold you that fake Gucci bag.

(As the line-up interrogation begins, we hear a short blast of loud feedback. This feedback repeats after each spoken line during the interrogation.)

SERGEANT *(Voice-over)*: Suspect #2. Yes you in the middle. Step forward please. Turn to your right. Turn to your left. Please repeat after me—Gucci, Rolex, Obsession, check it out. Best deal, check it out.

SUSPECT #2 *(Perry)*: Gucci, Rolex, Obsession, check it out. Best deal, check it out.

SERGEANT *(Voice-over)*: Uh, try it again...this time as if you're in Chinatown.

SUSPECT #2: Gucci, Rolex, Obsession, check it out. Best deal, check it out.

SERGEANT *(Voice-over)* Suspect #2 please try it again as a Chinese person.

SUSPECT #1 *(Wayland)*: Oh, hey, can I try? Gucci, Rolex, Obsession, check it out. Best deal, check it out. Heh heh! I do this all the time in auditions man. Check this out--If you can grab the pebbles from my hand you may leave the temple. The wind carries the lotus leaves across the ocean, the mountains, the deserts...*(He is interrupted by feedback.)*

SERGEANT *(Voice-over)*: Thank you suspect #1. Step back in the line-up please! Suspect #2, where were you at approximately 2:45 PM yesterday?

SUSPECT #2: Uh.. I was uh...well I went to the post office in the morning *(The other two actors exit.)* and checked my post office box. Then I went to have some coffee at the west side cafe over there on Chambers Street. Oh! 2:45 PM yesterday! I was rehearsing with my band Secret Asian Man. *(He reaches behind his back.)*

SERGEANT *(Voice-over)*: FREEZE! DON'T TRY IT!

SUSPECT #2:　　　　　　　Hey, it's just my flute man. I was rehearsing with my band. We're working on a new song..."Buddha Blues."

*(He begins playing the flute as the screen rises to reveal a rehearsal space. The other two actors join in with elec-
tric guitar, drums and percussion. The tune develops into a catchy rendition of a Grunge-Bluesy Peking Opera
interpretation of "Heartbreak Hotel." After the song ends, the screen descends gradually as SUSPECT #2 walks
back downstage to the line-up finishing up his last flute melody. The other two actors join him in the line-up.)*

SERGEANT *(Voice-over):*　　Thank you suspect #2. Relax gentlemen. *(Pause)* Now can you all
motion or gesture like you're trying to get someone into a shop. *(Each suspect executes sales hustler gestures interrupted by the voice-over.)* Thank you gentlemen. Suspect #3 step up to the line please. Turn to
the right. Turn to the left. Now do what you were doing and at the same time repeat—Gucci, Rolex,
Obsession, check it out. Best deal, check it out.

SUSPECT #3 *(Rick with an English accent):*　　Gucci, Rolex, Obsession, check it out. Best deal, check
it out.

SERGEANT *(Voice-over):*　　Were you at Mulberry and Bayard at 2:45 PM yesterday?

SUSPECT #3:　　　　　　　Well, yes. I was.

SERGEANT *(Voice-over):*　　Is that the way you always talk?

SUSPECT #3:　　　　　　　The way I talk. Yeah. I've been talking like this since I was 12, when I
saw my first James Bond film *Goldfinger. (The other two actors exit quietly.)* It drove my folks crazy. Still
does. Yeah, but when I saw him, Bond, James Bond, I said to myself that's what I want to be. He
was so cool. He had all those great gadgets, all those great cars, that great charisma, making love to
all those great-looking women. Oh yeah, he had a real great...accent. Yea, I know, people tell me it's
strange, you know, me being Asian talking with an English accent. Yeah, but I mean, who wanted to
be Asian. What like Odd Job? Or Dr. No?! Hell no! I wanted to get laid. Now there was Bruce Lee.
He was cool. He had charisma, presence, all those great moves. But did he ever get laid? Did he ever
screw? No. Never screwed in any of his films. That's probably why Asians got labeled with that word
"in-screw-table." Yea, well I never got laid either even with this accent. I began thinking that maybe
it was hormonal, you know, like it was my Asian testosterone that wasn't attracting women to me.
God knows it was making me horny enough. But maybe it just wasn't sending off the right signals,
like it was somehow stopping my pheromones from being released. Well, they say that Asian men
don't smell, maybe that's why I wasn't getting laid. I didn't stink enough. But then along came
JASON SCOTT LEE. Oh yea, in *Map of the Human Heart* making mad passionate love on top of that
huge blimp. And in Dragon where we finally see Bruce Lee getting laid. And in *Jungle Book* being
raised by wild animals, running, sweating naked through the steamy jungle. You know he had to be
smelling pretty good then. Jason Scott Lee gave me confidence, passion, lust, masculinity, got my
testosterone boiling, released my pheromones! I'm Man! I'm Asian!!! Smell me!!! Now if I could only
get rid of this bloody accent.

SERGEANT *(Voice-over):*   So you were at Mulberry and Bayard yesterday afternoon.

SUSPECT #3:   Oh yeah! Friday night, broccoli with garlic sauce and brown rice.

(SUSPECT #3 disappears behind the screen as the lights fade to black and the audience begins to hear little squeaky sounds, bells, horns and vocal noises in the dark. The screen rises as the lights come up revealing three Chinese food deliverymen on tricycles peddling around and chanting a guttural work rhythm. An a cappella song begins.)

NO MENUS PLEASE (THREE DELIVERY GUYS RIDING IN A CIR-CLE ON TRICYCLES)

(Rick) Through crowds of people I ride my bike,
Thousands are eating Chinese tonight,
Free delivery is my life, Send my money back to my wife,
To feed my family went overseas,
Only to read no menus please,
(All) No menus, No menus please *(repeat)*

*(Perry)*My tuition's due I don't get a break,
How much can I save how long will it take,
Two dollar tips are all that I get, Midterms are soon have to study yet,
I'm failing intro to Cantonese,
Should have took French,
(All) No menus, No menus please *(repeat)*

(All Chant) Soy sauce, and hot sauce, and duck sauce, Hooh!
Lobster sauce, fish sauce, and garlic sauce, Hooh!
White sauce, and brown sauce, and red sauce, Hooh!
Don't matter what color as long as it's good!
Don't matter what color as long as it's good!

(Wayland) I can't stand this goddamn bike,
I'd rather be boning my girl tonight,
Dad says the restaurant needs family, But handing out menus is not for me,
It's for the family I shiver and freeze,
But inside I scream no menus please,
(All) No menus, No menus please *(Repeat)*

(Break—Choreographed cycling, collision and slow motion falls...They sing the final verse at a slower tempo, coming downstage looking disheveled and holding food delivery bags.)

(Rick) Through snow and rain and gloom of night
(Perry) We bring to you your chicken delite
(Wayland) Nothing is ever quite as it seems
(All) We litter your halls with our family dreams,
Delivery is our opportunity
But all that we see is No menus please
No menus, No menus please *(Repeat)*

(Scene ends with the three holding out their hands for tips. One by one each leaves the stage, leaving the bags downstage in three pools of light.)

THREE ANOREXIC SUMO WRESTLERS

After "No Menus Please," the actors enter the stage one by one stripped down to black mawashis (Japanese sumo wrestling "jockstraps"). They execute a brief choreographed unison movement that takes them to the delivery bags that were left downstage in the pools of light from the previous scene. They immediately attack the bags of food, and with loud chewing, slurping and burping sounds, they devour noodles, except for JACK-SAN who is not eating. The three begin their conversation while eating and proceed through their daily ritual of warming up, stretching and wrestling.

TOM *(Perry)*: Hey Jack-san, you better finish up. We only have five more minutes.

(JACK pulls out a cheese sandwich.)

HARRY *(Rick)*: Jack-san! You're not even half-way done. You know how important it is for us to eat. The Oyakata says if we don't put on some pounds he's going to drop us from the stable.

JACK *(Wayland)*:I'm just not hungry.

HARRY: Hungry!? Hungry has nothing to do with it. We need poundage man.

TOM: Jack-san we've all been eating like maniacs for months, you can't fall off your diet now. Hey, look at Harry-san, he's got a nice belly going there.

HARRY: You think so?

TOM: Oh yeah, you're getting a real nice shape.

HARRY: Hey thanks man, I've been meaning to tell you that your butt's getting big.

TOM: Thanks. I thought I was getting bigger, but it's so hard to tell back there.

HARRY: Jack-san, eat. Listen, if you go up against someone like Kitanoumi you're going to need something between you and his 360 pounds. It's not like we got driver-side airbags.

JACK: Linda left me.

TOM & HARRY: Holy shit. No way.

OYAKATA *(Stablemaster Japanese voice-over)*: Meals over! Begin the warm up!

(All three clean up their bags of food, HARRY exits with the bags.)

JACK: I should have seen it coming. I came home last night, all her things were gone, and she left a note on the kitchen table. She even made me meatloaf before she left.

TOM: Your last supper huh?

JACK: She made six.

HARRY: *(Enters with a faux rubber sumo wig)* See on the way out the door even she wants you to eat. Keikoda!

ALL: Keikoda!

(They get into their respective positions in a circle, warming up.)

JACK: She said she couldn't take it anymore. All the practice. All the traveling for tournaments. She said she needed some stability.

HARRY: I thought she liked the road. Didn't she follow the tour around before you started dating?

JACK: Yeah, but that was three years ago. She said her biological clock was ticking and that she needed to settle down.

HARRY & TOM: Aaaah...the clock.

JACK: Yeah the clock. I told her just wait, baby. Just wait until I get moved up to the next ranking. Then I'll be making more money, I'll be home more, and I won't have to tour these farm towns anymore, just the majors.

HARRY: Can't argue with the clock. There's no snooze button for the nesting alarm.

TOM: Sanban.

ALL: Sanban.

(They reposition themselves and begin a ritualistic tilting movement.)

TOM: That's why I date young, man. The younger you date, the more time you have for your clock to catch up with hers.

(They move in a circle.)

HARRY: Like Biological Savings Time.

TOM: Yeah! Men fall back, women spring forward. Besides, what a lot of women are looking for in relationships are their fathers anyway.

HARRY: Just like a lot of men are looking for their mothers.

JACK: Yeah! My mom makes one hell of a meatloaf!

TOM: Despite all this "Woman of the '90s" stuff, women are still looking for the perfect provider, the bringer of the proverbial pork strips.

HARRY: Goban! (*HARRY signals TOM & JACK to begin wrestling.*)

ALL: Goban!

(*TOM & JACK execute a brief choreographed wrestling routine that ends with a "patty-cake" hand routine and butt slap.*)

HARRY: Yeah but women always go for the loner, the rebel, the inaccessible, the James Dean.

JACK: The Brad Pitt.

TOM: Elvis!

ALL: AH! Elvis-san! Soh-des! Thank you ma'am, thank you very much, thank you ma'am....

(*JACK breaks into hip-swiveling rendition of "Hound Dog" as HARRY and TOM begin wrestling.*)

OYAKATA (*Stablemaster Japanese voice-over*): Jack-san! Bakayaro! What the hell are you doing? Get back to work! Give me 20 push-ups.

JACK: Hai sensei! (*Begins doing push-ups*) Uno, dos, tres...

OYAKATA (*Stablemaster Japanese voice-over*): Count in Japanese!

JACK: Hai sensei! Ichi, ni, san, shih, go.

TOM: Elvis was the shits man. He had it all.

(*TOM & HARRY continue to wrestle.*)

HARRY: Women, fame, he had America in the palm of his hand.

TOM: Charisma, sex appeal, music, the moves. He definitely had what women wanted.

JACK: Yeah. My mother was into Elvis.

TOM: Yeah? My mom too. I grew up listening to her old 45s. "Hound Dog."

HARRY: "Jailhouse Rock." Hikake!

ALL: Hikake!

(HARRY is flung down by TOM)

JACK: Yeah, but when it comes down to an actual relationship that's exactly what women don't want. *(JACK & TOM collide & begin wrestling)* They want sensitivity, vulnerability, stability.

TOM: Elvis had that too. Remember "Love Me Tender," "Treat Me Nice," "Don't Be Cruel." Now there's sensitive and vulnerable.

(JACK throws TOM down.)

HARRY: Now that's what women want. The right combination of the spicy, the wild, the passionate, but watered down with stable, sensitive and vulnerable.

JACK: Sounds like Linda's meatloaf recipe!

(JACK breaks down sobbing uncontrollably like a big baby as HARRY & TOM look dumbfounded. Soon HARRY and TOM go over to JACK.)

HARRY: Hey! Hey! *(He grabs JACK.)*

JACK: What?!

HARRY: Would Elvis cry?

JACK: Nooooo...

HARRY: What would Elvis do?

JACK: I don't know.

TOM: He'd eat!

JACK: He'd eat?

HARRY: That's right! He'd eat! Burgers, fries!

ALL: Burgers, fries!

(By this time all three are massaging each other, JACK still kneeling on the floor, HARRY directly standing behind him kneading JACK's shoulders, Tom behind HARRY elbowing HARRYs shoulders.)

TOM: Elvis had it all!

ALL THREE: Soh-des!

OYAKATA *(Stablemaster Japanese voice-over)*: Warm-up is over. Hit the showers. *(They all respond with "Hai sensei!" bow and start to leave.)* Tom-san stay! Tom-san your butt's getting big.

TOM: Uh thanks sensei. I thought so but it's so hard to tell back there.

(End of scene. The screen slowly comes down.)

(TOM stays onstage and begins putting on clothes to transform into a tourist taking photos of the audience with a flash camera. He begins a monologue.)

THE TOURIST *(Perry)*:   I was in Venice, Italy this past summer with my lover. Venice is really beautiful. A city of canals, clean. I had to take a piss really bad and the thing about the Venice was that they had public urinals. There were "toilette" signs all over the place with arrows pointing to the nearest one. So we started following the signs but I really had to go. That's when I got homesick for New York City. Cuz if I was back home in the city I could just whip it out anywhere. We finally got to the toilet and Valentina paid our way in. Italian toilets are just like the ones in China. They don't waste any time sitting. They just squat, do the job, and split. So I'm finished and I'm outside leaning against a replica of Michealangelo's David when I noticed Valentina coming out. She looked a bit disturbed, actually, she was pissed. She came storming out and I chased after her. "Hey baby what's wrong? What's the matter?" She said, "Nothing, forget it!" I'm like come on what's wrong, what is it? It's nothing, forget it! Let it go! Let go of what? What's wrong? What is it? Then she slipped into her Italian mode."*Va bene va bene non valiente.*" Valentina's from the south of Italy. A real southern Italian woman and when she starts speaking Italian and says, "*Va bene va bene non valiente,*" I say forget what! So later on we were cruisin on a gondola through the canals. Vale's in my arms and she says, "*Senti...prima en el bagno...quando c'erano...quei ragazzi.*" Whoa Vale. You know my Italian's not that great. You know earlier at the toilette? Those guys taking the money, one of them said, "I wonder if she's fucking him?" And the other said, "What does it matter? You know Orientals can't fuck." Did they mean the women too? They used the masculine term UN-Orientale. They spoke in Sicilian dialect but I understood them quite clearly. "Aren't you angry?" she said. I said, "Vale, Americans talk about penis size all the time and how our sexuality is measured by the size of it. Black men have the biggest, Asian men have the smallest and everyone else is safely in between. Besides, how can I let a remark by a couple of Sicilian migrant workers taking money from peeing

Venice tourists bother me?" I told her of a saying I once heard from a wise old black man...Richard Pryor. He said, "Take a look at China. They've got 1.2 billion people. Someone over there is doing some serious fucking!"

(Blackout. Gradually the screen rises revealing a darkly-lit setting, we hear the sounds of drilling and hammering.)

Dr. Uehara's Waiting Room

Featuring a "non-traditional" casting:

THICK: A Texan
RODNEY: A recent Chinese immigrant
HOMEE: An African-American homeboy.

RODNEY is nervously pacing back and forth downstage as THICK is down and left of center in a chair facing diagonally up stage left. There is another chair up and right of center facing diagonally down stage right. The chairs are about 3-4 feet apart. Drill sounds continue for a few beats until lights come up.

THICK *(Wayland)*:   *(In a Texas drawl)* Been waitin long?

RODNEY *(Perry)*:   Huh?

THICK: I said have you been waitin long. Are you next?

RODNEY: *(In a Chinese accent)* I suppose to see the doctor at 3:00.

THICK: Listen, you mind if I see the doctor first?

RODNEY: You have appointment?

THICK: Nope, just droppin in.

RODNEY: Just dropping in? Sure, go ahead.

THICK: This your first time here, huh. My name's Johnny. But you can call me Thick.

RODNEY: My name is Wong. Wong Siu Long.

THICK: Shoe Who?

RODNEY: No, Wong Siu Long. I have an American name, Rodney. Yes, it's my first time.

(Drill sound/light flicks off and on and off and on- each time this happens RODNEY reacts jittery and jumpy.)

THICK: Boy, you're real nervous aren't you. Listen Rodney, the first time I came here I was real nervous too in fact worse than you. Yeah I understand cause it ain't like just gettin a nose job, your eyelids adjusted, or even gettin a breast enlargement. It's real serious reworkin' Willie!

RODNEY: (Quickly sits in chair) Willie? You been here before!

THICK: Yeah. I'm just here for a tune up.

(Drill sound/lights flicker to go off.)

RODNEY: Tune up? What you mean? Like car tune up...change the plugs, check the wires?

THICK: Yeah Rodney. 6 months or 600 fucks whichever comes first.

RODNEY: Aaahyaah. Unbelievable! You busier than Hong Kong stock exchange.

THICK: Yeah!

(Tool sound/lights flicker on and off and on.)

RODNEY: This doctor. Is he good?

THICK: Yup. Best in the business. He even worked on Schwarzenegger.

RODNEY: Arnold? Really? You mean *Kindergarten Cop*?

THICK: Yes sir. But you know all them steroids he took back when he was body-buildin really messed him up. Made him even smaller than us. Size of an espresso bean. Doctor's got photographs before and after. Picture this. You got his wife Maria smilin real big next to her new Arnold proudly holdin him up like a firehose. According to Doc, Maria wouldn't marry the man unless he did one of two things. Get an enlargement or become a liberal democrat.

RODNEY: Tough choice.

(Tool sounds/lights flicker.)

THICK: Rodney, Rodney don't worry there boy. You're in good hands.

RODNEY: I just want to be sure. I work real hard save my money for something special like today. Thick, all my friends tell me American girls, they like...ahh... (Motioning to THICKs crotch)

THICK: Big dick?

RODNEY: Yes yes. BEEG DEEK! In Chinese we say "Dai Lop Churng." You have girlfriend?

THICK: Yup.

RODNEY: American?

THICK: Yes sir. African-American.

RODNEY: She's Brack!? *(Breaks into Chinese—That's unbelievable!)* You brave! I wish I have American girlfriend, blonde goddess like Sharon Stone or nice Jewish girl with big mouth and sexy lips like Barbra Streisand. I tired of Chinese girls. Too traditional, old country, *(Pause)* except the ones from Brooklyn. I never been with brack woman.

THICK: Hey most of us haven't. It's a rare sight you know? Us guys with a black woman.

RODNEY: Yes, yes but maybe after my operation then I can get American girlfriend too!

THICK: You will buddy. Soon as Dr. U. works on you, you're going to have one big...hey boy, how is it you say big dick in Chinese again?

RODNEY: Dai Lop Churng.

THICK: Dai Lop Churng! With your new Dai Lop Churng you'll be fighting off truckloads of women.

RODNEY: Beeg Deek.

THICK: Dai Lop Churng.

RODNEY: Beeg Deek

THICK: Dai Lop Churng.

RODNEY & THICK: *(They get out of their chairs, move downstage and chant together:)* Big Dick, Dai Lop Churng, Big Dick, Dai Lop Churng *(Repeat as necessary)*

(HOMEE enters carrying a boom box, picks up the chant and continues until he has been chanting at least four times alone. By now the lights have come up even more brightly.)

HOMEE: *(In a thick African-American street accent)* Hey, dis must be the right place. Dat was fun. Why'd ya all stop?

THICK: *(Laughing at HOMEE)*

HOMEE: The name is Wong, HomerWong, but you can call me Homee.

THICK: *(Still laughing)* Homee?

RODNEY: (As THICK laughs) Homer Wong...hmmm.

HOMEE: What's so funny? You laughing at me, man?

THICK: Hey alright, alright boy! Do you have an appointment?

HOMEE: Yeah, I got an appointment! I'm a little late, but I got an appointment.

THICK: Hooowee! Irritable lil "homeboy" aren't you?

HOMEE: Dat's right Jethro.

RODNEY: (Breaking right in) Homer Wong. You the son of Ming-Wa Wong?

HOMEE: No. But I have an aunt named Ming-Wa Wong live ovah deah on Mulberry Shtreet.

RODNEY: Aayaah. This is unbelievable day. Must be destiny again. My name is Wong Siu Long. Rodney! Ming-Wa Wong is my auntie too!

HOMEE: No shit?! Oh you must be the guy dey told me about, some guy come ovah from Guangzhou owns a big Chinese restaurant. Dat's you?

RODNEY: Yeah! You must be my second cousin on auntie's side.

HOMEE: Oh no man. Actually her husband Jo-Long is my mother's older brother.

RODNEY: So then you not directly my second cousin from Ming-Wa. You my cousin still, though, from Jo-Long, brother of your mother, what her name?

HOMEE: Stephanie. Her Chinese name is Shu-Fen.

RODNEY: Ooooh. So your mother Shu-Fen...American name Stephanie, is younger sister of Jo-Long married to my auntie Ming-Wa, who is younger sister to my mother Cheng-Yu, wife of my father Hop Jai Wong.

HOMEE: Yeah, yeah I guess dat's right. I don't know all of dat, but yeah...

RODNEY: So, Homee, your English is so good. What you do? Are you a waiter?

HOMEE: No man. I do a lot of things. In fact I just came from helpin out some kids at the Police Activities League, kind of like the Big Brothers, Big Sisters Program only we call it the Big Homees, Little Homees Project for Disadvantaged Youth.

THICK: Volunteer work, huh? That's quite commendable! But uh, Homee, what is it you do for work?

HOMEE: You wanna know how I make my cash? Yo it's really none of your business! You probably think I deal drugs, rip people off or some shit like that, huh?

THICK: Well do you?

HOMEE: Fuck you. I'm a rap artiste!

RODNEY: Really! Sing something for me cousin.

HOMEE: Cuz, you gotta be shitting me? In this dress and cap?

RODNEY: I would be honored. I love the rap music, the urban feeling, so simple and strong like Cantonese opera. Make me feel, how you say, "like one bad motherfucka." Give it up Cousin Homee.

HOMEE: Alright, alright, alright. Let me see. Oh I got an idea! Hey Rodney, check dis out.*(Begin a vocal rhythm for a little while.)* Now keep this rhythm. Yeah dat's it. Here we go, but you gotta be ready for your turn alright? Yeah, dat's it. And keep that arm going like dat. Yeah, dat's good. Alright, here we go. *(Return to rhythm and then begin Rap)* Your mother Cheng Yu, wife of Hop Jai Wong, sister of Ming Wa, wife of Jo Long, whose sister is my mother, Shu Fen, Stephaneeeeeee, married to my father Frankie Wong, pick it up hey hey...

RODNEY: Hey, hey. My auntie Ming Wa, married to Jo Long, brother of Shu Fen, mother of my cousin, Homee, Homee, Homee, her name Stephaneee...

HOMEE: Ming Wa your auntie too, sister of Cheng Yu, wife of Hop Jai Wong, we the family Wong, bro we can't go wrong, *(RODNEY joins in and they keep rapping "we the family Wong, bro we can't go wrong" until THICK breaks in.)*...

THICK: Hey, hey, hey! Quit y'all. That rap music shit drives me crazy!

HOMEE: Chill man. You interruptin us. I don't always get to rap wit a real live fresh off the boat Chinaman. And rap music ain't shit. It's urban poetry, Jethro.

THICK: Urban poetry? That's bullshit! And by the way there boy, my name is not Jethro. You call me sir, alright?

HOMEE: Scuse me? You got some fuckin attitude Mr. Tootie-Fruttie. The only bullshit around here is the crap comin out your mouth.

THICK: You're a real insultin' bitch aren't you, you pathetic piece of street shit. *(THICK &*

HOMEE start circling as they trade verbal punches.)

HOMEE: Weak! Weak! Dat's the best you can do? Hit me again hillbilly boy.

THICK: I don't hit anybody in a dress!

HOMEE: Shit, what's that you wearin?! At least mine matches my cap!

RODNEY: Wait! Everybody relax! Chill! We all here for same pathetic reason!

HOMEE: Rodney, I ain't takin take no shit from this banana ass whitey wanna be.

THICK: You watch your pussy mouth there, homeboy wannabe.

HOMEE: Oh yeah? You wouldn't know a pussy from a fuckin bear rug.

THICK: I know you get no pussy with that little bitty tinkle of yours and
you talk like you got a fuckin egg roll up your skinny ass.

HOMEE: So show me what you can do you thick, cock-sucking motherfuckin mama's boy.

THICK: Alright boy. Let's go!

(THICK & HOMEE charge at each other as RODNEY is in the middle and pushes them apart.)

RODNEY: Wait, wait! Stop! I don't understand! *(Breaks into Chinese—Can't we just get along!)* We
all Asian! We all brothers! We all Small!

(Sexy female receptionist's voice-over breaks in—"NEXT!")

THICK & HOMEE: You're up Rodney.

RODNEY: Thick, Thick you want to go first?

THICK: You go on right ahead, Rodney. It's your day, boy!

RODNEY: Homee, you want to go first?

HOMEE: Sure! *(Begins to walk off and then turns around)* Hey Rodney, you really nervous about
this huh? Hey cuz what if we go in together at the same time?

THICK: Homee, that is a brilliant idea. Make it a family affair! After all—*(Begins rapping)* You
the family Wong, boys you can't go wrong, you wanna bigger dong, you want it one foot long, your

mama's in the john...

(*RODNEY & HOMEE cut THICK off*).

RODNEY: OK,OK, OK. Thick, Can Dr. U. work on both of us at the same time?

THICK: Yeah Rodney. Like I said he is the best in the business with his special procedure, he's got these big delicate hands to work with, plus he's got this dynamite looking ex-Dallas Cowboy cheerleader blonde assistant named Ingrid.

RODNEY & HOMEE: Let's go bro!

(*RODNEY & HOMEE run off excitedly. THICK pushes play button on the boom box and begins guitar-accompanied monologue.*)

THICK:
There was time when I was like those guys
Couldn't score with the ladies no matter how hard I tried
Then I thought I'd score better if I was different than
Your stereo-typical Asian American man...

I started making up stories, fantastical lies
About my background, my family, that I bungy jump and fly
But the ladies were unimpressed with my overzealous tries
Until desperately I boasted of my larger than average size

Then this long-legged lady at the end of the bar
Started slowly walking, down my way
I froze in my aroused fascination
As she whispered in my ear "Give me a first-hand examination"
And if what you say is true I'll take you up to my room
And make all of your wildest fantasies true too...

I backed down humiliated
I ran out of the bar extremely deflated
Down the street and onto the train
I wallowed in my self pitied pain...

Then I looked up and I saw a sign
Right next to the anal-wart 800 hot-line
All the answers to my problems my head raced as I read
All my hopes, all my dreams
And this is what it said...

(The Dr. U prelude is followed by the Dr. U. theme, sung and danced by all three characters accompanied by the tape player on stage. They enter the stage with phallus props strapped on.)

(Chorus)
Dr. U can do it for you
Dr. U can do it for you
He can make a tree out of a your stick
Dr. Yuhara's penis enlargement clinic.

You say you've got a little problem man
You want a bigger hot dog stand
Dr. U has got the foot-long bun to make you number one

(Repeat chorus)

(The song cycles as each actor comes downstage to do bits of an infomercial.)

INFOMERCIAL SPOKESMAN 1: Are you a man with a small penis? Or perhaps you know some-one. Well, your worries are over. Dr. Uehara has developed his exclusive PEEP system—the Penis Enlargement Effusion Procedure. These men have had their penises enlarged through PEEP and as a result they look and feel much younger.

HOMEE: Before I had the procedure, I used to wait until the gym shower was empty before I went in. Now I go straight in for a shower right after my workout. No more snickers and I can hang out with the brothers.

INFOMERCIAL SPOKESMAN 2: PEEP or the Penis Enlargement Effusion Procedure is a patented system that is completely safe and natural. It is a non-surgical, in-office procedure that will have you back at work the same day.

RODNEY: After I had PEEP my friends came up to me and asked, "Have you been on vacation? You look great!"

INFOMERCIAL SPOKESMAN 3: Once you've had the PEEP procedure there's no lengthy follow up visits. Just drop in for a tune-up and vitamins when you need to. The time varies depending upon individual usage.

THICK: Having PEEP done gave me back my self-esteem. Now my social life is all booked up. Bar-hopping with Reba on Wednesday, mud wrestling with Dolly on Thursday, and off to the ballet this weekend with Sarah!

(All three continue to sing and dance a ballet variation as the Dr. U song keeps playing, and they end with a big bang, pulling and detonating the party popper streamers from their phallus props.)
(Quick fadeout)
(The shadow screen drops down. Two actors stand behind, back-lit, with profiles of their shadows and phalluses still strapped on. They wave at each other and begin to attempt to shake hands in silence. Their big dicks get in the way. A little game of whose phallus is bigger begins as each takes turns stepping upstage to the back light to increase the size of the shadow phallus. The third actor returns with an object in hand that looks like a bigger phallus as the other two begin moving back downstage toward the screen shaking in fear. They all stop in back of the screen motionless.)

(The police sergeant's voice-over returns.)

SERGEANT *(Voice-over)*:   Well ma'am. I know it could be any one of them. Ah what the hell, book 'em!

(Original composed music begins as the third actor in the center turns on a chainsaw and begins to execute a cutting pattern with the chainsaw, and castrates each of the other two shadow phalluses.)
(Fade out lights)

(This is the beginning of a dance/partnering piece, with the actors' pants down around their ankles. It is a dance that is extremely physical, supported by driving percussive music interspersed with strains of Asian instruments and voices. At the end of the dance all three run downstage and stop, as the screen drops down quickly behind them.) (Blackout)

(Lights up for a bow.)

(As the audience applauds SLANT quickly sets up their musical instruments and perform "Secret Asian Man.")

END OF PLAY

THE LAST HAND LAUNDRY IN CHINATOWN

By Alvin Eng

"You used to have to buy-in, to be an American.
Now you've got to sell-out, to really get some clout."

Just as "What are we fighting for?" was the battle cry for social
change and awareness in the 1960s and '70s, in the down-sizing
'90s, that cry became "What are we working for?" Under the dark
shadow of the corporate cleansing of America (cum the world), where
the eventual outcome seems to be only one big (brother of a) con-
trolling corporation, almost every working person finds it difficult to build up any personal or professional equity and security.
In fact, most find themselves getting ousted from the very institutions to which they have dedicated themselves and built-up.

It is this ghostly landscape, in which America knows what it is
not, but is not exactly sure of-or afraid to admit-what it has
become, in which THE LAST HAND LAUNDRY IN CHINATOWN (A REQUIEM FOR AMERICAN
INDEPENDENTS) is set. Utilizing contemporary "vaudevillian rock &
roll" songs within a traditional musical narrative structure, the
piece focuses on the spiritual, financial and ethical effects of
gentrification on a second generation Chinese American family in
New York City's Chinatown-where ancient, supernatural Chinese spirits have a head-on collision with modern, gritty urban realities.
Within this framework, the musical also explores the legacy of the
pioneering hand laundrymen and women of Chinese America-of which my
parents were two.

ALVIN ENG

Concept, Book & Lyrics by Alvin Eng
Music by John Dunbar

THE LAST HAND LAUNDRY IN CHINATOWN was presented at La MaMa, E.T.C., May 9 - 18, 1996, with the following cast, crew and band

Cast *(In order of appearance):*
BO-GEE: Ming Lee
MARTHA/GHOST: Elizabeth Speck
GEORGE/GHOST: Gabriel Hernandez
JOSIE: Emy Baysic
DYLAN: Rick Ebihara
JUNE: Lori Tan Chinn
CRAZY TOM: Jojo Gonzalez

Director: Bevya Rosten
Musical Director: Miriam Daly
Stage Manager: Alexandra Lopez
Lighting Design: Howard Thies
Costume Design: Linda Keller
Set Design: Joey G. Mendoza
Mask Design: Madeline Slovenz-Low

Piano: Miriam Daly
Guitar/melodica: John Dunbar
Percussion: David Martinez

THE LAST HAND LAUNDRY IN CHINATOWN was first developed in the NYU/Tisch School of the Arts' Graduate Musical Theatre Writing Program.

Dedicated to the spirit of the Chinese Hand Laundry Alliance

Setting: Chinatown, NYC, mid-1990s

Characters
(all characters are Asian American)

DYLAN TOM, Male, mid-30s,

JUNE TOM, Dylan's mom, late 50s.

"CRAZY TOM" (everyone just calls him Tom), Dylan's father, early 60s

BO-GEE (means "newspaper" in Chinese), Late 50s, physically challenged newsstand owner and operator, Dylan's Uncle.

JOSIE TOM, Early-30s. Dylan's sister.

MARTHA & GEORGE / GHOSTS, Singing tourist couple, mid-40s, who also double as Crazy Tom's ghost friends.

Songs

Prologue

"Ballad Of Chinatown" - BO-GEE

Act I

Opening Medley: "Chinatown Suite (& Sour)" - TOURISTS & CAST
"Home Is Where It's Harshest" - DYLAN
"Ballad Of Chinatown" (Reprise) - BO-GEE
"I Tried" - JUNE
"Not For Sale" - CRAZY TOM, DYLAN
"Family" - BO-GEE, DYLAN
"Happy Birthday Lily" - BO-GEE
"Ballad Of Chinatown" (Reprise) - BO-GEE
"Stand Your Ground" - JOSIE, DYLAN
"Something For Me" - JUNE, CRAZY TOM
"Home" - CRAZY TOM

Entr'Acte

"Ballad Of Chinatown" *(Reprise)* - BO-GEE

Act II

"Things You Can't Forget" - CRAZY TOM, BO-GEE
"Like A Couple In A Great Old Movie" - JUNE, JOSIE
"The Last Hand Laundry In Chinatown" - CRAZY TOM, GHOSTS, DYLAN
"Lament" - CRAZY TOM
"Home" *(Reprise)* - CRAZY TOM, GHOSTS
"Where Is Home?" - JUNE
"Proclamation" - DYLAN, JUNE, JOSIE, BO-GEE

Epilogue

"Ballad Of Chinatown" *(Reprise)*

THE LAST HAND LAUNDRY IN CHINATOWN

(A REQUIEM FOR AMERICAN INDEPENDENTS)

PROLOGUE

Lights up on a rectangular newsstand on a Chinatown street. It is dawn and the street is empty save for a few bundles of newspapers. The newsstand's "window" opens and from inside, BO-GEE sings while opening up for business. As he sets up shop, he emerges from the newsstand in a wheelchair.

"BALLAD OF CHINATOWN"

BO-GEE: THE MORE WE TRY TO STAY THE SAME
THE MORE WE HAVE TO CHANGE
JUST LOOK AROUND OLD CHINATOWN
AND TELL ME WE'RE THE SAME
AND TELL ME WE'RE THE SAME

("Ballad" music continues as BO-GEE speaks:) This used to be a place called Chinatown. It was a small village of...convenience, shall we say. It was located near the southernmost tip of Manhattan, on the northeastern shore of America. The rest of the country used to think of Chinatown as exotic. But those of us who lived here knew otherwise. Our ancestors were barred from returning to our old homeland of China, yet never fully accepted here. So for them, while Chinatown wasn't quite home, it was the only place they had. So they made the best of it and prospered in spite of their outsider status. Many children were raised, and we got over our need to be accepted here...until recently.

(Lighting change—end of prologue)

ACT I - SCENE 1

"Tourists Music" starts. It is now mid-morning. MARTHA and GEORGE, two tourists enter. They clutch NYC tour guide books.

"CHINATOWN SUITE (AND SOUR)"

MARTHA: WELL IT LOOKS LIKE WE'VE FOUND CHINATOWN
             BOY, THAT CABBY TOOK A REALLY STRANGE ROUTE

GEORGE: LET'S GO AND FIND THAT FAMOUS HOLE IN THE GROUND

MARTHA & GEORGE:
             HERE IN CHINATOWN
             HERE IN CHINATOWN

("Tourists Music" continues as underscore.)

MARTHA: Excuse me, do you speak English?

BO-GEE: Only during business hours.

GEORGE: Sorry, we didn't mean to insult you, but we're just lost.

BO-GEE: I'll say.

MARTHA: Yes, this map is a little confusing... Can you tell us how to find Wo-Hop?

BO-GEE: Wo-Hop? You sure you don't mean the new IHOP?

MARTHA: You have an IHOP down here?

BO-GEE: Well, doesn't IHOP stand for <u>International</u> House of Pancakes?

MARTHA: I guess so, but we have one of them at home, and frankly we came down here to see just how different Chinatown really is.

GEORGE: Plus we've heard nothing but good things about that place. Like this book says, "For a great, cheap meal, you've got to check out that exquisite hole in the ground, Wo-Hop."

(JOSIE enters. Underscore changes to "Stand Your Ground.")

JOSIE: Hurry up, Bo-Gee I'm late!

BO-GEE: Sorry Josie, *The Wall Street Journal* is sold out this morning.

JOSIE: Typical. I'll just have to get one uptown. It's amazing how any business is conducted at all in Chinatown.

(Underscore returns to "Tourists Music.")

MARTHA: THE TRAVEL AGENT KEPT ASSURING US
          THAT CHINATOWN IS STILL A CURIOUS PLACE

GEORGE: MAYBE IT USED TO BE EXOTIC DOWN HERE
          BUT CHINATOWN HAS CHANGED
          CHINATOWN HAS CHANGED

(DYLAN enters. He sports "Hollywood sunglasses" and carries several suitcases. Underscore changes to "Home Is Where It's Harshest.")

DYLAN: Uncle Bo-Gee?

BO-GEE: Dylan!

DYLAN: It's been too long!

BO-GEE: Too long indeed... Hey, nice shades!

JOSIE: Why is it really my big brother, "Hollywood Dylan Tom?"

DYLAN: Why it's the outlaw Josie Tom! How the hell have you been?

BO-GEE: *(To tourists)* Then I hope you enjoy your visit, because Chinatown is really different now—

JOSIE: No, no, no! Chinatown is the same as where you come from, right Bo-Gee?

BO-GEE: Uh, right Josie.

(Underscore returns to "Tourists Music.")

JOSIE: PAY NO ATTENTION TO WHAT YOU'RE SEEING NOW
          THIS TIME NEXT YEAR THERE'LL BE A NEW CHINATOWN
          NO LONGER ROWS AND ROWS OF UGLY OLD STORES
          WE'LL HAVE BRAND NEW MALLS

(JOSIE shmoozes with MARTHA and GEORGE.)

JOSIE: Hi, I'm Josie Tom from the Chinatown Office of Development, C.O.D. for short. And if there's anything we can do to make your visit better just let us know. Here's my business card and our office is right here.

(Lights up on the Chinatown Office of Development, one floor above The People's Laundry. The "C.O.D." sign should overwhelm the Laundry's sign.)

JOSIE: When you come to Chinatown, no matter where you're from, we want you to feel at home. I wish I could show you around personally today, but I've got to run. But I'm sure Bo-Gee will show you all of the new things Chinatown has to offer. Have a wonderful visit!

MARTHA & GEORGE: Thank you.

(Tourists exit.)

JOSIE: Here, Dylan, you get a card too.

DYLAN: Give em hell, Josie!

JOSIE: Bo-Gee, have you given some thought to what me and Mom spoke to you about?

BO-GEE: Can't say I have.

JOSIE: Just remember, money isn't the only thing that's numbered around here. Well, Dylan, I've got to go to work now.

DYLAN: I thought we were in your office already.

JOSIE: Very funny, no wonder you never get any on-screen credit for your writing.

DYLAN: Low blow. But at least they pay me out there, not like the New York theatre world.

JOSIE: But seriously, are you free later? Maybe we can have a drink and catch up?

DYLAN: Well, don't we have that family dinner thing tonight?

JOSIE: Well, how about before that? I'd really like to talk a bit before we sit down with Mom and Dad.

DYLAN: And I'd really like to drink a bit before we sit down with them.

JOSIE: Great! Then why don't we meet at about 6:30 at Golden Palace?

DYLAN: Wow, that would be just like the old days.

JOSIE: Only this time, the drinks are on you, Mr. Hollywood.

(Underscore changes back to "Ballad Of Chinatown." DYLAN and JOSIE freeze, BO-GEE sings:)

BO-GEE: PEOPLE ALWAYS COME AND GO
            WHAT DO THEY HOPE TO FIND?
            ALTHOUGH WE LEAVE WE STILL MAY SEEK
            THE THINGS WE LEFT BEHIND
            THE THINGS WE LEFT BEHIND

(Underscore returns to "Tourists Music." JOSIE starts to exit.)

JOSIE: Save me a *Wall Street Journal* tomorrow!

(JOSIE exits.)

BO-GEE: So, I hear you're a Hollywood big shot now?

DYLAN: Yeah, if you can call selling one script—after seven years—that they immediately take your name off of and have someone else mutilate then yeah. But I'm getting divorced now, so maybe I'll finally fit in with Hollywood...

BO-GEE: I was very sorry to hear about that.

DYLAN: Thanks, but I think it's ultimately for the best.

BO-GEE: I hope so...So are you back here on business?

DYLAN: Yes, I'm back here to deal with the meanest, dirtiest, least-fulfilling business of all.

BO-GEE: Are you going to work for the Mayor?

DYLAN: No, nothing like that. I'm back here to deal with unfinished family business. Besides, I'm overdue for a visit...and, well, you know my mom. It seems like she writes me every month... and calls me every week!

(Underscore changes to "June's Music." Light comes up on JUNE, who is writing a letter. BO-GEE & DYLAN continue to speak.)

DYLAN: How's my Dad doing?

BO-GEE: Maybe it's best if you just see him yourself.

(A light comes up on CRAZY TOM, who sits near a wall of laundry. He seems to be counting them and talking to himself. Their singing overlaps.)

JUNE: EVERY DAY AND EVERY NIGHT
            HE SITS ALONE IN THE BASEMENT

CRAZY TOM:
            YIT, NGEE, SLOM SLEE *(1,2,3, 4 in Chinese)*
            PRETTY SOON, WE WILL BE FREE

JUNE: DOING GOD ONLY KNOWS WHAT

CRAZY TOM:
            YIT, NGEE, SLOM SLEE *(1,2,3, 4 in Chinese)*
            PRETTY SOON, WE WILL BE FREE

JUNE: I SIT UPSTAIRS WONDERING
            HOW THESE THINGS JUST FELL APART
            WHEN YOU WERE HERE
            THINGS ADDED UP

CRAZY TOM:
            YIT, NGEE, SLOM SLEE *(1,2,3, 4 in Chinese)*
            PRETTY SOON, WE WILL BE FREE

JUNE: NOW WITHOUT YOU
            THINGS SEEM WASHED UP
            I KNOW IT'S NOT YOUR BURDEN
            BUT CAN YOU PLEASE COME HOME?

DYLAN: So I know that taking care of this unfinished family business won't be sweet. But hopefully, it will be as short as possible.

(Blackout on JUNE and CRAZY TOM. Underscore returns to "Tourists Music." GEORGE & MARTHA enter.)

MARTHA: Excuse us again, uh...Mr. Budgie, is it?

BO-GEE: No, Bo-Gee. It means newspaper in Chinese.

GEORGE: Funny, we're Martha and George Carpenter, and my great granddaddy was a—

GEORGE & BO-GEE: Carpenter.

GEORGE: Isn't that something? I bet in all cultures, people's names are always derived from their trades.

MARTHA: George please! I'm sure he's not interested and neither am I.

GEORGE: Oh pardon us, sir, but are you from out of town also?

DYLAN: No, do I look it?

MARTHA: Not really...

DYLAN: Then what? Do I smell like I'm from out of town?

GEORGE: Nothing of the sort. We just saw your suitcases and all.

DYLAN: Well I live in L.A. now, but I grew up around here.

MARTHA: So this is home?

DYLAN: Right over there.

(Lights up on "The People's Laundry" exterior.)

GEORGE: You mean that little building that says "The People's Laundry?"

DYLAN: Yes, I'm afraid I come from a long line of stereotypes.

GEORGE: You know, I think I read something about The People's Laundry in one of the guide books and I thought that it was a museum about communism or something.

MARTHA: George, don't let everyone know we're from Columbus, Ohio.

GEORGE: Martha!

MARTHA: I'm sorry, but we just thought those things didn't exist anymore.

BO-GEE: Well, you're both sort of right. Years ago, laundry owners were the backbone of our community, and The People's Laundry was like Town Hall. But not anymore.

(Underscore changes to "Ballad of Chinatown." All freeze except for BO-GEE, who sings:)

BO-GEE: THIS LAUNDRY WAS A SOURCE OF PRIDE
          NOW IT'S FALLEN OUT OF GRACE
          NOW IT'S A FAMILY DIVIDE
          AND WHAT WILL TAKE ITS PLACE?
          AND WHAT WILL TAKE ITS PLACE?

BO-GEE: Yes, they don't make them like The People's Laundry anymore.

(Underscore returns to "Tourists Music.")

MARTHA: Well, as I was saying, Ball-Gee. That "People's Laundry" building over there looks kind of quaint.

DYLAN: Quaint? Yeah, come on into the kitchen, I'll introduce you to my uncle, Hop-Sing, you'll remember him, he used to be the cook on *Bonanza*, and—

(Underscore changes to "Home Is Where It's Harshest.")

MARTHA: All right! Perhaps quaint wasn't the right word, but I meant that as a compliment.

GEORGE: Oh let's go Martha he's just like our kids, no respect for his elders.

DYLAN: Yeah, run along Martha and enjoy your visit now.

GEORGE: Thanks, we will.

MARTHA: You try to enjoy your visit home, too.

(MARTHA and GEORGE exit. DYLAN sings:)

"HOME IS WHERE IT'S HARSHEST"

DYLAN: Home...Home... We'll see about that.
(Sings)

          I'M HOME...I'M HOME
          I'M HOME...IN THEORY
          AND WITH THEORY, ONE MUST ALWAYS BE
          A LITTLE LEERY
          LEERY OF THE FAILURE RATE LEERY OF THE PLANS YOU MADE
          BUT MOSTLY LEERY
          OF WHAT THE "EXPERTS" SAY

LIKE THEY SAY: "HOME; IS WHERE THE HEART IS"
BUT I SAY; "HOME; IS WHERE IT'S HARSHEST"

AT HOME; THERE'S NOWHERE TO HIDE
THEY KNOW ALL YOUR SECRETS AND THEY'RE HIP TO YOUR JIVE
YOU CAN'T PRETEND YOU'RE SOMEONE YOU'RE NOT
AND YOU HAVE TO CONTEND WITH THINGS
YOU WISH YOU FORGOT

SO IS HOME; REALLY WHERE THE HEART IS?
NO NO NO; "HOME; IS WHERE IT'S HARSHEST"

AND THERE'S OUR LAUNDRY
"THE PEOPLE'S LAUNDRY"
IT MAY BE THE PRIDE OF THE NEIGHBORHOOD
BUT TO ME, IT WILL ALWAYS BE
THE NEMESIS OF MY CHILDHOOD

STARCH THAT COLLAR
SCRUB THAT CUFF
IRON THOSE SLACKS
THEN WRAP 'EM ALL UP

PHONE CALL FOR ME?
NO I CAN'T GO TO THE MOVIES
I GOTTA WORK IN THE LAUNDRY
NO I CAN'T TRY OUT FOR THE FOOTBALL TEAM
I GOTTA WORK IN THE LAUNDRY
NO I CAN'T HAVE ANY DREAMS
I GOTTA WORK IN THE LAUNDRY

IF THIS SOUNDS LIKE A BAD B-MOVIE
BELIEVE ME, IT IS
SO WHY AM I IN THIS SEQUEL?
IT'S ALL PART OF MY MOTHER'S GUILT TRIPS;
AND BELIEVE ME, HER GUILT HAS NO EQUAL
HER GUILT TRIPS ALWAYS DO THE TRICK
AND WE'RE NOT EVEN JEWISH OR CATHOLIC!

MONEY MAY MAKE THE WORLD GO ROUND
AND LOVE MAY BE ALL YOU NEED
BUT GUILT IS THE TIE THAT BINDS
AND GUILT RULES MY FAMILY AND ME

LIKE I SAY; "HOME IS WHERE IT'S HARSHEST"
YES I SAY; "HOME IS WHERE IT'S HARSHEST"

(DYLAN sees his mother, JUNE, coming out of the laundry.)

THOUGH THAT STILL MAY BE
WHERE THE HEART IS

(Song ends. JUNE and DYLAN embrace.)

DYLAN: See you later, Bo-Gee.

(DYLAN and JUNE exit into the laundry. BO-GEE sings:)

"BALLAD OF CHINATOWN (Reprise)"

BO-GEE: DYLAN'S HOME SO NOW HE'LL SEE
THE WORLD HE LEFT BEHIND
READY OR NOT, IT'S HERE HE'LL MEET
THE FATE HE IS TO FIND
THE FATE HE IS TO FIND

(Blackout)

ACT I - SCENE 2

JUNE and DYLAN in "The People's Laundry."

JUNE: Dylan, you must be hungry.

DYLAN: No, I'm OK mom.

JUNE: Why don't you help yourself to some of those bows and don-tot on the table, while I wrap up these few packages, and we can keep talking.

DYLAN: Mom, I'm not hungry but why don't you let me help you while we talk?

JUNE: Oh, don't worry. I just do these three or four packages and that's it for the day.

DYLAN: That's it?

JUNE: That's it.

DYLAN: How long has business been this bad?

JUNE: A few years now. But Josie is doing some great work with the Chinatown Office of...Commerce, I think?

DYLAN: Development—C.O.D. I saw her in action this morning. She should run for Mayor.

JUNE: Yes, Josie is doing fine...and she can help us do fine.

DYLAN: Mom, look I have no time to play Truth or Dare; What's going on?

JUNE: Look, I keep telling your father we should get out.

DYLAN: Mom, you've been saying that since I was in grade school

JUNE: This time is different!

DYLAN: How?

JUNE: Well you know we never had much money, but now we owe a lot of money...And your father refuses to pay the rent.

DYLAN: So how do you stay here?

JUNE: Somehow, Josie, through her job, has been able to work out an extension.

DYLAN: Extension?

JUNE: The landlord wants to build a new mall here and a few years ago, he offered us a reloca-tion fee that was enough for a down payment on a small house...but your Dad always refuses. But that was before Josie came back. So now we're going to try and strike that deal again. But just in case, I was wondering if you could...

DYLAN: Give you some money, sure, but I could've easily done that from California.

JUNE: Dylan, this time I need more than your money; I need your support.

DYLAN: My support? When Dad practically disowned me when I left, where were you?

JUNE: Dylan...

DYLAN: You didn't face up to him then, just like you won't face up to him now! I know Dad has done a lot of damage; But you've always let him have his way!

JUNE: Dylan, don't.

(*JUNE gets upset. DYLAN comforts her.*)

DYLAN: Oh Mom, I'm sorry.

I TRIED

JUNE: OH LIVING'S TOUGH WHEN THERE'S NOT ENOUGH
          AND WORSE WHEN THAT LITTLE BIT IS GONE
          THAT'S THE WAY WE'VE ALWAYS LIVED
          I'M SURE YOU REMEMBER, MY SON

          THIS TAKES IT'S TOLL ON YOUR HEART AND SOUL
          YOU START TO DREAD EVERY COMING DAY
          I KNOW IN YOUR HEART THERE'S A HOLE
          THAT COMES FROM LIVING THIS WAY

          BUT SOMEHOW YOU MADE YOUR WAY THROUGH
          BUILT UP YOUR WRITING AND PRIDE
          THOUGH I WISH WE DID MORE FOR YOU
          JUST KNOW I TRIED

AND NOW WE'RE HERE WITH THE SAME OLD FEARS
THE STRINGS ATTACHED TO OUR HEARTS ARE CUT
NOT FACING EACH OTHER FOR YEARS
THEN HOPING THAT DOOR WOULD STAY SHUT

TO OPEN THE DOOR DOES NOT MEAN WAR
ALTHOUGH I WANT YOU TO TAKE MY SIDE
I FEEL THAT I'M UP FOR THE TASK
OF TURNING OUR FAMILY'S TIDE

SO LET'S TRY TO OPEN THAT DOOR
AND NOT KEEP OUR FEELINGS OUTSIDE
AS FAR AS CONVINCING YOUR DAD
YOU KNOW I TRIED

MAYBE WITHOUT THIS LAUNDRY
THE THREE OF US COULD FINALLY BE
SOMETHING THAT WE NEVER WERE; A FAMILY

(*JUNE takes DYLAN's hand.*)

TOGETHER WE CAN SEE THIS THROUGH
FROM US BOTH, YOUR FATHER CAN'T HIDE
IF ALL OUR WORST FEARS STILL COME TRUE
AT LEAST WE TRIED

DYLAN: OK Mom, I'll help you talk to Dad.

(*Blackout*)

ACT I - SCENE 3

CRAZY TOM sits in dim light of the laundry office, which looks more like an abandoned storage room. He is coughing and counting the packages on the wall. JUNE and DYLAN are just outside, knocking on the door.

CRAZY TOM: *(Sings)*
> YIT...NGEE...SLOM...SLEE *(1,2,3, 4 in Chinese)*
> PRETTY SOON, WE WILL BE FREE

JUNE: Tom, Dylan is here open up! Tom? Tom, Dylan is here, please open up!

CRAZY TOM: The door's always open.

(JUNE and DYLAN enter.)

DYLAN: Dad! *(Coughs)* Dad? Are you in here?

(CRAZY TOM turns on a lamp over his head. He is sitting on a stool, smoking a cigar and occasionally coughing.)

JUNE: Look Tom, Dylan is here!

CRAZY TOM: June, I think I can see that.

JUNE: Well, aren't you going to say something?

CRAZY TOM: When you give me a chance, I will.

JUNE: Tom, we haven't seen Dylan for so long and you're acting like you can't be bothered —

DYLAN: Mom, Dad, I don't know what to say. Except that it's good to see you two...together.

JUNE: Why don't I let you two talk?

CRAZY TOM: That would be a wonderful idea, my dear.

JUNE: See what I have to put up with Dylan?

(JUNE exits.)

CRAZY TOM: Welcome home, son...I'm sure you've noticed that things haven't changed much around here.

DYLAN: It's really good to see you.

CRAZY TOM: Good to see you too. Why don't you have a seat?

DYLAN: I guess it's been a while.

CRAZY TOM: Yes, it has.

DYLAN: Dad, why are you sitting here alone in the dark?

CRAZY TOM: This is where I always sit. The basement is good for my asthma.

DYLAN: But that cigar can't be helping.

CRAZY TOM: Well, like you told me, just before you left for college; you said I was "beyond help."

DYLAN: Dad, would you mind if I turned on another light?

CRAZY TOM: Make yourself at home, son.

(DYLAN searches a bit, then finally finds a light that illuminates the whole room and reveals a wall-size shelf of laundry packages.)

DYLAN: Whoa!...It's the "Great Wall of Laundry."

CRAZY TOM: You could call it that.

DYLAN: What is all of this...unclaimed laundry?

CRAZY TOM: Just some things my friends and colleagues have left behind.

DYLAN: It's almost like a cemetery.

CRAZY TOM: I prefer to think of it as a shrine.

DYLAN: A shrine!?...A shrine to what?

CRAZY TOM: Nobody's ever made a movie about this, so you wouldn't understand.

DYLAN: Dad, there's no need to be patronizing—

CRAZY TOM: I was just about to say the same thing.

DYLAN: Well...I guess I have been away too long.

CRAZY TOM: Five and a half years, but who's counting?

DYLAN: I guess it's been a really long time.

CRAZY TOM: The last time you were here the President didn't smoke pot.

DYLAN: Yeah, I think Bush was more of a Prozac kind of guy.

CRAZY TOM: Well, at least we agree on one thing. So what brings you back here?

DYLAN: Well, since you ask, I've been talking to Mom about that possible mall deal—

CRAZY TOM: OK, I get it now. My son, the big Hollywood big-shot, has come back to Chinatown to straighten his loser dad out.

DYLAN: Dad, no one's calling you a loser. But maybe we can get you to reconsider.

"NOT FOR SALE"

CRAZY TOM:

    SO NOW YOU'RE GONNA SHOW ME HOW TO LIVE?
    TREAT ME LIKE I'VE GOT NOTHING LEFT TO GIVE

    YOU MAY BE RICH, NOW
    WHILE I'M STILL POOR
    BUT THAT DOESN'T MEAN YOU HAVE EVERYTHING
    THAT I'VE STRIVED FOR

DYLAN: IT'S NOT ABOUT HAVE AND HAVE NOT
    THIS IS ABOUT WHY AND WHY NOT?
    I'M NOT SHOWING YOU HOW TO LIVE
    I'M JUST TRYING TO SHOW YOU HOW TO STOP DYING

CRAZY TOM:

    DYLAN, WE NEVER STOP DYING
    RIGHT FROM THE DAY WE ARE BORN
    DEATH IS A REWARD OF LIFE
    JUST AS PEACE IS A REWARD OF WAR

DYLAN: EVEN IN WAR THERE IS PEACE
    BETWEEN BATTLES THERE IS PEACE

            SO FOR ONCE, FOR US
            LET THERE BE PEACE

CRAZY TOM:
            I HEAR YOU SPEAKING OF PEACE
            BUT WANTING TO BUY MY STORE
            AND TO BUY ME OUT
            IS TO ENGAGE IN WAR

DYLAN: I DON'T WANT TO "BUY YOU OUT"
            I WANT TO HELP ALL OF US OUT

(*Spoken*) I know I haven't been around much. And I'll probably never be the son you wanted. But maybe it's time we cut our losses here.

CRAZY TOM:
            THE PEOPLE'S LAUNDRY'S NOT FOR SALE
            NOT TO YOU, NOT TO EMPIRE NATIONAL
            NOT TO ANYBODY
            WE'LL GET OUT OF THIS, ALL BY OURSELVES
            AS LONG AS CRAZY TOM'S AROUND,
            "OUR OWN LAW" WILL PREVAIL

DYLAN: Why are you bringing that up now?

CRAZY TOM:
            YOU CAN'T SELL OUT
            WHEN THE PRESSURE'S TOO GREAT
            YOU MUST PREVAIL AND CARRY YOUR WEIGHT
            ALWAYS CARRY YOUR WEIGHT
            THAT'S WHAT OUR OWN LAW'S ABOUT
            THAT'S WHAT CRAZY TOM IS ABOUT

CRAZY TOM: Dylan, do you remember The Laundry...Allied...Workers; what we used to call "Our Own LAW."

DYLAN: Of course I do! They used to meet right here. You'd stand before them, raising holy hell, like you were in the pulpit or something.

CRAZY TOM: That's right they even called me—

CRAZY TOM & DYLAN: Crazy Reverend Tom.

CRAZY TOM: But after a while, they dropped the Reverend— "Our own LAW" we were an ecu-menical bunch.

DYLAN: More like a maniacal bunch. What ever happened to all those guys of "Our Own LAW?"

CRAZY TOM: Well Dylan, this "great wall of laundry"—as you call it, is all that's left of "Our Own LAW."

DYLAN: This unclaimed laundry?

   "NOT FOR SALE (Reprise)"

CRAZY TOM:
          TO YOU, THIS IS UNCLAIMED LAUNDRY
          TO ME, A LEGACY
          THOSE LAUNDRIES ALL WENT DOWN
          NOW THEIR SPIRITS LIVE THROUGH ME
          YOU CAN'T SEE THIS
          CAUSE YOU'RE NOT LIKE ME
          BUT THIS UNCLAIMED LAUNDRY'S WORTH
          MORE THAN YOUR SCREENWRITING FEES
          YOU CAN'T BUY ME OUT
          BECAUSE I AM NOT FOR SALE
          NO, CRAZY TOM IS NOT FOR SALE
          NOT FOR SALE!

CRAZY TOM: Now, leave me alone, I have some work to do.

(DYLAN exits. Underscore: "Home.")

CRAZY TOM: We did well, boys, we did well. I mean, this is what you wanted, right? This is what you wanted, right! This is what you wanted, right!

(Blackout)

ACT I - SCENE 4

DYLAN comes out of the laundry. It is now dusk and BO-GEE is closing up his newsstand. DYLAN goes to help him. BO-GEE throws a magazine at him.

DYLAN: *Basketball Digest!*

BO-GEE: When you were a kid that was your favorite.

DYLAN: Between you and me, it still is. Hey, thanks a lot. It's the nicest present I've gotten since I've been back.

BO-GEE: Well, like they say, you can never go home again.

DYLAN: Well, whoever said that wasn't Chinese, cause when you're Chinese, you always have to go home again.

DYLAN: So, are you living in the same place?

BO-GEE: No, I've moved.

DYLAN: Oh great, so you've finally moved out of Chinatown?

BO-GEE: No, I live right there.

(BO-GEE points to the laundry.)

DYLAN: Uncle Bo-Gee, you're pointing to the laundry.

BO-GEE: That's where I live.

DYLAN: My god, I didn't know that.

BO-GEE: Yeah, my old building on Walker St. went co-op and I couldn't afford it—story of a lot of people around here. Luckily, your father took me in.

DYLAN: I'm glad he did.

BO-GEE: Me, too. "Crazy Tom" is like me, we hate to see what's happening to Chinatown. I bet if he could, "Crazy Tom" would take us all in.

DYLAN: He's always left me out in the cold—I don't know why I came back. In fact, my parents are the best argument I know for never getting married. But did I learn from them? No, of course not!

BO-GEE: Look, Dylan. I'm sure it was not easy for you to come back here. But believe me, despite all the problems, you should be thankful you still have a family to go to.

DYLAN: Oh, then take my family—please!

"FAMILY"

BO-GEE: FAMILY IS LIKE AIR
YOU CAN'T SEE IT, BUT YOU KNOW THAT IT'S THERE
IT FILLS YOUR LUNGS WITH PRIDE
IT'S HARD TO SWALLOW WHEN YOU CRY
AND YOU KNOW IT DOESN'T LEAVE TILL YOU DIE

DYLAN: *(Spoken)* No, Uncle Bo-Gee; *(Sings)*
FAMILY IS MORE LIKE A RECEIPT
YOU PUT IT AWAY, HOPING NO ONE NEEDS TO SEE IT
IT'S NICE TO KNOW YOU HAVE IT
BUT LET'S NOT MAKE IT A HABIT;
MORE THAN ONCE OR TWICE A YEAR—LIKE TAXES

BO-GEE: FAMILY IS A NEST TO US

DYLAN: NO, FAMILY IS A PEST TO US

BO-GEE: BUT IT'S BETTER TO HAVE, THAN HAVE NOT

DYLAN: YOU WOULDN'T SAY THAT WITH MY LOT!

BO-GEE & DYLAN:
AND THAT'S WHAT FAMILY MEANS TO ME

BO-GEE: *(Spoken)* All right, Dylan; *(Sings)*
FAMILY IS LIKE FOOD
AFTER YOU EAT IT; YOU ARE IN A GOOD MOOD
YEAH, YOU MAY SKIP A MEAL,
BUT INSIDE YOU'LL ALWAYS FEEL
THE NEED TO CHEW ON SOMETHING THAT'S REAL

DYLAN: *(Spoken)* No, Uncle Bo-Gee, you be for real. *(Sings)*
FAMILY IS LIKE GOING OUT TO EAT
IT'S TOO EXPENSIVE, AND UNCOMFORTABLE SEATS

THE ATMOSPHERE IS RAW
THE CONVERSATION'S A BORE
BUT WE'RE ALWAYS COMING BACK FOR MORE

BO-GEE: FAMILY IS A NEST TO US

DYLAN: NO, FAMILY IS A PEST TO US

BO-GEE: BUT IT'S BETTER TO HAVE, THAN HAVE NOT

DYLAN: MAYBE A LITTLE, BUT NOT A LOT

BO-GEE & DYLAN:
            WELL, THAT'S WHAT FAMILY MEANS TO ME

BO-GEE: Oh Dylan, you must like your family a little bit.

DYLAN: You know how I would like my family, Uncle Bo-Gee?

BO-GEE: How would you like your family, Dylan?

DYLAN: Over and easy; just like my morning eggs.

BO-GEE: Well, Dylan, then you better wake up and smell the tea.

(BO-GEE smacks DYLAN in the head and sings.)

BO-GEE: FAMILY IS A NEST TO US

DYLAN: NO, FAMILY IS A PEST TO US

BO-GEE: BUT IT'S BETTER TO HAVE, THAN HAVE NOT

DYLAN: JUST MAKE THE BEST OF WHAT YOU'VE GOT!

BO-GEE & DYLAN:
            WHY CAN'T FAMILY BE LIKE US?

(BO-GEE wheels back into his newsstand and then re-emerges with a table and duffel bag.)

BO-GEE: Come here, I want to show you something.

(BO-GEE pulls out incense sticks, oranges, snapshots and a bowl of sand from the bag, and starts arranging

them on the table.)

BO-GEE: I usually do this alone, but since we hardly see each other anymore. I'd like you to share this with me.

DYLAN: Sure.

BO-GEE: Today is your Aunt Lily's birthday. She would've been 49 today.

DYLAN: I'm sorry.

BO-GEE: She's been gone for almost six years now. And every year, on her birthday, I still write her a letter. And in "hung-ngen," Chinese tradition, I always write her a letter and burn it, so she can read it in heaven.

(BO-GEE lights six incense sticks. He hands three to DYLAN and holds three himself. BO-GEE looks at DYLAN, they both close their eyes and bow their head three times. BO-GEE stands the incense sticks in the bowl of sand and motions for DYLAN to do the same. He does BO-GEE pulls out a letter, which he sings.)

"HAPPY BIRTHDAY LILY"

BO-GEE: HAPPY BIRTHDAY LILY
            YOU WOULD'VE BEEN FORTY-NINE TODAY
            THOUGH IT'S BEEN A LONG TIME
            YOU'RE STILL ON MY MIND
            AND YOUR PICTURE'S NEVER FAR AWAY

            HAPPY BIRTHDAY LILY
            THE NEWSSTAND'S STILL DOING FINE
            THAT WAS YOUR IDEA
            AND NOW I'M STILL HERE
            BUT WHO KNEW WHAT WAS DOWN THE LINE?

            WE OPENED THE NEWSSTAND
            SO YOU COULD TAKE CARE OF ME
            AFTER I COULD NOT WALK
            THEN YOUR ILLNESS STRUCK
            AND YOU COULD NO LONGER SEE
            CARING FOR YOU TOOK ALL OUR TIME AND MONEY
            BUT I'D DO IT ALL OVER AGAIN, HONEY
            I'D DO IT ALL OVER AGAIN

            HAPPY BIRTHDAY LILY

HOPE YOU HAVE A GOOD TIME TODAY
DON'T THINK OF NEXT YEAR
JUST TAKE CARE OF WHAT'S NEAR
CAUSE MY LOVE, I'LL BE THERE SOMEDAY
MY LOVE, I'LL BE THERE SOMEDAY
HAPPY BIRTHDAY, LILY

(BO-GEE *burns the letter in the bowl next to the snapshot. He looks at* DYLAN, *they both close their eyes and bow their heads three times.*)

BO-GEE: Here, have some orange.

(*They eat oranges.* BO-GEE *starts packing up his things.*)

BO-GEE: Thank you for sharing this with me.

DYLAN: No, thank you. It certainly puts things into perspective.

BO-GEE: I'm glad I could be of help.

DYLAN: Life's just way too short for all of this bickering and bullshit. And Uncle Bo-Gee, I know I'll miss my parents one day, but for now, my parents—especially my Dad—make me as mad as when I was a little boy.

(*JOSIE enters.*)

JOSIE: Bo-Gee!

BO-GEE: Well, Dylan, I have to go now.

DYLAN: Hi, Josie!—(*To* BO-GEE) Where are you going?

BO-GEE: Excuse me, Dylan, but I really must be going.

JOSIE: Wait! Don't leave yet!

(*JOSIE and* DYLAN *freeze as* BO-GEE *sings:*)

"BALLAD OF CHINATOWN (Reprise)"

BO-GEE: WHEN JOSIE CAME BACK HERE TO STAY
SHE HAD TO GET HER WAY
TO GET HER WAY SHE'LL HAVE TO CHANGE

THE COURSE OF SOMEONE'S FATE

JOSIE: Bo-Gee, me and Mom really need an answer!

DYLAN: Josie, what's going on?

BO-GEE: I'll have to talk to you later!

JOSIE: Bo-Gee!

(BO-GEE gathers his bag and exits into his now closed newsstand.)

DYLAN: Why are you yelling at Uncle Bo-Gee?

JOSIE: Look, you've been away too long, you don't know what he's doing to Mom and Dad.

DYLAN: What on earth is he doing?

JOSIE: Even you must be able to see that the only reason Dad lets him live in the back room— for free—is just so he can use him as another excuse to stay in Chinatown.

DYLAN: Maybe they want to stay here.

JOSIE: Well, they sure don't act like it.

DYLAN: What are you talking about?

JOSIE: Dad doesn't even pay the rent and he has a little bit of money saved up—

DYLAN: Mom says they're broke!

JOSIE: Dad keeps it all away from her, and the only reason they haven't evicted his sorry ass is because I took out a loan to pay all the laundry's back rent.

DYLAN: Mom never mentioned this.

JOSIE: She's too proud. Besides, it's my contact with their landlord that's keeping them there at all. You see, their landlord wants to work with my company to redevelop this block into a mall.

DYLAN: So Dad is the only thing standing in the way of "The Great Mall of Chinatown?"

JOSIE: Hello? This is not a god-damned movie, this is real life! In fact, I'm even getting them to reconsider offering Mom and Dad a relocation fee if they get out this year. That's why we need you <u>and</u> Bo-Gee to talk to Dad about this.

DYLAN: Excuse me, but who died and left you in charge?

"STAND YOUR GROUND"

JOSIE: FOR SO LONG, THE CHINESE WERE PASSIVE
           ALTHOUGH, OUR NUMBERS SO MASSIVE
           WE SEE OURSELVES AS SECOND CLASS
           WE STEP ASIDE TO LET OTHERS PASS

           NOW LOOK WHERE THAT THINKING HAS TAKEN US
           THE CITY, HAS ALL BUT FORSAKEN US
           AS LONG AS IT'S KEPT IN OUR NEIGHBORHOOD
           AS LONG AS WE JUST DO WHAT WE SHOULD
           THEY DON'T GIVE A DAMN AND THEY NEVER EVER COULD

           YOU'VE GOT TO STAND YOUR GROUND
           OR ELSE ALL YOU'VE FOUND WILL BE LOST
           THEY'LL TAKE EVERYTHING YOU HAVE
           AND LOSING FACE WILL BE THE COST
           CAUSE YOU CAN'T TRUST PEOPLE
           NO MATTER HOW NICE THEY SOUND
           SO JUST SMILE AND BE CHARMING
           BUT INSIDE, ALWAYS STAND YOUR GROUND

JOSIE: THAT'S WHY I WORK IN THIS PLACE NOW
           TO HELP CHINATOWN SAVE FACE NOW
           BUSINESS BOOMED LIKE NEVER BEFORE
           HELPED DEVELOPERS TO OPEN NEW DOORS

           IF WE DON'T, THIS COULD BE A GHOST TOWN
           THESE STORES ARE ALL GONNA CLOSE DOWN
           WITH A NEW MALL, WE CAN STAND TALL
           WITH A NEW MALL, WE WILL NEVER FALL
           WITH A NEW MALL, THERE'S NO MORE GREAT WALL

           YOU'VE GOT TO STAND YOUR GROUND
           OR ELSE ALL YOU'VE FOUND WILL BE LOST
           THEY'LL TAKE EVERYTHING YOU HAVE
           AND LOSING FACE WILL BE THE COST
           CAUSE YOU CAN'T TRUST PEOPLE

NO MATTER HOW NICE THEY SOUND
SO JUST SMILE AND BE CHARMING
BUT INSIDE, ALWAYS STAND YOUR GROUND

JOSIE: HELP ME TO TAKE THIS STAND
HELP YOUR MOM CONVINCE YOUR OLD MAN
THAT THE LAUNDRY'S A THING OF THE PAST
AND NOW IT'S TIME TO LEAVE WHILE THEY STILL CAN

SOMETIMES TO STAND YOUR GROUND
YOU GIVE A LITTLE TO GAIN A LOT
AND THIS IS NOT JUST BUSINESS
I AM TALKING MATTERS OF THE HEART

JOSIE: Dylan...no one has to die for someone else to take charge. Will you help me talk to Dad tonight?

DYLAN: Let's go for that drink first.

(Blackout)

ACT I - SCENE 5

The Tom's dining room in "The People's Laundry." Entire cast is sitting around a dining room table. JUNE proposes a toast.

JUNE: Dylan, we're all glad to have you back. Even if it's just for a week.

BO-GEE: That's right!

DYLAN: Thank you!

JUNE: And hopefully, this will be the last time you have to visit us in this cramped, old place.

JOSIE: Amen!

BO-GEE: What do you mean "cramped, old place?"

JUNE: Excuse me, but am I making this toast or are you?

BO-GEE: Sorry I asked.

CRAZY TOM: Why don't we just drink already!

JUNE: Is that all you have to say?

CRAZY TOM: Well, I think you've said more than enough.

DYLAN: Let's just all calm down and finish dinner.

JOSIE: I guess I'll bring out the dessert.

(JOSIE exits.)

JUNE: Yes, Josie was nice enough to bring dessert.

BO-GEE: Just save mine. I'm sorry, everybody, but I'd like to be excused.

CRAZY TOM: Bo-Gee, you haven't missed a dessert in years.

DYLAN: And besides, the night is still young.

BO-GEE: Thanks for the great dinner, but I have to go back to my room.

DYLAN: Why don't you just stay through dessert?

JUNE: He wants to leave, so let him go!

BO-GEE: To tell you the truth, right about now you two always start to drink too much and say stupid things.

JUNE: I won't tolerate that from a lodger. Not a lodger, a freeloader!

CRAZY TOM: June!

BO-GEE: See what I mean? Goodnight everybody.

JUNE: Not so fast, Bo-Gee I am so tired of having no say in what goes on around here...so until we decide what we're doing I'm moving in with Josie!

DYLAN: Mom!

"SOMETHING FOR ME"

JUNE: I'VE PUT UP WITH HIM
FOR YEARS PUT UP WITH YOU TOO
FOR YEARS HELD SO MUCH BACK
BUT NOW MY SILENCE IS THROUGH

TOM, YOU KNOW I'VE ALWAYS STOOD BY YOU
IT'S THE PLACE I'VE ALWAYS CHOSE TO BE
NOW I'M ASKING; CAN WE DO SOMETHING FOR ME?

I KNOW THIS LAUNDRY
AND CHINATOWN YOU LOVE SO
BUT YOU HAVE TO REALIZE
THAT IT IS TIME WE MUST GO

TOM, I REALLY NEED TO GET OUT NOW
AND I THINK YOU NEED TO GET OUT NOW
AND WE HAVE TO ACT WHILE THERE'S STILL SOME WAY OUT

CRAZY TOM:
YOU FORGOT WHERE WE CAME FROM
YOU FORGOT THE BAD OLD DAYS
RIGHT BEFORE THE LAUNDRY CAME OUR WAY
STRUGGLING TO JUST GET BY

THE LAUNDRY GOT US RIGHT IN STRIDE
IT GAVE US A LIVING AND OUR PRIDE

REMEMBER HOW CHINESE WERE TREATED
EVEN THOUGH ALL OF US WERE BORN HERE
THEY STILL SAW US AS FOREIGNERS
AND LOWLY LEECHES THAT WAS MADE PERFECTLY CLEAR

WE SURVIVED WITH OUR OWN LAW
DON'T FORGET OUR OWN LAW NOW
WE SWORE TO IT LIKE A WEDDING VOW

THROUGH IT, WE BECAME SOMEONE
AND THROUGH OUR OWN LAW, WE EVEN RAISED A SON
THAT LEGACY IS WHAT WE'RE ALL ABOUT
SO JUNE, LET'S NOT THROW IT ALL AWAY NOW

JUNE: TOM THIS IS NOT AN EASY TASK
AND I'M NOT THE ONE TO SAY YOU'RE WRONG
BUT THIS HAS BEEN ONLY YOUR DREAM ALL ALONG
I HAVE BEEN WAITING PATIENTLY
IT'S AMAZING THAT YOU STILL CAN'T SEE
THAT I STILL NEED SOMETHING DESPERATELY FOR ME

(Spoken over underscore)

DYLAN: Mom, let's not be so hasty!

JUNE: THIS HAS BEEN BUILDING
FOR THIRTY YEARS NOW
SO I DON'T THINK THAT
YOU COULD CALL THAT FAST
BUT IT IS HERE NOW, THE TIME IS HERE NOW
AND I THINK FREEDOM'S REALLY GONNA LAST

JUNE: FOR MANY YEARS NOW, TOO MANY YEARS NOW

CRAZY TOM:
WE SURVIVED WITH OUR OWN LAW

JUNE: I'VE SACRIFICED ALL TILL THERE WAS NO MORE ME

CRAZY TOM:

DON'T FORGET OUR OWN LAW NOW

JUNE: BUT IT IS HERE NOW, THE TIME IS HERE NOW

CRAZY TOM:
            WE SWORE TO IT LIKE A WEDDING VOW

JUNE: AND I AM DOING SOMETHING JUST FOR ME
            SOMETHING JUST FOR ME

(As JUNE gets up from the table, JOSIE enters with dessert.)

CRAZY TOM:
            LET HER GO, JUST LET HER GO
            "CRAZY TOM" IS FINE ALONE
            SO WHY DON'T YOU ALL JUST GO HOME!

JOSIE: Maybe we should take a rain check on dessert?

DYLAN: Josie, how many different scams are you running?

JOSIE: (Pointing at CRAZY TOM) Maybe you should ask him that. Come on Mom. Dylan,
perhaps you should come too.

CRAZY TOM: Can everyone please leave the premises!

(JOSIE exits with JUNE, BO-GEE follows.)

DYLAN: Dad, don't worry, it's gonna be all right, I'm just gonna go get Mom settled at Josie's.
I'll be right back.

CRAZY TOM: So will she, you'll see; a bad penny always comes back.

DYLAN: Dad when will you stop!

(DYLAN exits. Music to "Home" starts. CRAZY TOM pours all of the unfinished drinks on the table into his
glass and drinks it in one sip. He starts toasting "The Great Wall of Laundry" by calling off his old friend's
names. After each name is called, a faceless figure dances out from behind the wall.)

CRAZY TOM: Chin! You're not forgotten. Wong! You're not forgotten. Yee! You're not forgotten.
Loo! You're not forgotten. "Our Own Law" is still upheld here. "Crazy Tom" calls a meeting of the
officers of the Laundry Allied Workers Society.

(CRAZY TOM dances with ghost friends and sings.)

"HOME"

CRAZY TOM:
      COME ON BOYS, GATHER 'ROUND
      CAUSE SOON WE'RE GOING TO LEAVE
      LITTLE OL' CHINATOWN

      CAUSE THE TIME WILL SOON COME
      WHEN THE MOON WILL OBLITERATE THE SUN
      THE SKY WILL COME CRASHING DOWN
      AND THE EARTH WILL COME UNDONE

      WHEN THAT DAY ARRIVES
      YOU WON'T SEE ME CRY
      I'LL SEE IT AS DESTINY FULFILLED
      AND MY CHANCE TO FINALLY GO HOME

      HOME; WHERE OUR OWN LAW
      IS ALWAYS UPHELD
      HOME; WHERE OUR OWN LAW
      IS ALWAYS UPHELD

      BOYS WE'RE HALFWAY HOME
      WE'VE WEATHERED MANY STORMS
      NOW THERE'S ONLY ONE MORE BIG ONE TO GO
      THEN IT'S TIME FOR US TO GO HOME

      HOME; WHERE OUR OWN LAW
      IS ALWAYS UPHELD
      HOME; WHERE OUR OWN LAW
      IS ALWAYS UPHELD

END OF ACT I

ENTR'ACTE

BO-GEE appears in a single spotlight.

       "BALLAD OF CHINATOWN" (Reprise)

BO-GEE: CHANGE IS A NECESSITY
             ABANDONMENT IS NOT
             BEFORE YOU MAKE A MAJOR CHANGE
             BE SURE OF WHAT YOU'VE GOT
             BE SURE OF WHAT YOU'VE GOT

(Blackout)

ACT II - SCENE 1

CRAZY TOM sits alone getting drunk in his office. BO-GEE enters.

BO-GEE: Tom, can I come in a moment?

CRAZY TOM: Sure, come on in. Want a drink?

BO-GEE: No, thank you. I'm sorry about what happened tonight, Tom.

CRAZY TOM: No need to be, Bo-Gee, no need to be.

BO-GEE: Well, I'll only stay a minute, but I just wanted to say, that if you think I'm becoming too much trouble, I can stay somewhere else.

CRAZY TOM: Nonsense! As long as I'm around, you're staying right here.

BO-GEE: You're a good man, Tom. Thank you.

CRAZY TOM: Sometimes. But I did some really stupid things tonight.

BO-GEE: But Tom, you always have, and—

CRAZY TOM: Thanks a lot, my old comrade in confidence.

BO-GEE: Tom, please don't take this the wrong way. What I meant is, everybody does stupid things, but you're one of the few who learn from their mistakes.

CRAZY TOM: That's very nice of you to say that, Bo-Gee.

BO-GEE: Well, it's true. You just have to do that now, to turn things around with June and Dylan.

CRAZY TOM: Well...what have I learned? I've learned that I've slaved here for twelve hours a day my whole life, while Dylan and Josie, and to some extent, June, were free to go see the world. I've never stopped them, and that's fine—that's why I've worked here. But they don't understand that this laundry is my world. It's all I know. And now they want to take that away from me...and if that happens I'll be just like my father and so many other guys here in Chinatown. They leave China, leave their world, come here and become zombies. Sure they make some money, go buy their houses on Long Island. But inside, they're dead...Bo-Gee, I'm not ready to leave my world yet.

BO-GEE: Come on Tom, no one's saying that.

CRAZY TOM: Well you saw tonight. Dylan, Josie and June...My wife and my kids were like complete strangers. They hate this place. They hate me...what have I worked for all these years? What have we lived for all of these years?...Bo-Gee, why go on?

BO-GEE: TOM!...It's going to be OK.

"THINGS THAT YOU CAN'T FORGET"

BO-GEE: I REMEMBER WHEN YOU WERE NINETEEN
YOUNG AND STUPID, EVEN MORE STUPID THAN NOW
AND SO NAIVE, YOU DOUBTED OUR FATHER'S WAYS
YOU WOULD NOT LISTEN TO WHAT HE HAD TO SAY
IN FACT, YOU DIDN'T EVEN WANT TO STAY

THINGS GOT SO BAD
YOU HAD ONE FOOT OUT THE DOOR
THAT'S WHEN I PULLED YOU ASIDE
AND SAID "WHAT ARE YOU DOING THIS FOR?"
GIVE YOUR OLD MAN A CHANCE
CAUSE YOU'RE ALL HE'S LIVING FOR"

CRAZY TOM:
I HAD A HEART TO HEART WITH OUR DAD
THOUGHT, "WELL THIS AIN'T SO BAD"
I STARTED HELPING WITH HIS LAUNDRY
NOW YOU KNOW IT'S BECOME ME
AND THAT'S SOMETHING YOU CAN'T FORGET

BO-GEE: YOU MUST BELIEVE THAT TOM
AND REMEMBER THOSE THINGS RIGHT NOW
YOU'VE GOT A WIFE AND SON
WHO REALLY ARE AWFULLY PROUD
AND WHEN THE TROUBLES START
YOU SAY THINGS THAT YOU JUST REGRET
THAT'S WHEN YOU SHOULD REMEMBER
THE THINGS THAT YOU CAN'T FORGET

LISTEN TO ME, TOM
TOGETHER WE'VE BEEN THROUGH A LOT
BUT HERE IS HOPING THAT
ALL THIS IS ONLY A START
CAUSE IF WE STICK TOGETHER
THERE IS NO NEED TO REGRET

THE THINGS THAT WE CAN'T FORGET
THE THINGS THAT WE CAN'T FORGET

CRAZY TOM & BO-GEE:
 AND IF WE STICK TOGETHER
 THERE IS NO NEED TO REGRET
 THE THINGS THAT WE CAN'T FORGET

BO-GEE: You just have to talk this way to June and Dylan.

CRAZY TOM: I've always said I would give my life for them. And I still would.

BO-GEE: They'd do the same for you, Tom.

CRAZY TOM: Ha! They don't even give me the time of day. They just laugh at me. Laugh at me all the time. Ha! Ha! Ha! Well I'll have the final laugh.

(DYLAN enters.)

DYLAN: Excuse me, was I interrupting...

BO-GEE: No, come in, come in. Good to see you. I was just having a word with your father

DYLAN: Are you sure?

CRAZY TOM: Hey it's Mr. Hollywood!

BO-GEE: Tom, take it easy! *(To DYLAN in a stage whisper)* He's had a few too many, give him some slack.

DYLAN: I only came back to get a few of Mom's things.

BO-GEE: Dylan, please stay a minute...for me.

DYLAN: Only for you, Uncle Bo-Gee.

BO-GEE: Thank you. So why don't I let you two talk...Good night all.

DYLAN, CRAZY TOM: Goodnight.

(BO-GEE exits.)

CRAZY TOM: I saw that awful movie you supposedly wrote—

DYLAN: Dad—

CRAZY TOM: I stayed to the very end, and your name wasn't even in the credits!

DYLAN: I became an uncredited ghost writer on that one.

CRAZY TOM: So what did you come back here for, to "ghost write" my life?

DYLAN: I just came back to get some things for Mom, that's all.

CRAZY TOM: What's your hurry, they gave out this year's Oscars already. Why don't you have a drink?

DYLAN: Haven't you had enough?

CRAZY TOM: I was feeling deprived.

"THE LAST HAND LAUNDRY IN CHINATOWN"

DYLAN: MOM STOOD BY YOU FOR THIRTY YEARS OR MORE
          NOW YOU'VE PUSHED HER OUT THE DOOR AND WHAT FOR?
          I OFFERED YOU SOME MONEY, BUT YOU TELL ME NO
          NOW I'M READY TO GO WITH MOM AND LEAVE YOU HERE ALONE

CRAZY TOM: Are you threatening me?

DYLAN: Threatening? No. *(Sings)*
          DAD, WHY DON'T YOU COOPERATE FOR A CHANGE?

CRAZY TOM:
          COOPERATE?
          FOR WHAT KIND OF CHANGE?
          FOR YOUR CHUMP CHANGE?
          THAT COOPERATION JUST MEANS CO-OPT
(Spoken) And co-opt means kaput!

DYLAN: So where are you now, that you can be so proud?

CRAZY TOM:
          DO YOU KNOW WHAT IT'S LIKE
          TO REALLY GIVE YOUR WHOLE LIFE
          TO SOMETHING THAT GIVES YOU NOTHING BACK?
          WELL I HAVE LIVED THAT LIFE

THAT LIFE HAS BEEN MY LIFE
FOR A VERY LONG TIME
SO UNLIKE YOU COMPANY BOYS
OR IN YOUR CASE, STUDIO BOYS
I KNOW HOW TO SURVIVE ON MY OWN
HOW TO TAKE A STAND ALL ALONE
FOR BETTER OR FOR WORSE
I'VE ALWAYS BEEN IN CONTROL
WHILE YOU COMPANY BOYS
MAY FALL INTO FAVOR EVERY ONCE IN A WHILE
MY HEART, MY GUTS ARE ALWAYS ON TRIAL

YOU USED TO HAVE TO BUY-IN, TO BE AN AMERICAN
NOW YOU HAVE TO SELL-OUT, TO REALLY GET SOME CLOUT
BUT I WILL DO NEITHER AS LONG AS I CAN BREATH
SO THE PEOPLE'S LAUNDRY WILL STAY FOREVER FREE
EVEN IF WE'RE THE LAST OF A DYING BREED

THE LAST HAND LAUNDRY IN CHINATOWN
MAY BE DOWN, BUT NEVER OUT
THE LAST HAND LAUNDRY IN CHINATOWN
WILL NEVER GO DOWN FOR THE COUNT

(As before, CRAZY TOM starts toasting "The Great Wall of Laundry" by calling off his old friend's names. After each name is called, a faceless figure dances out from behind the wall.)

CRAZY TOM:

> CHIN'S LAUNDRY; DOING FINE
> WONG & SONS; JUST DIVINE

DYLAN: What's going on?

(CRAZY TOM pays him no mind and carries on with his ceremony.)

CRAZY TOM:

> YEE'S HAND LAUNDRY; GOING STRONG
> LAUNDRY BY LOO; CAN DO NO WRONG
> BUT CRAZY TOM'S PEOPLE'S LAUNDRY
> IS STILL THE MIGHTIEST OF THEM ALL
> I'M STILL THE LEADER OF THE PACK! VROOM! VROOM!
>
> WITHOUT THE LAUNDRY WHERE WOULD I BE?

WHERE WOULD YOU BE? WHERE WOULD WE BE?
THE LAUNDRY HAS BEEN OUR HEART
THROUGH IT WE BREATH AND BLEED
IT'S ANSWERED ALL OF OUR QUESTIONS
PROVIDED ALL OF OUR NEEDS
FOR YOU, FOR YOUR MOTHER,
FOR YOUR GRANDPARENTS AND FOR ME

(CRAZY TOM and GHOST FRIENDS gesture for DYLAN to join them, he does.)

CRAZY TOM & DYLAN:
THE LAST HAND LAUNDRY IN CHINATOWN
MAY BE DOWN BUT NEVER OUT
THE LAST HAND LAUNDRY IN CHINATOWN
WILL NEVER GO DOWN FOR THE COUNT

CRAZY TOM, DYLAN & GHOST FRIENDS:
THE LAST HAND LAUNDRY IN CHINATOWN
MAY BE DOWN, BUT NEVER OUT
THE LAST HAND LAUNDRY IN CHINATOWN
WILL NEVER GO DOWN FOR THE COUNT

CRAZY TOM:
THAT'S ALL FOR TODAY, BOYS;
CAUSE SOON WE WILL BE HOME;
WHERE OUR OWN LAW IS ALWAYS UPHELD
YES SIR, SOON WE'LL BE HOME;
WHERE OUR OWN LAW IS ALWAYS UPHELD

(CRAZY TOM holds up two glasses, offering one to DYLAN.)

CRAZY TOM: Dylan, don't let them take away "Our Own LAW."

(DYLAN takes a glass and toasts CRAZY TOM. Blackout.)

ACT II - SCENE 2

JOSIE's apartment in a different part of Chinatown. JOSIE sits in her kitchen getting drunk. JUNE enters.

JUNE: You couldn't sleep too?

JOSIE: Nah, I'm the original insomniac...Oh, and uhm...I don't do this every night.

JUNE: Josie, Josie, this is your house. You're a grown-up now and you can do what you want.

JOSIE: I know, but well you know. You're still my Mom. Want to talk?

JUNE: Yes.

JOSIE: All right, don't mind if I have a drink or three? Would you like one?

JUNE: No, thank you, but you enjoy.

JOSIE: I guess I never thought it would come down to this. You staying here with me. Dad, Dylan and Bo-Gee back at the laundry.

JUNE: A lot of things don't turn out the way you think they will.

JOSIE: Maybe that cliché is true that you really don't know what you've got until it's gone.

JUNE: I think there's a lot of truth to that cliché. But on the flip side, you also don't know what you have until you actually have it—especially when it comes to marriage.

JOSIE: My marriage was not nearly as long as yours—and thank God we didn't have any kids—but I know what you mean. It couldn't have been easy for you.

JUNE: Marrying Tom, and now maybe leaving him, have been my two biggest leaps of doubt.

JOSIE: Mom, <u>that</u> cliché is "leap of faith."

JUNE: Whatever.

JOSIE: It's funny, well, not *funny*, but kind of ironic that now that Dylan's getting divorced, we're all in the same boat again. Maybe it's meant to be for us all to be back together in Chinatown.

JUNE: I feel very badly for Dylan. Because he's back in the middle of a struggle he thought he'd left behind years ago.

JOSIE: Let's make this the last cliché of this conversation, but sometimes you've got to go back and clean up where you started before you can move forward.

JUNE: Maybe so, but I look at some marriages and think what were they thinking when they got married.

JOSIE: Mom...can I ask what <u>you</u> were thinking?

"LIKE A COUPLE IN A GREAT OLD MOVIE"

JUNE: I USED TO SEE TOM AND ME
           LIKE A COUPLE IN A GREAT OLD MOVIE
           NEVER BROKE, NEVER LOW
           ALWAYS DRESSED UP WITH SOMEPLACE TO GO
           LIKE A COUPLE IN A GREAT OLD MOVIE

JOSIE: SO WHEN DID THE MOVIE END?
           MAYBE YOU'RE JUST CHANGING REELS?
           CAUSE IF THE MOVIE REALLY ENDS?
           WHOSE TO SAY YOU'LL FIND A NEW DEAL?

JUNE: WAS IT ONLY ME, WHO YEARNED TO BE
           LIKE A COUPLE IN A GREAT OLD MOVIE?

JOSIE: MAYBE WE SAW DIFFERENT MOVIES
           BUT WE SAW STARS ALL THE SAME
           I USED TO SEE PAUL AND ME
           GOWING OLD TOGETHER—POOR BUT HAPPY;
           NOT AS BAD AS MOM AND DAD
           MAKING MARRIAGE A JOKE THAT'S HAD
           BY A COUPLE IN A GREAT OLD MOVIE

           COULD IT BE MY FOLKS WERE RIGHT
           YOU CAN'T MARRY JUST FOR LOVE ITSELF
           TAKE A LOOK AT ME TONIGHT
           ALMOST FORTY AND ON THE SHELF

JUNE: SO MAYBE WE WON'T EVER BE
           IN A COUPLE LIKE A GREAT OLD MOVIE
           BUT THERE'S STILL TIME FOR YOU AND ME
           TO REMAKE SOME GREAT OLD MOVIES

JOSIE: (*Spoken*) No, we can still be in some great new movies!

JUNE AND JOSIE:*(Sung)*
    LET'S TRY AND MAKE SOME GREAT NEW MOVIES

(DYLAN enters.)

JUNE: Dylan!

JOSIE: Did you talk to Dad?

DYLAN: Well...Sort of!

JUNE: What do you mean, "Sort of?"

DYLAN: Mom, you can't leave Dad and the laundry yet.

JOSIE: Dylan, Mom's already left.

DYLAN: There's something important you're leaving behind. Please Mom, let's just go back to the laundry one more time.

JUNE: I'm never going back!

(JUNE runs out of the room.)

JOSIE: Dylan, how could you do this?

DYLAN: Josie, you don't understand—

JOSIE: No, Dylan, I understand. You choked and sold us out.

DYLAN: I sold out? Now wait a minute—

JOSIE: Look Dylan, I'm not happy with what has happened, but I can't apologize for what I'm trying to achieve for Mom.

DYLAN: There's a lot that you don't know about that laundry.

JOSIE: You left me holding the bag here nine years ago, and now you think you're gonna just waltz back in and take over? I don't think so.

DYLAN: Josie, this is not some real estate power play. This is Mom and Dad!

(JUNE comes back with her coat on.)

JOSIE: Mom!

DYLAN: Oh good, come on Mom.

JUNE: Oh Josie, I have to hear him out.

JOSIE: You're just going to throw away everything I've done for you?

JUNE: Josie, please don't be upset with me.

JOSIE: You should be upset with yourself. But go ahead, go back! Let him walk all over you
again!

DYLAN: Josie, that's enough.

(*JUNE and DYLAN exit. JOSIE pushes everything off of her kitchen table and lets out a scream of frustra-tion.*)

ACT II - SCENE 3

DYLAN and JUNE enter TOM's office and turn on the lights. CRAZY TOM is very drunk and singing to himself.

CRAZY TOM:
> HOME, WHERE OUR OWN LAW IS ALWAYS UPHELD

DYLAN: Dad, Mom wants to talk.

CRAZY TOM:
> Who's stopping her? It's a free country!

(Sings)
> HOME, WHERE OUR OWN LAW IS ALWAYS UPHELD
> HOME, WHERE OUR OWN LAW IS ALWAYS UPHELD

JUNE: See what I have to deal with Dylan!

(JUNE turns to go, DYLAN stops her.)

DYLAN: Please let's all just try and talk. DAD!

(CRAZY TOM stops singing.)

DYLAN: Dad, why don't you show Mom what you showed me earlier.

CRAZY TOM: Come on June, let's get this over with. You've been trying to get rid of me for years.

JUNE: And you've been ignoring me for years!

CRAZY TOM: You and Roy Orbison; "Only The Lonely" huh?

DYLAN: Dad, come on!

JUNE: Tom, I'm not coming back. I just came here to see if you'd reconsider the landlord's relocation offer.

CRAZY TOM: OK.

JUNE: Do you mean OK you'll reconsider?

CRAZY TOM: No, OK, let's take the God-damned deal. I don't want to hold anyone back.

DYLAN: Dad are you sure you don't want to show Mom what you showed me earlier?

CRAZY TOM: No, your Mom is right. Let's sell this useless place. Your Mom is strong, she can stand alone, right June?

JUNE: Tom, I don't want to be alone. I just want to get out of here, I just want to be free of this laundry.

CRAZY TOM: We all do June, We all do.

(CRAZY TOM tries to lift the wall, but it just comes crashing down on him. Music stops.)

DYLAN: Mom, call an ambulance!

CRAZY TOM: Don't call an ambulance!

JUNE: Tom, we must!

CRAZY TOM: PLEASE!...Don't call an ambulance...Just listen to me.

(DYLAN and JUNE finally get the wall partially off of him. DYLAN props him up on his lap, JUNE grasps his hand.)

"LAMENT"

CRAZY TOM:
          I HOPE YOU ALL KNOW
          I NEVER WANTED THIS LIFE
          I JUST WANTED TO BE
          GOOD TO YOU; MY FAMILY

          I GOT TOO CAUGHT UP
          WHEN LAUNDRY OWNERS HAD TO UNITE
          FOR IT WAS US AGAINST THE "NEW WORLD"
          IN A VERY, UNFAIR FIGHT

          SO WE MADE "OUR OWN LAW;"
          THE LAUNDRY ALLIED WORKERS IT WAS CALLED
          TOGETHER, OUR LITTLE VOICES
          MADE A SOUND SO GREAT
          AND THROUGH "OUR OWN LAW"
          SOON WE COULD CARRY OUR WEIGHT

US LAUNDRY OWNERS
HAVE NO MORE MUSIC AROUND
FOR LAUNDRY OWNERS
THERE'S JUST A FAINT SOUND
BUT LISTEN CLOSELY
WHILE THERE'S A CHANCE YOU CAN HEAR
BECAUSE THAT FAINT SOUND
SOON WILL JUST DISAPPEAR

(CRAZY TOM slides off of DYLAN's lap and lands on the floor. Suddenly, CRAZY TOM's GHOST FRIENDS appear and lift the wall entirely off of him. CRAZY TOM gets up and does a slow, processional dance with his GHOST FRIENDS as they escort him out the door. He sings)

"HOME" (Reprise)

CRAZY TOM:
MY BOYS WILL SEE ME HOME
LIKE THEY ALWAYS DO
THROUGH ALL I'VE DONE WRONG
THEY'VE SEEN ME THROUGH
WHEN DEATH HAS CALLED ME UP
 MY BOYS WOULD ALWAYS SAY
"I'M SORRY, HE'S NOT HOME TODAY"
BUT NOW THE TIME IS RIGHT
SO MY BOYS WILL SEE ME HOME

SO STEP ASIDE, MY LITTLE ONES
CAUSE WHERE I'M GONNA GO
THEY DON'T GIVE A DAMN OF WHERE YOU'VE BEEN
THEY JUST SAY "TAKE A LOAD OFF"
THEN LEAVE YOU THE HELL ALONE
SO DON'T WORRY ABOUT ME
CAUSE NOW MY BOYS WILL SEE ME HOME

HOME, WHERE OUR OWN LAW IS ALWAYS UPHELD
HOME, WHERE OUR OWN LAW IS ALWAYS UPHELD

(CRAZY TOM and GHOST FRIENDS exit. Blackout.)

EPILOGUE

One month later. DYLAN, carrying a bunch of laundry packages tied together, stands in front of the laundry with JUNE, JOSIE & BO-GEE. They watch as workers take down "The People's Laundry" sign and erect a huge "Empire National Mall" sign. After sign has been put and workers exit. DYLAN puts a small plaque on the wall. JUNE, JOSIE and BO-GEE set-up snapshots, incense and bowls of sand. Once incense is lit and distributed, JUNE comes forward with a letter.

"WHERE IS HOME?"

JUNE: WHERE IS HOME?
I USED TO KNOW
NOW IT'S TIME TO GO
TO ANOTHER HOME
WITHOUT YOU

WITHOUT YOU
I THOUGHT I WANTED TO BE
NOW IT'S SO HARD TO SEE
SO FAR GONE

SO FAR GONE
TOMORROW THAT'S WHERE I'LL BE
TODAY IS THE LAST FOR YOU AND ME
NOT FOR THE FAMILY
OUR FAMILY

HOME IS NOT JUST SOMEPLACE TO GO
HOME IS HAVING SOMETHING TO SHOW
HOME IS PLANTING SOMETHING TO GROW
AND WE'VE DONE THAT
AS LONG AS WE HAVE THAT
THEN YES, WE ARE HOME

(JUNE adds her letter to the fire, everyone joins hands and bows three times. Then, DYLAN comes forward to read his own letter.)

DYLAN: Dear Dad, We sold the laundry, cause there's no reason to stay here without you. I hope it's all right that I'm taking the remains of the "Great Wall of Laundry" back to L.A. with me. I'll set it up in my writing room as a shrine. Mom and Bo-Gee will be working in the mall...I don't think you would've liked that, but it's the best we can do right now. I'm sure Mom will be O.K., but I'll be coming back to New York regularly to take good care of her. Finally, we're putting a plaque on the building for you. I hope you like it. It says:

"PROCLAMATION"

DYLAN: *(Spoken)* You may say
THIS WAS JUST ANOTHER LAUNDRY
JUST ANOTHER MOM AND POP STORE
JUST ANOTHER FAILED SMALL BUSINESS
JUST LIKE THE ONE BEFORE
BUT THIS ONE WAS REALLY DIFFERENT
UNLIKE ANY OTHER STORE
THIS WAS THE LAST HAND LAUNDRY IN CHINATOWN
AND YOU WON'T SEE IT ANYMORE

JUNE: YOU WON'T SEE THE FAMILIES TOGETHER
GENERATIONS SIDE BY SIDE

JOSIE: GENERATIONS TEACHING EACH OTHER
GENERATIONS SHARING PRIDE

BO-GEE: PEOPLE CARING FOR EACH OTHER
OPENING UP WITH NOTHING TO HIDE
PUTTING THE FAMILY BEFORE THEMSELVES
WITHOUT THINKING IT'S A SACRIFICE

DYLAN: NOW I CAN'T SAY I DID THAT
BUT MY PARENTS AND GRANDPARENTS DID
AND IN MY FATHER'S DYING PLEA
HE SAID THESE WORDS TO ME;

DYLAN, BO-GEE, JUNE AND JOSIE:
    "YES, THIS WAS 'THE PEOPLE'S LAUNDRY'
RUN BY THAT TROUBLE-MAKER, 'CRAZY TOM'
AND EVEN WHEN I'M DEAD AND GONE
MY SPIRIT WILL LIVE ON
THE SPIRIT OF INDEPENDENCE
THE SPIRIT TO BE FREE
THE SPIRIT OF OUR OWN LAW
THE SPIRIT OF THE PEOPLE'S LAUNDRY
HAND LAUNDRIES USED TO BE EVERYWHERE
NOW THERE'S NONE TO BE FOUND
SO WHEN YOU READ THIS, REMEMBER:
THE LAST HAND LAUNDRY IN CHINATOWN"

DYLAN: THIS MAY NOT BE OUR HOME, ANYMORE
           BUT IN OUR HEARTS,
           OUR OWN LAW WILL ALWAYS PREVAIL
           IN OUR HEARTS,
           OUR OWN LAW WILL ALWAYS PREVAIL
           AND THAT IS WHERE I WILL CALL HOME

DYLAN: Goodbye Dad. I'll really miss you. Your son, Dylan.

(DYLAN burns letter and places it in bowl near the incense, oranges and snapshots. DYLAN, BO-GEE, JUNE and JOSIE all join hands and bow three times. DYLAN bids goodbye to everyone and exits. JUNE and JOSIE exit into the mall. BO-GEE starts putting away the ritual apparatus.)

BO-GEE: Yes friends, this used to be Chinatown.

           "BALLAD OF CHINATOWN" (Reprise)

BO GEE: THE MORE WE TRY TO STAY THE SAME
           THE MORE WE HAVE TO CHANGE
           JUST LOOK AROUND OLD CHINATOWN
           AND TELL ME WE'RE THE SAME
           AND TELL ME WE'RE THE SAME

           PEOPLE ALWAYS COME AND GO
           WHAT DO THEY HOPE TO FIND?

(CRAZY TOM & GHOST FRIENDS enter and begin to sing with BO-GEE.)

BO-GEE, CRAZY TOM & GHOST FRIENDS:
           ALTHOUGH WE LEAVE WE STILL SHALL SEEK
           THE THINGS WE LEFT BEHIND
           THE THINGS WE LEFT BEHIND

(BO-GEE starts to exit into the mall.)

CRAZY TOM & GHOST FRIENDS:
           FATES FULFILLED COME ONLY ONCE
           AND THEN THAT TIME IS GONE
           BUT TIME AND SPACE CANNOT ERASE
           THE FAITH WE CARRY ON
           THE FAITH WE CARRY ON

           SO DEAR FRIENDS OUR STORY ENDS

BUT THAT'S THE SIMPLE PART
AS WE ADVANCE WE MUST RETAIN
THE MEANING IN OUR HEARTS
THE MEANING IN OUR HEARTS

(BO-GEE, CRAZY TOM & GHOST FRIENDS enter the mall.)

END OF PLAY

SLUTFORART

By Ping Chong & Muna Tseng

In 1990, my older brother and photographer Tseng Kwong Chi died of AIDS at the age of 39. I was suddenly robbed of an idyllic Chinese childhood we had growing up in Hong Kong, the misery of adolescence spent as immigrants in Canada, and our unspoken, steely alliance as working artists in New York, far away from the disapproving looks of our parents.

SLUTFORART began as an idea of an homage to a brother, and it has taken nine years to realize it. I began collaborating with theater director Ping Chong three years ago, and I asked him to help me with this new visual dance-theater piece. The visuals are built around projections of the now-famous iconic "tourist" snapshots series of photographs Tseng Kwong Chi took of himself, dressed in a Mao uniform, posing as a Chinese ambassador in front of highly recognized landmarks around the world. The text is culled from the hours of interviews with friends and colleagues of my brother's, all movers and shakers of the New York downtown art scene of the 1980s. The music is from his favorite music: from dad's 1950's mambos, to Nino Rota's Fellini hits, to Brooklyn caplypsos.

The choreography is mine, peppered with the insouciant poses and elegant hauteur I recall from a "first-born, number one Chinese son," the first of the last emperors.

The new work includes 98.6:- A CONVERGENCE IN 15 MINUTES, my first collaboration with Ping Chong, which serves as an intro. to SLUTFORART.

MUNA TSENG

SLUTFORART had its World Premiere at Playhouse 91 in New York City, March 2,3,4,6 & 7, 1999 in a joint presentation by The 92nd Street Y Harkness Dance Project, and Muna Tseng Dance Projects in association with Ping Chong & Company.

SLUTFORART Scene list:
1. Mock 98.6
2. Jenny and Hong Kong
3. 1st Cable Release
4. 1st Dance For My Brother
5. 2nd Cable Release
6. Party of the Year
7. Things My Frere Liked Dance
8. 3rd Cable Release
9. Interview with Tseng Kwong Chi
10. Expeditionary Series
11: Last Dance For My Brother/Monologue
Epilogue

with the voices of:
Interviewees:
> ANN MAGNUSON, actress/performance artist/friend of Kwong Chi
> KENNY SCHARF, visual artist/friend of Kwong Chi
> RICHARD MARTIN, Curator of Fashion, Metropolitan Museum of Art
> KRISTOFFER HAYNES, companion
> BILL T. JONES, choreographer worked with Keith Haring & Kwong Chi
> TIMOTHY GREENFIELD-SANDERS, fellow photographer
> JENNY YEE, cousin
> MUNA TSENG, sister

Interviewer: PING CHONG

Choreography & Performance by Muna Tseng
Conceived & Directed by Ping Chong
Projection Design: Jan Hartley
Light Design: Mark London
Sound Design: Brian Hallas
Music Collage: Hong Kong Pop, Nino Rota, Perez Perado, Eartha Kitt, Gustave Mahler
Costume Design: Han Feng
Mao Suit Tailor: Carol Ann Pelletier
Production Stage Manager: Courtney Golden
Stagehand: Hitoshi Yoshiki
Assistant to Ping Chong: Edith James
Assistant to Muna Tseng: Marcello Picone

SLUTFORART

Scene 1: Mock 98.6

PING *(Voice-over)*:   The things they share
The full mystery of an Other

Eyes, ears, nose, mouth,
The ability to breathe, breath.
You know, the givens:

Billions of cells working in unison
To create a walking, prancing, dancing
Likely to function
Likely to not,
Full fledged, miraculous being,
Him, her, us, them, you, me.

The full mystery of an Other
The things they share.

(MUNA enters)

PING *(Voice-over)*:   She's 5'1/2" tall, dark eyes, short hair
What one would describe as petite,
Seeming to need protection,
Seeming to not,
Seeming to be assured
And seeming to not,
Hesitating and seeming to not,
Not to be that is.
One thing's for sure: she moves with a buttery grace.

The things they share.

MUNA: An alliance at the altar of Art

PING *(Voice-over)*:   The full mystery of an Other.

MUNA: He was my idol. He was my guru.

He was impossible, but I loved him.
He was my brother.

PING *(Voice-over):*   The things they share.

MUNA: The solace in Art as a refuge from pain.

PING *(Voice-over):*   The full mystery of an Other.

(Blackout/Slide out. MUNA exits as soon as blackout occurs. Stagehand removes drum stools.)

Scene 2: Jenny and Hong Kong

Music: Chinese pop from the '50s. Slides: Black & White Hong Kong slide fades up turns to color. After Hong Kong image turns to color along the top of the image appears over the course of the scene Black & White portraits/close-ups of Kwong Chi. During this scene the whole image may flutter once or twice like a flag.

PING *(Voice-over)*: You're cousins?

JENNY *(Voice-over)*: Yes, we're cousins.

PING *(Voice-over)*: What kind of cousins?

JENNY *(Voice-over)*: My mother is number 19 and Kwong Chi's father is number 14, because there are so many aunts and aunties, we don't call names; first of all no respect. And secondly you just couldn't remember so we all call number by number. And there's number 10, number 14, number 13, number 19, number 8, there are more close, you know. My mother And Kwong Chi's father had the same father but different mother. Kwong Chi's father is number 2 wife son. My mother is number 3 wife.

PING *(Voice-over)*: OK, I think that's enough. I don't think anybody can keep up with that.

JENNY *(Voice-over)*: At that time Kwong Chi, Muna, they all lived there in that big mansion. So here goes summer time, party time. I remember Kwong Chi then was very like delicate and very fragile. Kwong Chi's mother, my aunt, is always the nervous type paranoid. Kwong Chi can't do this, Kwong Chi gotta take a nap, he can't do—you know, Kwong Chi cannot play with you guys, you know, very restricted. But the minute my number 14 aunt is out the door, like to go shopping, then we would be dancing and singing, you know. I remember particularly, we were all chasing each other, running up the stairs with the rest of the cousins, he fell. Big deal, right? You know just tumble down a little bit, no big deal. At that very moment my number 4 aunt walked in from shopping or something, walked right in. Boy, she freaked out. Everybody got punished and screamed at.

I remember, we used to take Chinese painting together near where he lived and he loved to eat. One time and we here are sitting with this painting teacher, he's an old guy, he real slow and asking us to do the—I think we were drawing crabs you know in Chinese painting and he was instructing us how to do it. Here Kwong Chi and I look at the water we've got to go, you know, finish it up so we can eat our noodles and rush home in time, in a decent time. So I think our mind was off as a result, the crab I think is supposed to have eight legs or something like that—I don't know how many legs we draw. We draw like 20 legs, you know, keep drawing legs you know and the painting teacher looks at us and says what is this? You know? I remember we go crazy like how many legs does a crab have?

PING *(Voice-over)*: How would you describe his personality?

JENNY *(Voice-over)*: Just fun-loving, you know—just loved to play. And even when he was a teenager, same thing. Any time he can have fun he would go for it. He loved to laugh I remember—he was always laughing. He always enjoyed life, I think that's his nature. He's the type that you know, do it today and forget about tomorrow.

(MUNA enters in red dress with cable release.)

JENNY *(Voice-over)*:   I think he's very rebellious against his mother, at least that's the impression I got. His mother is always a pusher—push, push, push—his mother is very intellectual. I think that's what she want Kwong Chi to be, an intellectual like her. You know she never want him to be a photographer or an artist. But his father, I think they are very close. Whatever Jojo want, Jojo get. I tell you I really miss him. Every time I go to New York I say gee, I wish Jo was here, especially when you do something crazy—gee I wish he was there, he would have liked this.

(Blackout)

Scene 3: 1st Cable Release

Slides: Squares of light. MUNA is on stage in red dress with cable release.

PING *(Voice-over)*:   How did you meet Kwong Chi, when and how?

KRISTOFFER *(Voice-over)*: We met at Twilight, the only gay Asian bar in NYC at the time.

BILL *(Voice-over)*:   I think I saw Kwong's pictures before I met him.

PING *(Voice-over)*:   What's your earliest memory of Kwong Chi?

MUNA *(Voice-over)*:   I think I remember playing with him and then in the garden, in my grandfather's house in Hong Kong.

ANN *(Voice-over)*:   I can't remember the exact moment when I met him, but I remember we did a photo shoot and it was when I was running Club 57.

PING *(Voice-over)*:   Where and when did you first meet Kwong Chi?

TIMOTHY *(Voice-over)*:   I imagine I met him first—I imagine that I met Kwong Chi first through his photographs. I think he was along with Keith Haring one of the early people in the East Village scene in the mid-'80s.

RICHARD *(Voice-over)*:   I'm not sure actually when I first met Kwong Chi. I remember the first time when we had a really sustained conversation which was the show he did at Semaphore gallery of the, I think, first group of Expeditionary photographs.

KENNY *(Voice-over)*:   I think I met Kwong Chi at Club 57.

ANN *(Voice-over)*:   I was running Club 57 between First and Second, it was underneath the Polish National Church. We had a juke box in the corner...so it was a mixture of Motown, old Ventures, singles and new stuff like The Flying Lizard and Devo and X-Ray Spex—that kind of stuff. And Kwong was there, dancing away. I seem to have an image of him with a joint in his hand, kind of swaying around and laughing and just being delighted by everybody. We had a "Tribute to Lawrence Welk" night, we had a hay ride hootenanny. We had an Elvis memorial night and there's a good picture of Kwong with a giant Elvis head. He was very inventive and also everything was always done very professionally, very slick. Nothing Kwong Chi did was shabby!

MUNA *(Voice-over)*: Uh, there was a lot of drugs.

(Stagehand enters and takes cable release from MUNA. MUNA starts to dance.)

ANN *(Voice-over)*:   Cabaret Voltaire and Dadaism and Andy Warhol's Factory...

PING *(Voice-over)*:   It was kind of an innocent time.

KENNY *(Voice-over)* Very innocent! You know, Kwong would just break out dancing. He was always hysterically laughing and making me laugh...it's all like big mush of great feelings. Oh god, he would walk in the room and go like hiiiii B does that sound like him, Muna?

TIMOTHY *(Voice-over)*: But I kind of remember him particularly for his elegance—you know Kwong Chi always dressed so differently from the rest of the scene.

ANN *(Voice-over)*:   He was I think just maybe a few years older than us, I'm not sure, just a couple, but he seemed so worldly. I mean he had so much knowledge both as a professional photographer and as a connoisseur of *(Laughs)* food mostly, of fashion, of beautiful, young people and of life, of music. I think his studio was the first place I heard the sound track of "La Dolce Vita," all the Nino Rota music. Oh god there's so much now all starting to flood back.

(Music: Nino Rota)

Scene 4: 1st Dance For My Brother

Music: Nino Rota. Text slides: Start of identity fugue text

An eternal tourist
A solitary figure
A solitary figure in shades
A deadpan in a Mao suit with shades
A displaced person sugared by privilege
A downtown art scamp
A throw away insouciance
A fixture of the East Village scene in the 80's
A party animal
Mao Tse Tung amid the pines, the glaciers, the snow smeared mountains
A walking cartoon guaranteed to activate stock associations of...
An Oriental
A slippage in geopolitical history
A party animal
Court photographer for Keith Haring
A reflection of...
A mirror of...
An enigmatic knight of one Billion plus
An ambiguous emissary
An objective witness
A subjective interpreter
A robotic Chinese avatar
A Chinese power doll (batteries not included)
A Joseph Tseng who is also a Tseng Kwong Chi
A latter day Caspar Friedrich Monk
An icon of the Cold War
A caricature of the yellow peril
An alter ego
A doppelganger
A SlutForArt
A photographer for Vogue and Gentlemen's Quarterly
An Asian American
An Asian American in a costume
An Asian American in a costume reproaching assimilation

A gay man or a bachelor bystander
A footnote to Keith Haring
A signifier signifying

A fixture upon which a pair of sunglasses rest
A friction between place and person
A figure upon a landscape
A prince in the funk

(MUNA *freezes then gestures to stagehand to bring her cable release.*)

Scene 5: 2nd Cable Release

Start second cable release scene voice-over just before music ends from previous scene. Slides: Continue identity fugue text then squares of light with Keith Haring subway documentation photographs and denizens of the '80s photos appearing in the squares of light.

RICHARD *(Voice-over)*:   You know...you know as one looks back...you know as one looks back on the '80s art world, there were such extraordinary things that happened.

MUNA *(Voice-over)*   One day Kwong Chi just said, "Oh I met this really cool guy and his name is Keith Haring and we met on First Avenue."

RICHARD *(Voice-over)*:   There were young artists...

PING *(Voice-over)*:   For example.

MUNA *(Voice-over)*:   Keith was a student at the School of Visual Arts at that time.

RICHARD *(Voice-over)*:   There were young artists...

PING *(Voice-over)*:   For example

RICHARD *(Voice-over)*:   Keith Haring is someone/thing like that—who was immediately catapulted into a kind of fame and recognition.

MUNA *(Voice-over)*:   Then he started drawing on the subways on the blank, black paper, before the advertising was put on. Kwong Chi decided that this was such historical, monumental work that Keith was giving to the people of New York and so Kwong Chi started to document and photograph this body of work.

MUNA *(Voice-over)*:   Keith was very savvy because the first line he did was the E & F that went through the 53rd Street and 5th Avenue stop, because that's the Museum of Modern Art stop.

RICHARD*(Voice-over)*:   Keith Haring is someone/something like that—who was immediately catapulted into a kind of fame and recognition.

ANN *(Voice-over)*:   Suddenly we were in Keith's limousine, you know, going off to fabulous parties and, getting to meet Andy Warhol and going to Mr. Chow's.

TIMOTHY *(Voice-over)*:   Artists were stars and the art world blossomed.

ANN *(Voice-over)*: It was just like eight different events every night so you were always.

RICHARD *(Voice-over)*:   He seemingly happened to be there at the right place at the right...

TIMOTHY *(Voice-over)*:   And Wall Street was powerful...

ANN *(Voice-over)*:   Jumping in a cab, hooking up with people somewhere...

TIMOTHY *(Voice-over)*:   And there was money everywhere.

RICHARD *(Voice-over)*:There were these sort of jokes about the youngest artist to be seen in the East Village.

ANN *(Voice-over)*:   It was very exhilarating, very intoxicating.

RICHARD *(Voice-over)*:   In a sense it is one of those great times in which one has a sense of art can be anything...

TIMOTHY *(Voice-over)*:   And there was money everywhere that was the shiny side of the coin and the dark side of the coin was AIDS.

(Music slowly fade up during this scene and with the word AIDS it bumps out. Also with the word AIDS the squares of light flutters and as it flutters—dissolve into Manchu robes in Black & White still fluttering and then the flutter settles and title for next scene comes up.)

Scene 6: Party of the Year

Slide: Identity fugue text continues into this scene. Following text slide appears over Manchu robes image which goes from Black & White to color.

THE MANCHU DRAGON
Costumes of the Ch'ing Dynasty 1644 - 1912

(Fades out. Fades in.)

A Party of the Year.

(Slides of the party appear in a choreographed slide sequence.)

RICHARD *(Voice-over)*:   The Metropolitan Museum party photographs I think are extremely important because it was a party/part of the year for the Chinese costume exhibition that Mrs. Vreeland had done and so in part it was—everybody was dressed up or many of the people were—Adele Simpson and others—in a kind of New York Chinoiserie in which they were trying to sort of emulate this-sort-of world in China. Kwong Chi comes to the party as a representative of "The SOHO Weekly News." He shows up there in the Mao suit and I think no one knows whether this is a member of the press, whether this is, you know, an emissary from the Chinese government.

(MUNA exits)

PING *(Voice-over)*:   Cabinet

RICHARD *(Voice-over)*:   Right! Exactly! Like an emissary from Cathay in an 18th Century European court. Here are all the Europeans or the Americans here, who are dressed up in this extravagant way—trying to be as Chinese as possible and there's this young man who walks among them who is innately and in a way, intrudes upon them and yet is at the same time—you know the one who is observing them, inasmuch as they're dressed up they must have been more captivated by him and by his mystery—than anything that they could, put together as those sort of fake Chinoserie outfits.

KENNY *(Voice-over)*: I remember I wanted to learn Chinese and I was very into Chinese culture and I had made up this language, was part of my paintings and I had made up this big dance with this scarf. It was like a Chinese scarf dance and I was like, you know Kwong was part of that. I would make sounds like—when I would be making a mark, you know? Like crazy. I'd do stuff in Japanese scroll style, like paper scrolls and Chinese landscapes, you know misty watercolors and then you know how they'd have the Chinese writing, telling the story? Well I had my own writing, telling my own story, that kind of thing? And it looked a little, it didn't really look Chinese, it looked Chinese and space age or I don't know. Telegraphic. Do you remember that, Muna?

MUNA *(Voice-over)*:   I remember some of those, yeah. You were really crazy.

KRISTOFFER *(Voice-over)*: I don't think that he really enjoyed being Asian so much. Anytime that I mentioned doing anything related to Asian or Chinese culture he would just put it down, he didn't want to have anything to do with it.

MUNA *(Voice-over)*:   In 1988 my parents wanted to have a family trip back to China and this was the first trip back to China, since they left in 1948. I took it to be a very important trip of a pilgrimage to my native land and to accompany my parents back from exile after a 40 year absence—to see my mother's sister, who she hadn't seen for 40 years. I thought that Kwong Chi would very much want to come along on this pilgrimage, but Kwong Chi didn't go! And he didn't, he didn't seem to think that was such a missed opportunity.

PING *(Voice-over)*:   How did you meet Kwong Chi? When and how?

KRISTOFFER *(Voice-over)*: We met at Twilight, the only gay Asian bar at the time.

PING *(Voice-over)*:   What's Twilight like?

KRISTOFFER *(Voice-over)*: Asian men go there to meet Caucasian men and Caucasian men go there to meet Asian men and people drink and try to pick each other up. I thought he looked very sexy in his Mao suit.

BILL *(Voice-over)*:   I think he described himself to me once as a snow queen, any person of color who prefers white men and but yet by the same token, he was very aware of the races and the way in which Asian people were viewed, and I think that's what I saw a lot in his work. He was taken aback that I was in a way, before people were really talking about identity politics.

MUNA *(Voice-over)*:   He did not want to be identified as an Asian-American artist, he hated that. He said I'm an artist.

BILL *(Voice-over)*:   However, his imagery was always the curious, blank Chinese tourist. I would say to Kwong that you don't fool me. I, I know, I can sense protest when I see it. This is a rough conversation we were having, that this blankness was the way in which this culture at large expected him, as an Asian man, to—to exist. So he became a kind of a cipher, a smooth surface that because it was so impenetrable, this persona, it reflected everything!

ANN *(Voice-over)*:   I remember going with him to the Vietnam Vets parade, the one that the country finally gave the Vets, you know, like twenty years too late and him photographing. I mean, there was this Asian fellow at a Vietnam Vet parade? In a Chinese Communist uniform? He'd get in the middle of the street and wait till like the last possible second they were as close as they could be before he took the picture. He was fearless. Absolutely fearless!

PING *(Voice-over)*:   You said that he knew that he couldn't pass.

BILL *(Voice-over)*:   ...but we started this by saying if you have in fact, as a bright, intelligent let's say Asian person or even Indian or whatever and you are a nuclear physicist, right? You have tenure at Yale or Princeton. You have everything, the best that the society could offer you, but what you don't have is inclusion in that, that you are not white. And I think now to be white means to be powerful. See that's what I was saying before.

PING *(Voice-over)*:   To be entitled, immediately!

BILL *(Voice-over)*:   Um hum. This young man, educated, I think from a pretty affluent background, right?

PING *(Voice-over)*:   Um hum.

BILL *(Voice-over)*:   What was it that he still didn't have from the culture at large? And it's that inclusion, that's what the question was—why is that fucking inclusion so important to us? Because it represents power, but I'm saying you have power! You have economic power. Intellectual power. What power don't you have? And you're saying there is, there is, there is this entitlement. This I think we can feel it, but he was trying to express it, I think, by this retreat if you will, of maybe this appropriation of this official Other, this stranger, a stranger...He can't be hurt, he needs nothing, he is completely self-contained, he is just moving through. I am just a tourist here, right?

MUNA *(Voice-over)*:   Well this persona in this official uniform gave him access to those various worlds of white power, the first one being the costume, the party of the year at the Met.

BILL *(Voice-over)*:   —Yes, that's right!

MUNA *(Voice-over)*:   I think it was Yves St. Laurent or yeah—Yves St. Laurent said to him because they were speaking in French and he says, you must be an ambassador from China *(BILL laughs.)* to speak French so well!

BILL *(Voice-over)*:   Ah hah!

MUNA *(Voice-over)*:   So there again, it's the whole play of why is this yellow person speaking French so well.

PING *(Voice-over)*:   ...Or English.

MUNA *(Voice-over)*:   Or English.

BILL *(Voice-over)*:   Well, there was something of an aristocrat in his strategy. You know the way that the eccentricities of most of the English aristocrats. They are set apart, they are maybe not comfortable where they come from, they have a—when you're up that high, this is a metaphor—you have a pretty wide view, you know. But by the same token, you're somewhat isolated and off the ground. That's the aristocrat's dilemma in a way. So in a way he made the art feel almost like the art of an aristocrat.

Scene 7: Things My Frere Liked Dance

Music: Eartha Kitt

Slide text: Things Kwong Chi liked plus other layers from previous scene which may be dissolving underneath. This text below is not in presentation order! Just a rough list. MUNA enters dressed in grey Mao suit.

Sole picasso
Federico Fellini's *La Dolce Vita*
Early morning mist, Vermont Lake
Falling foliage
Drunken crabs at Double Happiness
Rita Hayworth's brows
Soca in Brooklyn
Black truffle omelette
7 Lonely Days
Dancing all night at Bahia Carnivale
Marilyn Monroe
Bill T. Jones' physique
Kenny's beach, Ilheus, Brazil
Everything about Elvis Presley
Dinner parties at Mr. Chow's
Noodles
Keith Haring's subway forays
Guilietta Masina
Jean Cocteau's hands
Di Roberti's espresso
Rue du Dragon
Theatre 80's double features, remember Theatre 80?
Maria Callas
Noodles
Montblanc cakes at Patesserie Claude
Je ne regrette rien
DJ'ing at the Michael Todd Room, Palladium
Fred Astaire
Roma
New York
Paris
Afternoons at Cafe de Flore
Whole suckling pig on Chinese New Year
Peres Prado's Mambos
Mighty Sparrow

Gertrude Stein
Buffet lunches at the Mandarin Hotel in Hong Kong
Labor Day Calypso Parade
Brigitte Bardot
Nino Rota
Les Enfants du Paradise

Scene 8: 3rd Cable Release

MUNA remains on stage, stagehand brings on cable release and hands it to MUNA. Slides: Squares of light, text slides from previous scene may still be up. Slide: KENNY SCHARF's installation image comes up.

KENNY *(Voice-over)*: Well he'd always take us out to Chinatown. I remember having the most incredible Chinese food and Kwong would take this whole group of East Village weirdos and we'd all go to this totally Chinese restaurant and this big table and he ordered in Chinese, that was always a fun ritual. We were just such freaks for all the Chinese people in the restaurant.

KENNY *(Voice-over)*: Well, I think he had difficulties with his father. The whole gay thing. I think was really hard on your dad, right Muna?

MUNA *(Voice-over)*: Yeah.

KENNY *(Voice-over)*: Yeah, that was a big issue all through his life, all the way until the end and hey, Kwong was gay! I mean, come on, I mean! I wish that his dad, your dad could have been more...

MUNA *(Voice-over)*: Yeah, he never, I don't think he ever understood it or

KENNY *(Voice-over)*: He never did.

MUNA *(Voice-over)*: ...wanted to understand or accept it, you know.

KENNY *(Voice-over):* That's always a hard thing, but most of us we're like almost misfits in a way and outcasts from our communities and our families, for whatever reason. And that was, we had adopted each other as our, as family.

(Stagehand brings chair on stage and places it. Then exits.)

KENNY *(Voice-over)*: Yes, he talked about Paris and I think he learned a lot living there and he spoke French very well and it just made him just so much more sophisticated than he already was. Kwong liked the finer things! Didn't he?

MUNA *(Voice-over)*: He demanded the finer things.

PING *(Voice-over)*: But he was also comfortable with a lot of different kinds of people though? He wasn't..

KENNY *(Voice-over)*: Oh yeah, he'd be fine in the jungle, you know, eating bug eyes with, you know Indians.

MUNA *(Voice-over)*: Coconuts

KENNY (*Voice-over*): He'd be equally happy at the Ritz. He was very, very adaptable and you know, had that Chinese thing like he'd go anywhere in the world and just be fine.

KENNY (*Voice-over*): Well, I mean God I spent so much time with Kwong...Kwong was always very into music and anything tropical, in fact Kwong was a very tropical person. He kind of adopted the tropics, the Caribbean and Brazil.

KENNY (*Voice-over*): I remember when, I just had this memory of him in Carnival, everyone dresses up and he was like green. He had a green wig on and a green dress on and we called him—it was such a funny name like China green or I don't remember. And we were just running through the streets, screaming and you know, dancing—it was just fun.

(*MUNA hands cable release to stagehand who comes on to take it off.*)

KENNY (*Voice-over*): I'm very happy to see Kwong getting, finally, what he should have had during his lifetime, which is recognition of his art work. I think it was very frustrating for him—I know it was—especially because everyone was focusing on you know, Keith, John Michel, and me. He really wasn't getting the respect that he deserved. I realized that it's hard to have to listen to someone go on about all the great things that are happening and recognition and then not getting yourself and I could feel that was affecting his, you know, mood. It was, it's hard.

(*MUNA sits in chair with back to audience.*)

PING (*Voice-over*):   Where were you toward the end of his life? Were you still close at that point?

KENNY (*Voice-over*): Yes, I was close and this is the hard, I mean it really-it was very, very difficult, you know, being with him you know every step of the way—all the way, you know I hadn't thought about that for a while. It was very hard.

KENNY (*Voice-over*): I just think he was always celebrating, you know, just life in general. He was such an alive person.

KENNY (*Voice-over*): God I just miss him so much, he's still around in my life!

Scene 9: Interview with Tseng Kwong Chi

Slide: Square of light behind MUNA which turns into the expeditionary series photographs starting with the little house in Provincetown.

MUNA: I take pictures of myself because it is easier for me than having to direct somebody. On the other hand, I always set up my photos by composing perfectly the situation in advance. After that, I can get in front of the camera knowing the rest of the picture is what I want it to be; it leaves me the freedom to do what I wish within that frame, take chances. Also, you must have noticed that on these photos, I wear mirror glasses to block out my eyes; when you can't read the eyes, you become an object; it gives the picture a neutral impact, a kind of surrealistic quality I'm looking for.

The whole idea got started when I read that Nixon was going to China and open a dialogue with my country; a real cultural exchange was supposed to take place between the East and the West, but after a year or so, everything had stayed on a very official level and nothing substantial had been done. Today, the only Americans who are allowed in China are not so much the rich, but the people who, somehow belong to an elite; the visa is given to famous artists, musicians, scientists, politicians. So, I really got disappointed by all this and I thought it would be a good idea to make a statement about it.

(Slide: Provincetown image appears here beginning Expeditionary series images.)

MUNA: In 1979, I went to Provincetown, and I ran into a funny beach house; I happened to have my Chinese costume with me and that is how I did my first self-portrait; then, I took a trip around the USA and being interested in finding out what Americans worship in their country. I followed the trail of the typical places they love to visit. I find the architecture of American monuments quite wonderful; these monuments pretend to be authentic and their perfect realization brings out a kind of beauty; yet, we know they are the imitations of the real thing somewhere in Europe and that brings out the tacky note. The Parthenon in Nashville is a good illustration of my comment.

There's no prerequisite to taste in this country, something which would be unthinkable in Europe. Americans acquire what they want without questioning anything: that is certainly one of the reasons why the country is so dynamic. I find especially fascinating but also alienating in many ways the futuristic quality of their environment, like these new cities. Miami, Dallas or Las Vegas while holding on to very conventional and traditional social values.

When Diana Vreeland's Chinese Costume Show was about to have its opening, I learned that nobody was going to cover it! So, I immediately called their public relations and I explained my project to them. They got very excited over the idea. I put my Chinese national uniform on and I went to the opening taking with me a tape recorder. I interviewed many famous people that evening; I asked them what they were wearing, who had designed their dresses and what they thought of the show; it was the first time I did interviews and I got a good kick out of it. It was very entertaining. Paloma Picasso got her costume all wrong; she has a Japanese kimono on; Nancy Kissinger had purchased for the occasion a $5,000 dress designed by Adolfo and she ran into a woman who was wearing the exact same one. The interesting thing is the attitude they adopt under such circumstances. In France, a woman would feel terribly embarrassed and offended. In this country, they take it rather graciously. I took a picture of those two ladies with me in the middle and they thought nothing of it. I believe a sort of silent complicity took place between them, because wearing the same dress means they belong to the same crowd; it is reassuring.

I would like to go on the road again, but, in a more luxurious way! Perhaps with a mobile home, spacious and comfortable; also, take as much time as I want. There is a trip I hope I will do very soon. I want to go to EPCOT, Experimental prototype Community Of Tomorrow in Florida, the last born project of Walt Disney. Practically everything on Earth has been reproduced in that city: I will be able to do my self-portraits without the burden of real traveling: no taxis, no airports, no jet lag! And it will cost a lot less.

(MUNA exits. Stagehand removes drum stool.)

Scene 10: Expeditionary Series

Slides: The expeditionary series continues without voice-over or anything else. Then the voice-overs begin.

RICHARD *(Voice-over)*:   I think it was about two things. I think it was about two things happening at once, the sense of Kwong Chi himself as the artist who is moving through the world and not really a part of it.

ANN *(Voice-over)*:   I guess in Disneyland, didn't they think he was from Communist China?

MUNA *(Voice-over)*:   Yeah, especially when he had the ID badge on that said, "SlutForArt."

TIMOTHY *(Voice-over)*:   How did he do that? How did he get into some far location, trigger a camera? I mean technically they were incredibly accomplished. Did he have time release shutters?

KRISTOFFER *(Voice-over)*:   That trip was when he first stopped using the squeezing thing and he was so excited he ran down a hill to scout out a location and he lost that squeezing thing and that's when he went further away from the camera because he no longer needed that cord.

ANN *(Voice-over)*:   I think he had more of an understanding of America, had more appreciation of America than most Americans.

BILL *(Voice-over)*:   The world changed in light of this one persona, not the persona changed in the light of the world.

RICHARD *(Voice-over)*:   It's strange that as someone who admired the work and made that admiration clear, in terms of writing about it on a number of occasions and being very enthusiastic about it, I always found that I was more enthusiastic about his work than he was. I was the one overwhelmed and he was barely whelmed.

KENNY *(Voice-over)*:   We would all be out and whatever—doing, looking, exploring, and we'd see the elephant and go, "Oh my god" and he'd stop and he'd set up and do me and the elephant.

MUNA *(Voice-over)*:   So he always had his suit with him and things like that?

KENNY *(Voice-over)*:   Oh, in the trunk of the car, yeah.

MUNA *(Voice-over)*:   And his camera equipment?

KENNY *(Voice-over)*:   Everything!

ANN *(Voice-over)*:   Then when everyone started dying, I felt that I was really operating through a nervous breakdown and it seemed like the whole world was falling apart.

TIMOTHY *(Voice-over)*:   Of course, they were very beautiful—the way that frame them. The way that the light...he captured the light of the environment. They were kind of like Ansel Adams taken to a new level.

RICHARD *(Voice-over)*:   In my experience Kwong Chi was not the 80s artist out to establish his own reputation, at all. If anything he was almost the polar opposite of that.

TIMOTHY *(Voice-over)*:   And then that scene essentially, as Robert Pinkus Whiton said, "That scene turned on a dime." And that scene ended almost over night.

MUNA *(Voice-over)*:   His figure in the last works became smaller and smaller, like Chinese paintings, the classical paintings, man did not matter so much in this, in the wonder of nature.

ANN *(Voice-over)*:   He really unlocked a lot of doors, opened up a lot of windows. I guess as a little hick girl from West Virginia, who, strangely enough, I do get a little timid about going into new territories, and he certainly was an inspiration that way.

ANN *(Voice-over)*:   I remember, I remember Kitty called me up to tell me that he died. I remember where I was exactly. I had an old phone and I remember sitting on the ground just crying, just sobbing, you know. And looking out at the California sunshine and just feeling just such, this bottomless pit of sorrow that everyone died.

TIMOTHY *(Voice-over)*:   You're used to your parents dying, or your grandparents dying, but you're not used to your best friends dying! And, that I think was devastating for a lot of people.

KRISTOFFER *(Voice-over)*:   I get the feeling that he's at peace with himself, and more comfortable with being Chinese, and having his picture taken with that suit on.

(Slide fades out.)

Scene 11: Last Dance For My Brother/Monologue

No slides. Music: Mahler. MUNA enters after music starts, begins dance until music fades. MUNA on floor upstage left.

MUNA: When his eyesight started to go it really freaked him out. He needed his eyes. He was still talking about all these photographs he was going to shoot in Alaska. He was fighting so hard for life, for something to live for. When his left eye started to go he said, "Oh, thank god I focus with my right eye!"

One day I was cooking him lunch in the hospital, no hospital food for Kwong Chi, and tears were streaming down his face. I said, "What's the matter?" He said, "Oh I just love that song!" It was Edith Piaf singing "Je Ne Regret Rien."

Then on March 10, 1990, in his apartment at 14 Maiden Lane at 4 AM, Kwong Chi died of AIDS. He wanted to be cremated and have his ashes scattered into New York harbour from the Statue of Liberty which made me realize how much he loved New York. At Very Special Flowers on 10th Street, I found some beautiful, Shaker cedar boxes so I bought one, but when I tried to put the ashes into the box it didn't fit. I didn't know a person could make so much ash.

I think Kwong Chi never looked back much. I don't think he thought about the future much either. He always lived intensely in the moment like right here, right now celebrating all that life had to offer.

(Fade to black. MUNA exits. Sound of wind in a canyon.)

Epilogue

(Slide: Slide fades up of image from the expeditionary series of KWONG CHI with his back to the camera look-ing into the Grand Canyon. The image establishes itself, then Kwong Chi vanishes from the landscape. After a beat or two, Kwong Chi's full name appears on top of the image, dead center and the date of his birth and death, the names of celebrities and friends who died of AIDS in the last decade and a half appear around the image of the Grand Canyon. The memorial names stay up and the Grand Canyon fades away. The house lights go up.)

List of names for AIDS Memorial

Jim Thomas

David Lusby

Gin Louie

John Bernd

Lee Connor

Bill Anselmo

Bob Carroll

Michael Mathews

Robert Sterns

Arnie Zane

Michael Ciccarelli

Julio Galindo

Robert Labiak

Mario Saboya

Charles Ludlum

Georg Osterman

Chip Elwell

Bernard Samilon

Robert & Carole Wolfe

James Driver

Fidelio Bartolomea

Frank McDermott

Frank Moss

James Chumbley

Bill Ford

Gordon Bonwell

Rudolf Nureyev

Huck Snyder

Peter Anderson

Roland Roux

Wayne Springer

Daniel Mahoney

Robert Stark

John DeMonico

Ari Darom

Manuel Alum

Keith Haring

Michael Schwartz

John Sex

Dan Friedman

David Wojnarowicz

Tom Rubnitz

Robert Mapplethorpe

END OF PLAY

III THE VERBAL MURAL

PROLOGUE:
IN THE BEGINNING...

I started what is now called "Asian American theatre" in New York in 1970 with La MaMa Chinatown. Ching Yeh and Wu Gingi, who were a part of La MaMa, told me that they wanted very much to have something in Chinatown. They told me that the only thing in Chinatown was an occasional traveling troupe doing Beijing opera and not really anything else, and would I come and do something? So I did. We were able to get the basement of the Transfiguration Church on Mott Street, and the first La MaMa Chinatown show was THREE TRAVELERS WATCH THE SUNRISE by Wallace Stevens on August 6, 1970. In 1972, we changed the name of La MaMa Chinatown to La MaMa Asian Repertory Theatre. Then in 1976, they asked if they could call themselves Pan Asian Repertory Theatre; I trained Tisa Chang. So I can't say that somebody else wouldn't have come along and started Asian American theatre, but I was the one.

ELLEN STEWART

Out of respect for Ping Chong, I think he was the first Asian American to be produced in New York . I think that same year 1972 he had had something done at La MaMa off-off Broadway. He's been pissed at me for laying claim to being the first Chinese American playwright to be produced in NYC , when he was really the first (laughs). THE CHICKENCOOP CHINAMAN was maybe the first Asian American play produced a step up from off-off-Broadway, but not that much. But if you've ever read THREE TIMES I-BOW by this writer named Carl Crow, he writes that he had gotten a Workcore grant in the '30s to put together a theatre company, I think, called the Jung Wah Players, in New York's Chinatown. He writes that these Chinese Americans were anxious to put on a translation of a Chinese opera. A member of that group, Wood Moy, was a printer in San Francisco and then joined my theatre group Asian American Theatre Workshop in the '70s. Wood said that it was Carl Crow's idea to do this opera and that they were all American born and knew nothing really about China or Chinese opera. They were interested in doing American stuff - whatever that was.

FRANK CHIN

I don't know what he's talking about. Frank Chin is completely paranoid. How could I be mad at him for being the first Asian American produced in New York when I don't give a shit about that stuff! In fact, I think he's the pioneer...on that coast. The first time I ever had any contact with him was when a Chinese journalist said to me, "Frank Chin says that you are an expatriate," and I've never even met this man! So I laughed and said to the journalist, "How can I be an expatriate when I've never even been to China?" I'm a New Yorker. I grew up in Chinatown and went from a public school that was 99 percent Chinese kids to a junior high school that was half Chinese and half Italian kids, to a high school where I was the only Chinese kid and graduated as one of only four Asian kids. Then I went to Pratt Institute where again I was pretty much on my own. So basically that arc, that journey, was one of adjustment of growing up in a very enclosed cultural community to one that I really didn't understand. By the time I started working with Meredith Monk in 1971, and then doing my own pieces starting in '72, I was still working that out and I didn't have any kind of support group or anything because Asian American movements and all that stuff was just starting. It was a very difficult time for me because I was negotiating this identity schism on my own. So from the very beginning, my work was always about the issue of culture and the Other. When I finally met Frank Chin years later, he starts to rant, which is very Frank Chin, and he says "Your friend Erika Monk...blah, blah, blah," I don't remember exactly what he said. But I said "My friend Erica Monk? I'm not a friend of Erica Monk." So he immediately starts off being hostile. Then he goes, "Amy Tan is not Asian American, she's a Baptist." So I said, "Well, you're the first Asian American bigot I've ever met."

PING CHONG

I wrote the THE CHICKENCOOP CHINAMAN to get off Maui. I was on Maui with a bunch of other acid casualty friends. We were doing construction and we were all just too stoned too long and accidents started to happen and I had to find a way off. So I read about

East West Players' in Los Angeles playwrighting contest, wrote The Chickencoop Chinaman, won the contest and got off the island. East West said the play was too difficult to do, or beyond their technical capabilities, so they didn't do it. A friend of mine, Ishmael Reed, sent it to Harry Belafonte Enterprises, and the producer there, Chiz Schultz, sent it to Wynn Handman. Handman called me up and said let's do it.

FRANK CHIN

Since I started the American Place Theatre in the early '60s I had one phrase that guided me: to put voices worth hearing on the stage. So I didn't think that I was doing the first Asian American or Chinese American play on stage. When you do these things you don't know that you're making history. Chiz Schultz was on my advisory board and he sent me The Chickencoop Chinaman's Pregnant Pause—that was the original title—by Frank Chin because he knew it would be one of my type of plays. It may not have been as fat as the Manhattan phone book, but it was at least as fat as the Queens or Brooklyn phone book. So we proceeded to bring Frank in from California, because we had to get this play down to some size that was manageable, but Frank was a hard man to manage. He had and still has so much talent and anger and fury in him and such a wild imagination that it creates a turbulence that just keeps exploding. So when you ask him to change something in a scene, he comes back with a long prologue when you don't need a prologue. I haven't thought about this for a long time, but ironically, Frank stayed in the apartment of Harold Ickes, on the Upper West Side. We knew Harold, who's now my son-in-law, because he ran the New York state campaign for Eugene McCarthy in 1968, and his father was the Secretary of the Interior for F.D.R.'s administrations known as "The Curmudgeon." The Curmudgeon was the only one in the Roosevelt administration who openly opposed the incarceration of Japanese Americans. My father-in-law would be a hero to Frank...These were my original notes from when I first read Frank's script: "The talent is squandered because the scenes are too loose and drawn out. The writing is excessive. The audience will be too worn out by the time the play is less than half over. It needs focusing, tightening and cutting, but the talent is abundant, original, genuine and full of force needed for drama. This is the 'Chinese Look Back in Anger.' You must know that what we do to minority groups will ultimately produce its anger and then its violence, even with the Chinaman."

WYNN HANDMAN

In the early days, the 70s, it was quite a pejorative term to be called "minority theatre" or "ethnic theatre." Then we got the terms, "ethnic-specific" or "multi-cultural," and that sort of softened it or made us legitimate. I guess in the early days Asian American theatre felt like the step-child; we were not really fairly dealt with in terms of funding, recognition, press. I think much of that changed due to our Pan Asian Repertory Theater's success. When I started Pan Asian Rep, I just wanted to do something really meaningful to expand the American theatre. American theatre was very much dominated by a WASP mentality since the turn of the 20th century. By the 1970s, I thought we want to have a little chance because we are Americans! I thought the definition of American theatre was a little narrow if you limit it to everybody that's in the Antoinette Perry Awards. So I wanted to expand it to also include the very enriching traditions of the master works of China, Japan and India, but in a way that bridged both Asian and American cultures. Because at that time, the traditional Asian arts were always these pieces that foreign troupes would bring over and you would see them in a museum or lecture hall setting and it was rather boring. I'm not putting the Asia Society down, but I thought why don't I put these works in a truly integrated theatrical environment? So I guess in a way, I was a little revolutionary. And this was way before Peter Sellars and his "Peony Pavilion."

TISA CHANG

By the mid-'70s, things like the National Endowment for the Arts and the New York State Council on the arts and a lot of the foundations that had been giving to the arts were really established for a decade. Once that happened, there were a lot of forms to fill out and in a lot of the narratives for these grant proposals you had to justify why you were getting these grants. And part of this justification had

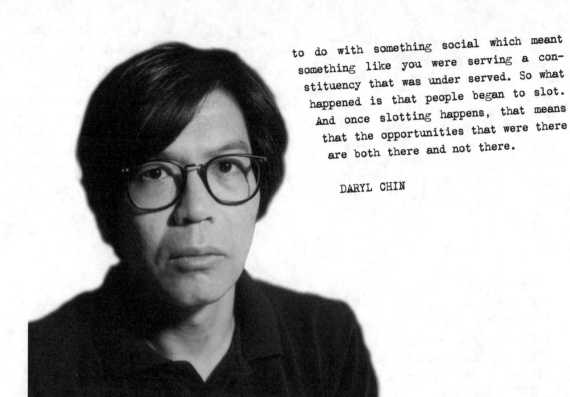

to do with something social which meant
something like you were serving a con-
stituency that was under served. So what
happened is that people began to slot.
And once slotting happens, that means
that the opportunities that were there
are both there and not there.

DARYL CHIN

Act I:
WHAT BECOMES ASIAN AMERICAN THEATRE MOST?

1. How far have we come?

There are more playwrights now that we can speak about, but I don't know how many more people are getting produced since that 1972 splash when Frank Chin's play came out. David Henry Hwang had his huge success in 1988 with M. BUTTERFLY, and not that Broadway has to be the barometer, because it's such a rarefied arena for anybody, white, yellow, black or brown because the stakes are so high in terms of money. So I'm certainly not expecting all of us to make it there. But there hasn't really been a huge, huge success for an Asian American playwright since then, and that was over ten years ago!

JESSICA HAGEDORN

Having gone through that period now where it's no longer a radical thing for New York theatrical audiences to see a play about the black or Asian experience or whatever, it's important that theatrical institutions and artistic directors begin to understand the context of the work they are dealing with to present it in the best way. The same way that if you were to do Shakespeare that you wouldn't do it without knowledge of the period or meter. You have to have a point of view about it. Theatres that program these ethnic works for token reasons are doing a disservice to their audiences, to themselves and ultimately to the artists and communities from where the plays come. And that probably can be attributed to a degree of tokenism in that the artistic directors of institutions do not feel sufficiently connected or committed to the work of an Asian American author to make that commitment irrespective of how a given work performs critically or commercially.

DAVID HENRY HWANG

SAKINA'S RESTAURANT was written by a student of mine, Aasif Mandvi. He developed all these characters in my class. It ran for 202 performances here and it was very gratifying to see how that audience became more and more Indian. By the time we closed, well over half and sometimes 75 percent of the audience was Indian. I so wanted them to come, because when the experience is shared-the recognition, the laughter, the tears-in an audience between people of different races, the race that is not being represented on the stage learns something about the other people.

WYNN HANDMAN

Now, with large white companies putting Asian American plays into their season once a year how that effects us is that Pan Asian, which is a small to medium theatre with four people on our staff, still cannot compete with The Public Theater in terms of promotion and marketing. When they have an Asian American play, they have a theatre that can sustain it. We still rent our theatre space and we're locked into schedules at St. Clement's. We're locked into what unions will allow us on the contract that we're able to afford. We don't have an 18-million dollar budget like The Public Theater does. In that way I feel a little frustrated. I feel that most of ethnic-specific, multicultural theatres are small to medium-size, and for the price of independence and the price of that originality, hand carved originality, we've given up a lot.

TISA CHANG

Asian Americans have had little or lack of representation within the theatre community. There are only a few major institutions that actually produce and support Asian American works like, for example, The Public Theatre. But they only do one Asian American play a year and other institutions don't even have an Asian American "slot" so to speak. I'm really disappointed that as we approach the millennium, I sense a lack of cohesion between mainstream institutions and the Asian American community because there a lot of talented playwrights, directors and artists who are forced to play in tiny venues where only people from within their own community will see them-be it at the Asian American Writers' Workshop, P.S. 122 or La MaMa. What I notice even more is that what gets presented as Asian American work in mainstream institutions in particular doesn't represent the current stuff that is out there by Asian American artists who try to push the envelope. I think what happens then is that we start to lose our voice even more because we see the one play that goes up. Then when it's not good because it's riddled with issues or it's an immigration story which a lot of folks think is old news, or it's catering to the white audience, no one in the community supports that. Then the mainstream audience sees this and says, "Wow this is really bad. Why am I going to support this crap? I could go see a black play or a Jewish play and it would be much more fascinating than an Asian American play." It's a pretty sad state of reality when David Henry Hwang is not known to the arts community and then he is our only representative. We should have ten people like him. I feel we're in a pretty crappy place, I have to say, compared to other people and artists of color-especially in New York, the center of our culture and theatre.

GARY SAN ANGEL

Benefiting from the groundwork having been laid by the previous generation of superior crafts people, my generation has the latitude to play more. We have a tradition to respond to. The earlier generation, like David Henry Hwang, Philip Gotanda, Jessica Hagedorn, felt the responsibility to first present images of Asian Americans and say "We are here." And I think it is my generation who's going to say, "We are weird."

DIANA SON

2. What does being an Asian American theatre artist mean to you?

Asian American theatre is a relatively new concept if you think about it. We only go back 20-30 years, so we have all of those issues to work through-chief of which is the immigrant experience. Writers need to get this out of their system. It's their most immediate experience of all; growing up, family, generations, racism, gender. We have to get through that before we start getting into all the other iterations of American life. It takes a certain amount of maturity as a writer to hone in on the nitty gritty of relationships and look at other situations, and as we develop Asian American theatre that'll happen.

RALPH B. PEÑA

We have an opportunity that no other people have: to tell people who we are. To show ourselves who we are and we haven't done it. Instead we're saying we're just like you, we're something Other. We're not. We have not looked at our history, and we believe that there are human beings and then there are minorities. No! Any real writer of any worth writes as if "I am the fucking universal man! Anyone who knows less than me is stupid!" Green, yellow, purple, whatever, any real writer writes from that point of view. But here we all are writing in this Christian form of confessional autobiography, pitching, "Please, puh-lease, puh-lease forgive me for being an Asian. Puh-lease I am really a human being." Fuck that.

FRANK CHIN

I'm not a "professional Asian American" so I've dealt with it in my own personal way. I've never been a joiner of any one group. By personality or choice I've always been Other. People say he's part of the avant-garde, well the white avant-garde never really academically accepted me. Like with Performing Arts Journal, I never really fit their white theories. Then some Asian American organizations might say, "Oh, he's not really part of the Asian American scene." But then because I have visibility and am needed, then I'm part of the Asian American scene. There's a lot of bullshit in the Asian American scene. The funny thing is that sometimes the people who are saying to me, "You're not Asian American," don't even speak their own language. They're completely American pie really and I don't judge that cause that's just a circumstance of fate. If they happen to be born here and they're third generation, am I supposed to judge them because they don't know anything about their culture? Yet they say to me, "You're not Asian American."

PING CHONG

I'm really not sure what value there is in identifying a writer by their ethnicity. For me, it's mostly an institutional commodity that a theatre can point to and say, "We're producing a play by so and so, who's an African American playwright." It's sort of like a peacock feather. When I see Asian American before the words, "playwright Diana Son," I really question why. My instincts say they are trying to relegate me and make assumptions about what I write about, i.e. generational differences, culture clashes. I am more interested in people who came to New York City from small towns to reinvent themselves as very different from the image that people had of them in their small towns. That comes out of my very specific experience, growing up Korean American in a small American rural town. But for me, it doesn't have to have a Korean American face in order for that story to be told.

DIANA SON

While I'm thankful for the recognition that SAKINA'S RESTAURANT has received, it gives me pause to be thought of as some kind of pioneer in bringing South Asian representation to the stage, because that is not my mission statement. It cannot be, because if it is, then it limits what I do. There's nothing wrong with the label, Asian American. I think it comes from the outside and it's necessary on one level for people, because we need to categorize things. The label just cannot come from the source. I cannot label myself as a South Asian writer because if I start doing that, then it's death for me and it's death for my work. And it's death for any writer or performer or anybody who starts labeling himself after arbitrary things like ethnicity, gender, sexual orientation, whatever.

AASIF MANDVI

There will always be writers exploring issues of identity, whether it's transgender or transcultural or transnational. Some people really have a satisfying life writing for a particular audience and a particular vision. They are not interested in writing color-blind stories. They want to write about what they know well. They're happy doing it and they do it well, so why the hell not? What's wrong with that label on some level? Maybe they don't mind being pigeon-holed or tagged or whatever.

JESSICA HAGEDORN

I was born in Hong Kong, spent my high school and university years in Vancouver, Canada, and then moved to New York to be a professional artist. That was a good twenty years ago. I didn't start thinking of myself as an Asian American artist until 1989 when I went back to China with my parents for the first time to visit "my mother land." When I came back from that trip, I wasn't searching, but this piece, "Post Revolutionary Girl," just poured out. That was the first autobiographical piece I did using my family history as fertile ground for making a dance theatre piece. And I used text for the first time in that piece. H.T. Chen said, "Why don't you do a piece at the Mulberry Street theatre?" As you know, that's smack dab in the middle of Chinatown. So I said yes. I had never connected with a Chinese audience before that. So that was the beginning of my consciousness as an Asian American artist. I was not trained in anything Chinese like Beijing opera, so my methodology and my conceptual thinking is Western, yet I had to find a way of linking that with my source material. I spent many years making work that did not really ring true from a center, or maybe it did at that time. But as I'm getting older and reflecting more and more about my heritage, and how I see life, that whole perspective of being a Chinese person living in the West and being in exile in a way... these issues come out. I think I'm finally reaching a place where I can freely weave the East and the West in me and I like that very much. But I still get calls from people saying, "Oh, can you come and do the 'Dragon Ribbon Dance' on Chinese New Year's?" And I just say thank you very much but I don't do that. So where do you place my work? It's not ethnic as such, but it comes from a place that is clearly from the perspective of a Chinese born.

MUNA TSENG

I don't call myself an Asian American playwright but I don't deny other people the opportunity to do so. It's just occupation modified by race to inform the consumer about the plays I write. But Sam Shepard isn't called a white playwright. He may not be called a white playwright but there are probably other adjectives that precede his description as a playwright. On the minus side, there's a connotation to

"Asian American playwright" of inferior quality, second rate. That's the unacknowl-
edged, unofficial reading of that descriptive. It's just not going to be fashionable
to be an Asian American playwright until a playwright comes along who easily shrugs
off the label, says "Why not?" and has some modicum of glamour to him. No one is
going to own up to being "Asian American" because it's just not a sexy enough term—that's what it all boils down to. And I'd like to think that I'm that figure—I'm just kidding. No I'm not kid-ding...Who cares?

HAN ONG

If you can't be proud of being an Asian American artist then you need to check yourself. We are not being pigeonholed by claiming and honoring who we are as peo-ple. Because all our work, all of our lives have been about sup-pressing and putting down any-thing valuable about how we feel about being Asian American. We've squashed it down so much that it's become a negative connota-tion. Now, when we have the
opportunity as leaders in the community or respected artists, we shy away from that.
I think it says more about the problematic issues within our community about self-
hate, about not really seeing that what we have to offer is so unique and valuable
and so beautiful that we should claim being Asian American artists 100 percent. By
doing that, we are creating no limitations. It doesn't mean that all of your work is
going to be about immigration because let's be frank, we've seen a lot of those plays
and we do need to move forward. But it really means honoring all that history and
then pushing forward.

GARY SAN ANGEL

3. If a play is written by an Asian American, but does not feature Asian American characters or "Asian American themes" is it still an Asian American play?

That's a phony question. A play is defined by its authorship. If you're an Asian American and you write a play it's an Asian American play. Shakespeare is British. He writes a play about Italians, calls it "Othello." Is it still a British play? But it's set in Italy. Why were the blacks pissed off at William Styron for winning the Pulitzer Prize for THE DIARY OF NAT TURNER? Because he's not black.

FRANK CHIN

One argument is that you're an Asian American playwright and you are part of the Asian American tradition because you are Asian American. But then would you likewise say that "Stop Kiss" does not belong in the canon of gay and lesbian literature because I personally am not living a lesbian lifestyle? I think it's very complex...What are you identifying? The personal life of the playwright or the piece of literature that they've created?

DIANA SON

This is where, frankly, the term "Asian American theatre/culture" needs to become more elastic. The community has changed a whole lot since the term was invented, and we've never really used it very precisely. The original arguments were a) we're going to use the term "Asian" because "Oriental" was colonialist, and b) it was unspecific because "where is the Orient?" But we ended up inventing this term Asian American and we're using it as unspecifically as the old Oriental term was used. Because as we deal increasingly with multiplicity of ethnicities in our community, the spirit of Asian American culture may continue to evolve, but the term may become less and less necessary or useful.

DAVID HENRY HWANG

It's Asian American, you don't have a choice. Your point of view, whether politically correct or not, whether it's of the majority view or not, it's uniquely yours as an Asian American. So when you write something, the roots of the material are Asian American regardless of whether or not your play has Asian American characters in it or if you're talking about an Asian American theme.

RALPH B. PEÑA

Is this a trick question? (*laughs*)

WAYLAND QUINTERO

I can understand the baggage that the term "Asian American plays" carries since we don't refer to mainstream plays as "white American plays."

CHIORI MIYAGAWA

The definition of Asian American theatre has broadened. I certainly think that if the characters are not written for Asian Americans, but the playwright is Asian American, that playwright should absolutely be represented in an Asian American theatre's repertoire. It's an individual case and it depends very much on what the playwright and the theatre want to accomplish and the synergy between those two.

TISA CHANG

I have a really hard time calling anything an "Asian American play" or a "black play." I don't have a clear answer because honestly, I'm almost not interested in that. But if you have to have an answer I guess it depends on the theme of the play and how the audience interprets what's going on on the stage.

AASIF MANDVI

Using painting for an example, everyone says, "That's a Van Gogh." No one says, "Oh, that's a Dutch painting."

RICK EBIHARA

As far as I'm concerned, if you're an Asian American, you have some consciousness about that, and you're writing a play and your characters are not Asian American then it's still an Asian American play. But the key, I think, is consciousness about being Asian American. Cause if you don't know the issues or what it means to struggle with that identity then what you're writing is just like any other play and it doesn't have the heart.

GARY SAN ANGEL

To me, that's not a very important question.

HAN ONG

It's a question of opportunity. In other words, if an Asian American writes it, that's what qualifies it, simply because there aren't too many opportunities out there for anybody. So if that's the only way that people can get their work done, fine. But what that leads to, though, is that there are so many plays that are supposed to be about "the Asian American experience." Then, what does that mean? It's actually a very diverse thing. But from the outside, a lot of regional theatres' definition of Asian Americanism is founded on a very clear idea that they already have from almost stereotyped images of oh, people in Chinatown that always have their extended families and on and on. So you find that they are either consciously or unconsciously looking for those kinds of plays. But what if you wrote about, for example, the fact that out on Long Island there's been these Asian Americans who have lived there for a long time in this almost country club environment that has gone on since the '50s? If you wrote about that, I don't think that that play would get produced, because that's not what people can stretch their imaginations to imagine the Asian American experience as.

DARYL CHIN

It's who the writer is and what that writer's vision is. It's always terribly interesting to see that vision and I think we need to contend with that and include it (Asian American plays) that don't feature Asian American characters or themes. Otherwise, we're all just going to segregate ourselves into nothing. It's going to get so narrow and so tunnelvisioned for everyone -- including white people.

JESSICA HAGEDORN

ACT II:
WHAT'S NEW YORK GOT TO DO WITH IT?

New York is the only place in America where you can work in the theatre and sort of feel like you're in show-biz. If you do theatre in L.A., you're definitely doing art. Because of Broadway and the influence of the commercial theatre here there is a show-biz entertainment aspect which doesn't exist in the other cities. When I started off, I had no idea that I would end up being a Broadway playwright. I just assumed that no serious work gets done on Broadway -- which is, by and large, true. But because I had a Broadway hit it changed my perception of the degree to which theatre can be a part of popular culture and this has changed my approach to writing. Therefore, I probably write more to that now which has its advantages and disadvantages. Struggling to try and create another hit is not a very productive artistic thing to think about. One should really focus on the truth of your work because you can't control if it's going to be a hit or a flop anyway. Yet that virus is part of me for better or worse, and that has affected the way I write.

DAVID HENRY HWANG

I don't think "The Chickencoop Chinaman" reached an Asian American audience in New York . I don't think there was an Asian American audience. I still don't think there's an Asian American audience. I don't think there are very many Asian American writers because everything they write is as if yellow is a disease or an affliction that they have to get over and that really they're white and they're just begging to be white and be accepted as white. Well, more power to them, but they're not Asian American. So whatever they have to say about Asian America is that they despise it. They despise themselves. They despise their history, they don't know it. They make a point of pride in not knowing it. Certainly they won't stand up for it. So here we have Asian American writers writing as if playing to the stereotype as if it's true, as if a yellow having sex with another yellow is an unnatural act, and that's New York. It's exclusive to New York. It begins in New York...Ms. Magazine... the chickens go to New York.

FRANK CHIN

Everyone and anyone is an artist in New York and I truly believe that. If you're in New York you're an artist in your own heart whether you're a doctor or a stock broker because there is this need, there is this hunger, to write your stories and get up and perform on stage, and there's no other place like it. So you have all these people who hunger for this. So when you create a space like PEELING THE BANANA, where it's about being able to tell your stories and share them openly and honestly with the community, as vulnerable as that is, anyone and everyone can be a performer. The workshops that inspired PEELING THE BANANA started in Los Angeles and we even did them on the East Coast in Philly and Boston. But New York is the only place where this work has continued.

GARY SAN ANGEL

We just got a rejection letter the other day from a regional theatre saying that the artistic director thought STOP KISS was "too New York." This is hilarious to me because I will never think of myself as a New Yorker. I always will be the country mouse in the big city.

DIANA SON

If you're a young man of any kind of ambition and you're not from New York and your ambition is to be a writer, sooner or later it will do you well to move out here. There's a certain competitiveness in the air...it's very Darwinian, and I think that, for the most part, it changes your writing for the better. But the best part of living in New York is that I don't have to think about living in New York anymore. It's always this mythic "going to" place. Now that I'm here, it frees my mind up to think about other things. I don't have to constantly think about "one day, I'm going to move to New York."

HAN ONG

When I was living in Florida, I was one of only two Indian kids in my whole school and I was always on the outside of a very white or black world. Coming to New York, there are lots of people who look like me and it maybe a clich , but New York is a city where you can be exactly what you are and nobody's going to judge you for it. It's a great place to experience everything there is to experience about different peoples and cultures and everything down the line. SAKINA'S RESTAURANT is seen as kind of an edgy play in other cities, and it's not necessarily edgy in New York.

AASIF MANDVI

I'm not a big fan of theatre in New York, I think the worst theatre I've ever seen in the world has been in New York and I've seen lots of it. The thing about New York is it makes fun of other places and other regions of the country, and cites very specific regional flavors as a way of demeaning the tastes of other parts of the country. But New York is the most regional place I've been in -- your plays have to have a certain bent to it. If you're Jewish; you have a guaranteed audience. If you're gay; you have a guaranteed audience. If you write about older people with older, more conservative concerns, you have a guaranteed audience. And I think the producers now are getting more conservative. Not as conservative as they were in the early '90s when arts funding was getting cut. The New York Times has a lot do with that. It's not really an arts organ, for me it's like a consumer report. It's like Ralph Nader going, "I've tested this battery and if you want to drive 10,000 miles..." That's all it really is. There's nothing artsy about it. In San Francisco I did two productions of mine that were lambasted by this critic who used to be a sports writer and in a way, I feel that a lot of theatre reviewers in NY and in this country are sports reviewers. They're like, "If I don't see a ball then...the ball has to be here and then it has to go there, and someone has to hit it back," and that's really the extent of theatre reviewing.

HAN ONG

New York put muscle in my work. Just because people here have seen a lot and they're a much more demanding theatre audience because this is one of the few places in America where theatre is taken seriously. More of your peers see your work so there are higher stakes. It also made me reassess my work and myself; is this what I really wanted to do? Do I really want to live here? Because it's a struggle to live here, as we all know, so every artist who decides to stick it out had better love it because it ain't about the landscape.

JESSICA HAGEDORN

Pan Asian would not have survived anywhere else except for New York, simply because in New York you are scrutinized and the expectation for excellence and professionalism is so high, and the competition is world class. There are 300 events going on every night in New York. So you really have to be quite competitive and stay on your toes. I sometimes feel like I'm a pit-bull. I gotta stay as fighting and as fit as a pit-bull walking on a tight rope.

TISA CHANG

I like that the disgustingly rich are right next to the homeless here. That kind of interaction of all these different class levels is a big inspiration for work. Like one thing that's unique to New York are all the Chinese delivery guys, they're like this unsung labor force. And one night I'm cruising along on my bike, you know I have my long hair, my leather jacket. Then this Chinese delivery guy rides up next to me and he says in Cantonese, "Hey, you working late tonight?" I thought, Whoa, he thinks I'm a delivery guy! Then everyone on the street thinks I'm a delivery guy! I thought I look nothing like this guy, yet I felt this connection with him. So I just kind of stuttered back in Cantonese, "No, I'm not actually working tonight." I was so embarrassed, I didn't know what to say. But that really inspired the idea for "No Menus Please" in BIG DICKS, ASIAN MEN. Because I was suddenly connected to them and their plight of what they have to face every day, which is essentially trying to do their job in front of signs that say, "Don't come here."

PERRY YUNG

2. How is the experience of the NYC Asian American theatre artist the same, and different, from other artists of color?

Like other artists of color, we expect to be in the mix, but we've also gotten used to dealing with ourselves as invisible people in the stories that we hear through popular mediums like film, theatre and music-although it's not so true in literature. In this country, there's been a longer and more distinguished history of African Americans and Latinos in the theatre, and subsequently there's been more of an audience and theatre going tradition in those communities. It's been difficult for those artists, but they have a certain visibility and a sense of themselves as part of the theatre. I think we're still scratching the surface.

JESSICA HAGEDORN

I went to see a performance by the Alvin Ailey Company up in Harlem and there was such incredible support from the community. It was a sold-out house that was so enthusiastic to see their friends and neighbors, sons and daughters up there on stage. We lack that as an Asian American community. I remember thinking, it's going to be a long time until we have this kind of support for our own kin. Asians are just not very supportive of the arts, especially not contemporary arts, except for a few classical music prodigies like Yo-Yo Ma or Sarah Chang or Midori.

MUNA TSENG

As far as other folks of color...I think we all need to realize that there's a hierarchy; and the reality is that if you're black, you have a much stronger chance of getting your work out there because this culture is basically black and white. There are just two races, and whether you're Latino or Asian you have figure out your own path. In many senses, I feel like the Latino community is just as lost even though they have much more of a presence culturally than Asian Americans-especially in New York, the heart of a lot of Asian American activism.

GARY SAN ANGEL

I think one thing all writers of color share is this expectation from the mainstream to deliver something culturally specific, and I think this is an obstacle especially because this expectation comes from the mainstream so it's not very enlightened about different cultures to begin with. The difference at this point lies in the critical mass of African American writers and artists as opposed to the very small pool of Asian American writers who are working in the mass media. Because of that, I think it's more likely that a theatre will view Asian American work in a spirit of Tokenism.

CHIORI MIYAGAWA

Initially the similarities are more striking than the differences. Certainly, Asian American political consciousness, out of which the Asian American theatrical movement initially stemmed, was an outgrowth of Third World and African American mentalities and ideologies. Therefore, it's not surprising that a lot of early models drew on African American work, like "The Chickencoop Chinaman" with the Black Jap Kenji character. So, seeing African Americans starting to define their own identities through literature and being an alternative to mainstream theatre is what kicked off a lot of the Asian American theatrical movement. As far as the differences, I think it comes down to the different ways in which different ethnic groups are stereotyped. So with Asian Americans, you end up having more of a sense of what the mainstream audience expects, which is more artistic, more beautiful, more poetic and more exotic than what they expect from plays about the African American experience, which is more sort of street. One of the biggest recent changes, and this actually applies more in film, is that Asian American artists, at least those behind the camera, have been able to crossover much more easily than other artists of color . Directors like Ang Lee, Wayne Wang and John Woo are basically just considered directors now, they're not considered Asian American directors even though a lot of their early work began either in terms of dealing with Asian American themes, as in Wayne's case, or Asian themes in Ang Lee and John Woo's cases. It's often been curious to me why the establishment has not allowed African American or Latino directors to do work that does not deal with their ethnicity. And to me, it seems as if that has to do with the ways in which the stereotype of Asian Americans, as being more purely artistic and more assimilated, works to our advantage at least in this narrow sense.

DAVID HENRY HWANG

3. How is the NYC Asian American Theatre community the same and different from other Asian American communities?

The New York community is, in a funny way, more traditional and more tied to root culture and root culture forms than some of the west coast communities. There are more immigrant groups in New York that maintain a community identity apart from assimilating into the mainstream community. And that means that you have more indigenous theatre groups. The city is supporting more Asian American theatre companies than are supported, to my knowledge, in Los Angeles, San Francisco or Seattle. There's more Asian American theatre going on here of a more diverse nature than on the West Coast, which is odd in a way. You always think of the West Coast as Asians having more influence and a lot stuff comes out of the West Coast, and both of those things are true. A lot of powerful stuff came out of San Francisco in the '70s and '80s, and there's been a great rejuvenation of East West Players under Tim Dang, but there's still a greater variety and greater number of companies here in New York.

DAVID HENRY HWANG

Asian Americans on the West Coast seem a little closer. In Hawaii and California there's a lot of film and TV, and everybody wants to be a celebrity and a star and a beauty queen. Here in New York, you just do your work and if by chance you get to a certain status, great. While the money's great, I can take or leave stardom—whereas in Hawaii and California, it seems to be more of the thing to go for.

WAYLAND QUINTERO

More than in other Asian American communities, the level of training and professionalism here is more exacting. The actors get more experience doing everything from theatre to TV to cabaret to improv, soaps, industrials, etc., so you don't get stuck in a certain mode. You're able to exercise your talents and skill more. Some of the other cities have a slower pace but that can also be an advantage as they have a greater gestation time for developing plays.

TISA CHANG

With the theatre and dance people I worked with in California, the sense that I got is that their work is more content, narrative driven. It's more about conventional plays and it's more about the story. Here in New York, I find that a lot of Asian Americans aren't as concerned with content as they are with form. I see that because there are a lot of Asians from Asia and you don't really understand what they're saying but you see their form of dance or music and how they're approaching their craft. It's like they're investigating how to tell the story more than what the story is.

PERRY YUNG

The Asian American communities on the west coast are much more cohesive than they are on the east coast. In San Francisco, for example, there is a real palpable Asian American community. You know where they are, so arts programming and arts development in theatre is much more community-rooted than it would be here. But the realities of the business in New York make it a completely different animal than it would be on the west coast. Here, we certainly enjoy support from the community, but here, the term "community theatre" is a pejorative term. It means that you're less than par and amateurish and I don't think there's that connotation on the West Coast. In Los Angeles there's no crossover. If you do a Chinese play you only get the Chinese community. If you do a Filipino play you only get the Filipino American community. When FLIPZOIDS was presented in Seattle the audiences were primarily Filipino Americans. We didn't get the other Asian American communities coming to see the play. That crossover we get more in New York simply because the nature and tradition of New York is just so mixed and exposed to the idea of going to the theatre.

RALPH B. PEÑA

4. Did the MISS SAIGON protests change anything?

When I look back on 1990, when the "Miss Saigon" protests erupted, I really feel
a little sad because I think we were very misunderstood. 1990 was fifteen, twenty
years after we first started picketing and things hadn't improved that much. If
the producers had just simply wanted the original actor, Jonathan Pryce, to play
the role they should have just said so instead of besmirching Asian American talent by saying, "there is no Asian American actor capable of playing the role." Once
that went into print in The New York Times we of course got into arms. The bone
of contention by the Asian American community was that we have an equal opportunity to audition and be seen in the lead role of the Amer/Asian character. Somewhere
I also feel a little bit manipulated about that whole thing because all of the con-
troversy and P.R. gave that show an awful lot of free advertising and we got a
black eye. Pan Asian certainly got a black eye in the commercial arena because we
were misunderstood. To this day, I still cannot get the rights to certain mainstream properties.

TISA CHANG

When they went out against "Miss Saigon" they admitted it was a racist play, and
what did they want? They wanted Asian America to stand-up for the right of Asian
American actors to play racist stereotypes. If they had any sense at all, they
would have encouraged a boycott of Asian American actors from that play. It's a
racist play so let the white racists play it all! But we won't do that because
we're chicken shit. We have become the stereotype.

　　FRANK CHIN

The protests were confounding to me. We're fighting for the right to be in these
plays? But it was an instance where Asians and Asian Americans were not seen as just
taking shit. We went out there and gave people headaches and that's good.

JESSICA HAGEDORN

We lost the battle but won the war. For what it's worth Cameron MacIntosh has subsequently always cast that role with Asian actors. Another long term benefit is any producer knows that if they cast a white actor as an Asian they will get a lot of shit.

DAVID HENRY HWANG

To me, the main issue was not just Jonathan Pryce playing an Asian. It was the fact that playing prostitutes in bikinis were still the only roles that Asian women could get on Broadway.

CHIORI MIYAGAWA

ENTR'ACTE:
GROWING UP: ASIAN AMERICAN THEATRE THROUGH THE YEARS

What was your first Asian American theatre experience as an audience member?

Until I was seventeen I only saw Chinese opera because I come from a family of Chinese opera performers.

PING CHONG

There was no such thing as Asian American theatre. There were church groups, and amateur productions of white works. I guess the only thing that could be called Asian American theatre was the Cantonese opera that was big in every Chinatown.

FRANK CHIN

A workshop that Frank Chin ran at A.C.T. in San Francisco.

JESSICA HAGEDORN

Menotti's THE MEDIUM at East West Players in L.A. in 1967. My mother was the pianist.

DAVID HENRY HWANG

I don't remember what it was, but the first time I saw Chinese performers in the West, I remember thinking, "Wow Chinese people can be on stage and not be ashamed." (*laughs*)

MUNA TSENG

SOUTH PACIFIC at the Dorothy Chandler Pavilion in Hollywood when I was seven. I saw two Asian kids on stage-back then I probably called them "Orientals"-and I actually felt proud. I thought, there are kids like me and they're on stage.

GARY SAN ANGEL

A Pan Asian Rep. production. I don't remember which one, but I went to see some of their shows when I was in college.

CHIORI MIYAGAWA

Local Asian American actors trying to do kabuki in high school in Hawaii.

WAYLAND QUINTERO

David Henry Hwang's FAMILY DEVOTIONS or Philip Gotanda's YANKEE DAWG YOU DIE during the early '80s in college in San Francisco.

PERRY YUNG

In San Francisco during college I saw Philip Gotanda's SONG FOR A NISEI FISHERMAN, and in New York it was Stephen Sondheim's PACIFIC OVERTURES which I consider to be an Asian American work.

RICK EBIHARA

M. BUTTERFLY on Broadway.

RALPH B. PEÑA

Act III:

SUMMATION: NYC ASIAN AMERICAN THEATRE 2000, A NEW DIVERSITY OR THE SAME OL' TOKENISM?

1. What has, and has not surprised you about how NYC Asian American theatre has evolved?

In the '70s there was a real excitement surrounding Asian American theatre -- particularly when Pan Asian Rep. was doing its first productions under the wing of La MaMa. It was new, they were doing new plays, adaptations of classics -- there was a real buzz around it and then that went away because we wore out our novelty. Nobody rode that wave into the next logical step to really establish a solid repertoire of original Asian American works. I don't know what happened. Either the artists lost interest or whatever, but that wave was not seen to its full potential. Now, we're almost starting from scratch again. Part of it was that the initiative was co-opted by the more established theatres. By somehow validating us, they weakened the initiative. Once they said, "Oh yes that is a viable form, we're going to start including you," all of a sudden, within the community was this feeling of "Well now that they're doing it on a much bigger and better scale then we don't have to push as hard." So right now, there's no solid development program out there. That's what's surprising and not surprising. I just thought that at this stage of the game that we'd be so much farther ahead.

RALPH B. PEÑA

I think some of the theatre we see now is what I call "comfortable theatre." It's like people see theatre as this 9-5 thing and you don't really see the blood, sweat and tears and the same degree and intensity of dedication and sacrifice. You don't quite flagellate yourself so hard to get it done. Now I'm not advocating that you flagellate yourself-you'll bleed to death!-but sometimes I'm a little disappointed with the 20-somethings and 30-somethings. Maybe they're just smarter. But I don't think anything that's really worthwhile can be achieved without some bloodletting, without some sacrifice, without something extreme.

TISA CHANG

To me it doesn't really surprise me that there are no Asian American theatre people. What surprises me is that there are. Because I don't think it's part of the acculturation. I never grew up with that which is why, for me, being in the theatre is a very tenuous proposition. I always expect the worst in human nature and most times I'm proven right. I'm mystified by why my plays are not often produced and what it is about the earlier generation of playwrights that makes them as often produced as they are? What is that people see in those works which I find very inferior?

HAN ONG

It's definitely grown to be much more of an identity and a force in giving people voices. I think it's important not to ghettoize ourselves by saying "I'm an Asian American artist and I always make work with that identity and keep it in the community." I guess the ethnic thing is a double edged sword. You've got to use it, but use it to break out of your own ethnicity and get out there and have a bigger voice so people will listen to you whether you're an Asian American or if they don't give a damn that you are.

MUNA TSENG

Young Asian American writers are still writing like Christian missionary schoolboys. All the stereotypes that the Christians had put down, if any of them had any guts, they would test the stereotype instead of accepting it. Go out, find the history. See if it's true. But they don't dare do that because deep down in their Christian souls they believe, they buh-lieve! that the stereotype is real. That they are that. And year after year, play after play, autobiography after autobiography that's all they have to say. What happens to those who say, "I am a human being, I am white." Then they write about whites. Then they are white, they live white and we never hear about them, do we? There are these writers out there who've taken white names and don't write about yellow people. Nobody knows that they're yellow from their authorship or the author's name or the subject matter of their book and nobody knows who they are... and who gives a shit? But there they are, supposedly the best of us. Supposedly what we want to achieve. This racial anonymity and just my good looks and my talent alone will lead me to my success. And what kind of success do we have?...Anonymity? The only difference was me. I was the change. I test the history, I don't play the stereotype. I stand up for Chinese culture, I don't tolerate the fake and I am not Christian. I made the change and the theatre got so fucking scared of me that they brought back the stereotype and created Maxine Hong Kingston.

FRANK CHIN

Often times it's perplexing that with Asian Americans and other ethnic groups, like blacks, the form they've chosen to make their theatre with is completely white. So their subject matter might be radical, controversial, whatever, but the form is completely traditional white theatre. So I find it very ironic and funny that there's all this stuff about what I do. Some of my detractors even say I jumped on the Asian American bandwagon because in '89 I started doing all these Asian pieces. I've never had any use for Western theatre, it's never had any influence on me. The biggest influence on my work is Chinese theatre. That's why I find it ironic when people don't recognize that where I'm coming from is not a Western thing.

PING CHONG

What surprises me is that we're still around and that we still want to do this. What it comes down to is who's still writing for the theatre anyway? Why would young people want to write for the theatre? More and more they're drawn to film where you can make a living without ever being produced-you can doctor scripts or something-whereas theatre is really a labor of love. They already know that they're not going to get widely produced so who's going to be attracted to that? You have to be some sort of lunatic to want to do this and put up with all this shit.

JESSICA HAGEDORN

The most surprising thing, and this is true about Asian American literature in general, is that we never expected the literature to become this popular. While at the same time, another thing that's surprising in a negative sense is that there hasn't been another kind of Asian American straight play commercial success since "M Butterfly" by me or somebody else. So the longevity of the footprint of "M Butterfly" in a commercial Broadway sense didn't happen -- it didn't have legs so to speak. Even given that, the popularity of Asian American literature is very surprising. The idea that this sort of subject could end up having mainstream appeal is something that we didn't imagine would happen when things first got going in the '70s and '80s.

DAVID HENRY HWANG

2. Is this the beginning of a new diversity or just the same ol' tokenism?

Han Ong, Alice Tuan, Chay Yew and I joke about who got "The Chink Slot" this year at what theatre. But for me, I really question whether or not I fulfill "The Chink Slot." Was STOP KISS the Asian American play of the season at The Public Theater? Is it an Asian American play because I wrote it? Is it an Asian American play because Sandra Oh was in it? The dominant theme of the play was sexuality, sexual identity and committing and not ethnic identity. So I don't know or care if it fulfills that spot. I would hope that they chose to produce STOP KISS because it was a good play. I can't imagine anyone who would feel satisfied that they got in because they fulfilled "The Chink Slot."

DIANA SON

There's certainly tokenism involved in the programming of these large commercial theatres and there is probably some attempt to diversify the programming of their season. But look at who's getting produced. We're talking about David Henry Hwang, Philip Gotanda, and Chay Yew and once in a while you'll see Diana Son or Alice Tuan slip in there. And what are we doing to insure that there's this continuous flow of work for these theatres or us smaller Asian American theatres to do? Nothing. So what's happening is theatres are taking a very passive approach and letting writers sort of self-develop themselves to the point where they become commercially viable or artistically exciting for these venues so you have to do it yourself.

RALPH B. PEÑA

It's the same old, same old. It's just contingent upon a new batch of people who haven't been beaten down yet by the system to come up and have the hubris to write their play and think, "History will make an exception and reward me because I'm so special," which is the way I thought when I first came along. But all of this is pretty privileged carping because the MacArthur ("genius" grant) has made it possible to remove myself from the to-ing and fro-ing of having to make a living and shaping my plays to meet a certain box office demand. Which is probably why I remain, over the past few years, unproduced.

HAN ONG

To have just one Asian American play in your season is complete tokenism. In some ways, what needs to happen is there needs to be an institution in New York like East West Players that serves the Asian American community and is an umbrella for a huge plethora of work, from experimental to straight plays to musicals. In some ways, Pan Asian is that in New York. But they don't have a home, so that forces them to be in all these other theatres and in some ways that's a metaphor for Asian American artists in New York. We're forced to bring our work to all these other theatres because we have no home.

GARY SAN ANGEL

There's some kind of unspoken quota or formula they're going after. They'll call it a balanced season and I'm sure that it stems from a genuine place. Unfortunately, sometimes the sensibility that selects those plays and the criteria for their choosing it is just, to me, a little whacko or off-kilter. There's no question that someone who's not schooled deeply in Asian American work and artists really can't do a very good job of selecting what is a great script. They'll generally play it safe and do a David Henry Hwang or a Philip Gotanda play.

TISA CHANG

You can argue that affirmative action, if used carelessly, can promote tokenism. But there's also a degree to which tokenism can open doors, but it tends to only open doors to a very small room.

DAVID HENRY HWANG

Token interest? They have no interest. It's a racist industry, it always has been and that's no surprise. They don't care about what we have to say. All they care about is making money and the stereotype makes money. And we have played that game.

FRANK CHIN

There's always room for more Asian/South Asian American plays. It's great that they're doing one play per season and they should do more. So even if it is just a token, so what? If it's good, has value, needs to be seen and it is seen, then who cares?

AASIF MANDVI

It's tokenism on another level because they'll do the one Asian American play a year, but they will not look at the play as merely an American play, but as "the one black play," "the Asian play" "the Latino play." It's better than nothing, but I truly don't like it. I love multiculturalism but I don't think it's been practiced. What I envision for multiculturalism is not like bringing out the "black play" for February or the "Asian play" for April and all that crap. For me, multiculturalism is a vision of how you relook at America and how the land-scape is constantly evolving. When you say America now, you can't assume that it's coming from a blonde, blue-eyed perspective. You have to include the constantly changing communities around you and the fact that America is now composed of these many cultures coming together, colliding, colluding, conflicting but vibrant, alive. There's no pat solution like then it's going to stop and we're going to close the doors to anybody new-although they're trying that. I think that when you look at a theatre season I wish it was no big deal if they would just decide to do plays that reflected this changing mosaic-and I hate to use that word because it makes me think of Mayor Dinkins, but it's a beautiful word. It's just been used to death by politicians. This country and what's wonderful about it on some level is that we're all here, and those collisions make for interesting theatre. Why can't Chay's play simply be part of the season? And why couldn't they do Chay and Han? I mean what's the weirdness of doing three Asian plays in one season instead of the one and making theatergoers deal with it instead of going, "Here's a spe-cial treat now, here's our Asian project for the whole year." Or, "Now we're doing the Latinos because we just did the Asians last year." And I really resent that because I feel like my work is not being looked at for the right reasons. Tokenism is alive and well, not just in the theatre but in everything.

JESSICA HAGEDORN

EPILOGUE:
IN THE FUTURE...

In the '70s '80s and 90s we did a good job of defining ourselves. Now the legitimacy is there, and in the 21st century we need to strengthen and empower ourselves, and take control in every way, and not just artistically... Maybe we need to take some tips from Jessie Ventura!

TISA CHANG

Once at the Playwrights Center in Minneapolis this Asian American moderator was putting me through the grill saying things like, "How come your company is all white? How come you don't work with the Asian American theatres? My answer was, "Cause nobody's asked me! If they ask me, I'll do it."

PING CHONG

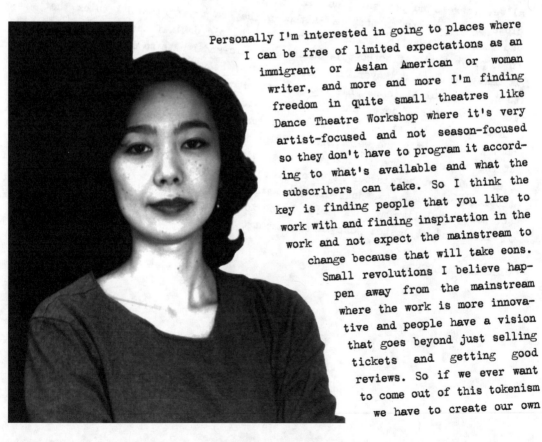

Personally I'm interested in going to places where I can be free of limited expectations as an immigrant or Asian American or woman writer, and more and more I'm finding freedom in quite small theatres like Dance Theatre Workshop where it's very artist-focused and not season-focused so they don't have to program it according to what's available and what the subscribers can take. So I think the key is finding people that you like to work with and finding inspiration in the work and not expect the mainstream to change because that will take eons. Small revolutions I believe happen away from the mainstream where the work is more innovative and people have a vision that goes beyond just selling tickets and getting good reviews. So if we ever want to come out of this tokenism we have to create our own world and not copy the mainstream and not try to be admitted as a member of the main-stream and not make that a priority and make the work a priority.

CHIORI MIYAGAWA

The future is going to be much more global and getting out of tribal mentalities and into a global and universal language. At the same time, individual artists are just going to have to be stronger on their own identity. Because given the scope of how easy and open communication and travel is, I think it's important that, somehow, we don't get all homogenized. That we still hold on to our own strengths and identities and at the same time be more open to each other.

MUNA TSENG

The opportunities that exist are a double-edged sword. The larger institutional theatres have to look for Asian American plays . Because of the foundation grants they have to look for diversification. It's good because it will allow people to work, but it's also problematic because often people are just targeted as a token and there's no development that goes beyond that. So far there's not been a single Asian American playwright or director in the theatre that's had a sustained developing career with a major institutional theatre. And I think that's a real problem because if that happened, a playwright could write something specifically Asian American and then experiment with something that was not and all sorts of other themes and ideas, and still find that they would have a place where there would at least be readings and development of their work. But there are more opportunities now.

DARYL CHIN

Asian American theatre never was, and never will be, a token at La MaMa.

ELLEN STEWART

I think tokenism will always be around, but we'll get away from tokenism as we understand it now-based on the particular racial categories that are currently existent; black, Latino, Asian. For instance, there's this whole theory about "The Browning of America" perhaps with the degree of multiracialism it's going to break down into this white/brown mix but there's still going to be African Americans. If so, there will be a tokenism that comes out of that-positive and negative. Both, tokenism in terms of trying to do things, however well meaning, but doing them badly for people who are perceived to be disadvantaged, and also the backlash of hatred and racism and other negative things. It's human nature to divide people into categories, but I think that those categories may change over time into things that we can't anticipate today.

DAVID HENRY HWANG

I think we are very close to the point where we won't be needing these "slots."

DIANA SON

I see no Asian American theatre on the horizon, ahead of me or behind me. Not in my lifetime, definitely not. We're all too busy kissing white ass and that's not Asian American theatre and that's not what passes for Asian American theatre. If Asian American theatre doesn't stand for Asian America, it stands for nothing. And it stands for nothing. I'm not holding the whites responsible for Asian American theatre, Asian Americans are responsible for Asian American theatre. I expect whites to be white racists, now and forever. They will always have their reasons and their reason will always be to make money their way. It is we ourselves who have no confidence in ourselves to make theatre. If there is no Asian American theatre, it is not the white man's fault. It is our fault, period.

FRANK CHIN

IV Contributors

TISA CHANG is the Founder and Artistic Producing Director of the Pan Asian Repertory Theatre. She began her career as a dancer and actress on Broadway and in films. In the early '70s, she started directing at La MaMa, E.T.C., where she specialized in bilingual productions such as RETURN OF THE PHOENIX (later premiered on CBS-TV's "Festival of Lively Arts"), A MIDSUMMER NIGHT'S DREAM, THE ORPHAN OF CHAO and innovative adaptations such as HOTEL PARADISO, THE SERVANT OF TWO MASTERS, and for Buffalo's Studio Arena, THE LEGEND OF WU CHANG. Memorable Pan Asian productions include Cao Yu's THUNDERSTORM, Momoko Iko's FLOWERS AND HOUSEHOLD GODS, Wakako Yamauchi's AND THE SOUL SHALL DANCE, Vijay Tendulkar's GHASHIRAM KOTWAL, Lao She's TEAHOUSE, Kan & Stewart's SHANGHAI LIL'S, and Ernest Abuba's AN AMERICAN STORY, EAT A BOWL OF TEA, CAMBODIA AGONISTES. Tisa is also on the Executive Board of Society of Stage Directors & Choreographers.

DARYL CHIN is a performance/theatre artist who created over 30 works between 1975-1984. Since then, he has worked in a variety of production capacities on independent film projects. In 1977, he cofounded the Asian American International Film Festival; in 1982, he cofounded the Asian American International Video Festival. At present, he is Associate Editor of "PAJ: A Journal of Performance and Art."

FRANK CHIN is a playwright, novelist and screenwriter known for his uncompromising portrayals of Chinese Americans, and for his outspokenness and controversial views on other Asian American authors. His plays, THE CHICKENCOOP CHINAMAN and THE YEAR OF THE DRAGON, were presented at The American Place Theatre in 1972 and 1974, and were the first Asian American plays to be produced on a NYC Off-Broadway stage. His fiction works include the novels, DONALD DUK and GUNGA DIN HIGHWAY, and the short story collection, CHINAMAN PACIFIC & FRISCO R.R. CO, which received the American Book Award from the Before Columbus Foundation. He is also an editor of AIIIEEEEE! AN ANTHOLOGY OF ASIAN AMERICAN WRITERS and THE YARDBIRD READER, VOLUME 3. He is the recipient of the Joseph Henry Jackson and James T. Phelan fiction awards, the East West Players Playwriting Prize, a Rockefeller Foundation and National Endowment for the Arts' Playwright's Grants. He is also the founder of the Asian American Theatre Workshop in San Francisco and was the first Chinese American brakemen on the Southern Pacific Railroad.

PING CHONG is a theatre director, choreographer, video and installation artist. He was born in Toronto, Canada and raised in New York City's Chinatown. He is the recipient of an OBIE Award, six National Endowment for the Arts Fellowships, a Playwrights USA Award, a Guggenheim Fellowship, a TCG/Pew Charitable Trust National Theatre Arts Residency Program Fellowship, a National Institute for Music Theatre Award and a 1992 ("Bessie") Award for Sustained Achievement. Since 1972, he has created over 30 works for the stage including NUIT BLANCHE, NOSFERATU, A RACE, THE GAMES (with Meredith Monk), ANGELS OF SWEDENBORG, KIND NESS, SNOW, NOIRESQUE, BRIGHTNESS, 4AM AMERICA and ELEPHANT MEMORIES. KIND NESS received the 1988 USA Playwrights Award and was published in TCG's PLAYS IN PROCESS and in NEW PLAYS USA. NUIT BLANCHE was published by TCG in BETWEEN WORLDS. SNOW was also published in PLAYS IN PROCESS. At NYC's Artists Space in 1992, Ping created the first production of UNDESIRABLE ELEMENTS, an on-going series of works exploring the effects of history, culture and ethnicity on the lives of individuals living in a particular community. He has created other versions of this throughout the world. It's Tokyo production, entitled GAIJIN or "foreigners" received a "Best Play of 1995" award from the Yomiuri News Company. Ping Chong created an audio version of UNDESIRABLE

ELEMENTS with sound artist Jordan Davis, that is currently available on CD.

ALVIN ENG is a native NYC playwright, lyricist, storyteller and journalist. Eng's stage works include MAO ZEDONG: JEALOUS SON (AN ABSTRACT PORTRAIT), an opera he wrote with composer Yoav Gal, the musical, THE LAST HAND LAUNDRY IN CHINATOWN, written with composer John Dunbar; the solo performance/monologue plays, MORE STORIES FROM THE PAGAN PAGODA and OVER THE COUNTER CULTURE; and THE GOONG HAY KID, his play with rock and rap songs. His plays have been presented throughout the country at venues including La MaMa, E.T.C., The Nuyorican Poets Cafe and Performance Space 122 (NYC), Theatre Mu (Minneapolis), The Group Theatre (Seattle), among others. THE GOONG HAY KID was published in the anthology, ACTION: THE NUYORICAN POETS CAFE THEATER FESTIVAL (Touchstone/Simon & Schuster). Excerpts from THE FLUSHING CYCLE, his autobiographical storytelling play, were published in THE SECOND WORD THURSDAYS ANTHOLOGY from Bright Hill Press. In '89, Eng wrote and co-directed a short film, THE 20TH ANNIVERSARY REUNION CONCERT OF BIG CHARACTER POSTER, in collaboration with Melissa Cahill. His honors include fellowships from the New York Foundation for the Arts, the Corporation For Public Broadcasting and The Harburg Foundation among others. He holds an MFA in Musical Theatre Writing from NYU/Tisch School of the Arts and was named after the Chipmunk cartoon character.

JESSICA HAGEDORN is the author of THE GANGSTER OF LOVE and DOGEATERS, both novels; a collection of poetry and prose, DANGER AND BEAUTY; and the editor of CHARLIE CHAN IS DEAD: AN ANTHOLOGY OF CONTEMPORARY ASIAN AMERICAN FICTION. Plays and collaborative multimedia theatre pieces include MANGO TANGO, HOLY FOOD, TEENY TOWN (with Laurie Carlos and Robbie McCauley), and AIRPORT MUSIC (with Han Ong). Hagedorn adopted DOGEATERS into a play for a 1998 production at La Jolla Playhouse. She is working on her third novel.

WYNN HANDMAN is the Artistic Director of The American Place Theatre, which he cofounded with Sidney Lanier in 1963. The American Place Theatre presented the World Premieres of the Frank Chin plays, THE CHICKENCOOP CHINAMAN and THE YEAR OF THE DRAGON, in 1972 and 1974 respectively, and of Aasif Mandvi's SAKINA'S RESTAURANT in 1998. Mr. Handman has been instrumental in bringing to the stage the early work of many of America's finest playwrights including Ed Bullins, Maria Irene Fornes, Frank Gagliano, Jonathan Reynolds, Ronald Ribman, Sam Shepard and Steve Tesich. The writer/performers Bill Irwin, Eric Bogosian and John Leguizamo also received early recognition for their work at The American Place Theatre. He is a recipient of two AUDELCO Awards for Recognition for Excellence In Black Theatre, the Lucille Lortel Lifetime Achievement Award from the league of Off-Broadway Theatres, a Rosetta Le Noire Award from Actor's Equity Association the Carnegie Mellon Drama Commitment to Playwriting, The Townshend Harris Medal, and The Working Theatre's Sanford Meisner Service Award for leadership in disseminating the arts to working people, among others.

DAVID HENRY HWANG is a playwright, screenwriter and librettist. Best known as the author of M. BUTTERFLY, the first Asian American play to be produced on Broadway, the play ran for two years and won the 1988 Tony, Drama Desk, John Gassner and Outer Critics Circle Awards as well as the 1991 L.A. Drama Critics Circle Award. The play also enjoyed a one-year run on London's West End, and has been produced in over three dozen countries to date. His most recent play, GOLDEN CHILD, premiered off-

Broadway at the Joseph Papp Public Theater, received a 1997 OBIE Award for playwriting and subsequently moved to Broadway where it received 1998 Tony and Outer Critics Circle Nominations for Best Play. Mr. Hwang's other plays include FOB (1981 OBIE Award), THE DANCE & THE RAILROAD (1982 Drama Desk Nomination), THE HOUSE OF SLEEPING BEAUTIES (1983), THE SOUND OF A VOICE (1983), BONDAGE (1992), FACE VALUE (1993), and TRYING TO FIND CHINATOWN (1996). His plays are published by Plume, Theatre Communications Group and Dramatists Play Service. He is currently rewriting Rodgers & Hammerstein's FLOWER DRUM SONG into a new version to be directed by Robert Longbottom, and working on a new play about Paul Gauguin to star actor Armand Assante. Mr. Hwang graduated from Stanford University, attended the Yale School of Drama, and has been awarded an honorary doctorate from Columbia College in Chicago. He lives in NYC with his wife, actress Kathryn Layng, and their son, Noah.

AASIF MANDVI is a writer and performer who was born in Bombay and raised in the north of England, where he began acting at the age of 10. Aasif moved with his family to the United States fifteen years ago. His New York stage credits include DEATH DEFYING ACTS, SUBURBIA and CROSSCURRENTS. His film and television credits include ANALYZE THIS, THE SIEGE, DIE HARD WITH A VENGEANCE, LAW AND ORDER, NY UNDERCOVER, NASH BRIDGES, THE COSBY MYSTERIES and MIAMI VICE among others. SAKINA'S RESTAURANT played for six and a half months Off Broadway at the American Place Theatre before touring various cities around North America and Europe. It is Mr Mandvi's first published work and the recipient of two 1999 OBIE awards.

CHIORI MIYAGAWA is an Artistic Associate of New York Theatre Workshop, where she manages the Writers Fellowship program for emerging playwrights of color, and a resident artist at Dance Theater Workshop, NYC. Her plays include JAMAICA AVENUE (1998 New York International Fringe Festival), FIREDANCE (Voice&Vision Theater), NOTHING FOREVER (New York Theatre Workshop and New Georges at HERE), YESTERDAY'S WINDOW (New York Theatre Workshop), AMERICA DREAMING (directed by Michael Mayer, produced by Music-Theatre Group and Vineyard Theater) and BROKEN MORNING (Dallas Theater Center). She has received support for her work from McNight Fellowship, Binekie Playwright in Residence at Yale School of Drama, Rockefeller Multi-Arts Production Grant, Jerome Foundation, New York Foundation for the Arts Playwriting Fellowship, New York Council for the Arts, NEA, TCG Extended Collaboration grant and others. Prior to becoming a playwright, she was a dramaturg for such major theaters as Arena Stage, Actors Theatre of Louisville, Berkeley Rep, American Conservatory Theater, and The Public Theater. She is a Binekie Visiting Professor at Yale School of Drama and also teaches playwriting at New York University and Bard College.

HAN ONG was named a 1997 MacArthur "Genius" Foundation Fellow at age 29, one of the youngest to ever achieve this distinction. A playwright and performer whose works include THE L.A. PLAYS, THE CHANG FRAGMENTS, SWOONY PLANET, PLAY OF FATHER AND JUNIOR, and WATCHER. His plays have been presented in prestigious venues across the country and abroad, including American Repertory Theatre (Harvard), The Public Theater (NYC) and the Almeida Theatre (London). His writings has been published in CONJUNCTIONS: THE NEW AMERICAN THEATRE and CHARLIE CHAN IS DEAD: AN ANTHOLOGY OF CONTEMPORARY ASIAN AMERICAN FICTION, edited by Jessica Hagedorn. He is the author of the screenplay for a short film broadcast on Los Angeles public television called NOT X.L., and a full-length screenplay called CANTONESE POP STAR, which he is currently preparing to direct. A high school dropout, Mr. Ong was born and raised in The Philippines and came to the United States as a teenager.

PEELING THE BANANA is a New York City based pan-Asian American performing arts ensemble started in 1995 by performance artist Gary San Angel. It uses autobiography and community building as departure points for performance. Peeling the Banana aims to explore various ways to present written work through public performances, ultimately with the goal of digging deep into issues that concern Asian Americans as artists and as members of a larger multi-racial community. The collective has actively sought to include previously under-represented groups in every step of its process focusing on communities traditionally marginalized in the discourse(s) of Asian American art, Peeling the Banana includes Filipino, Indian, Korean, Pakistani, and Thai members, as well as queer and multiple-heritage identified members. Prior performances have included the Joseph Papp Public Theater, Second Stage Theater, Highways Performance Space in Los Angeles, and the Desh Pardesh Festival in Toronto. Peeling the Banana is currently housed within the Asian American Writers' Workshop. Regardless of the physical space where it meets or performs, Peeling the Banana creates a metaphorical space where each participant feels safe enough to challenge themselves both artistically and emotionally. It is a place where individuals are respected. New participants are received enthusiastically without judgment or condemnation, and everyone is encouraged to take risks. It provides, quite simply, a home where participants can explore and express who they really are.

RALPH B. PEÑA is a playwright and actor. Ralph began his theatre training as an actor at the University of the Philippines in Diliman, and continued at the University of California in Los Angeles and at the Circle in the Square Professional Actor's Conservatory in New York as a Birch Foundation scholar. His plays include CINEMA VERITE, KAPE BARAKO, DECEMBER, FLIPZOIDS, and most recently, LOOSE LEAF BINDINGS. His plays have been presented at Theatre For The New City, Henry Street Settlement, The Joseph Papp Public Theater, all in NYC, the New WORLD Theatre in Amherst, Massachusetts, Northwest Asian American Theatre in Seattle, and at the Kumu Kahua Theatre in Honolulu. He is the recipient of a Playwright's Commission from South Coast Repertory Theatre and a panelist for the New York State Council on the Arts. He currently serves as Artistic Director for the New York-based Ma-Yi Theatre Company.

GARY SAN ANGEL is a New York-based Fil-Am performance artist and director. He is also the artistic director and founder of the Peeling the Banana performance troupe. Gary's collaborative performance creations have been performed across the country from Los Angeles to New York. He was a Van Lier Fellow at the Second Stage Theatre in directing and integrates visual art, theater, music, words, and movement to achieve a balance of aesthetic concerns with social consciousness. His work has been seen at the Joseph Papp Public Theater, Smithsonian, Second Stage Theatre, East West Players, Teatro Ng Tanan (TNT), Highways Performance Space, Asian American Theater Company, Japanese American National Museum, and South Coast Repertory.

SLANT is the New York City trio ensemble of RICK EBIHARA, WAYLAND QUINTERO and PERRY YUNG. As a resident company of the world-renowned La Mama Experimental Theater Club, SLANT's work is an original and dynamic tapestry of theatrical satire, live amplified, acoustic and a cappella music, dance, puppetry, and shadow play. Themes and stories derive from pop culture stereotypes, urban and ethnic myths, from stories and visions of previous generations, from contemporary experiences of their very American upbringing while paying homage to the guiding influences of their Asian heritage. Starting with their 1995 debut, BIG DICKS, ASIAN MEN, SLANT has gone on to create 4 more original pieces, THE SECOND COMING, SQUEAL LIKE A PIG, HOTEL CALIFORNIA, and WETSPOT, which they have performed throughout the world. SLANT's self-titled CD of songs and scenes from BIG DICKS, ASIAN MEN and THE SECOND COMING, was independently released in February 1998. SLANT is currently recording their second CD and was recently commissioned by The Joseph Papp Public Theater for a play.

DIANA SON is a playwright whose most recent play, STOP KISS, premiered at The Public Theater, NYC, in December 1998, where it ran for nearly four months. Originally commissioned by Playwrights Horizons/Amblin-Dreamworks, it will be published as a trade paperback by Overland Press/Penguin Press in late 1999. Diana's play, BOY premiered at La Jolla Playhouse in 1996 under the direction of Michael Greif. FISHES premiered at New Georges (NYC) in 1998 and was subsequently produced by the People's Light and Theatre Company. R.A.W. ('CAUSE I'M A WOMAN) appears in TAKE TEN: NEW TEN-MINUTE PLAYS published by Vintage Press and CONTEMPORARY PLAYS BY WOMEN OF COLOR by Routledge Press. Diana currently has works commissioned by The Public Theater and the Honolulu Theatre for Youth. Diana was the recipient of the Brooks Atkinson exchange/Max Weitzenhoffer Fellowship through New Dramatists (of which she is a member).

ELLEN STEWART is the Founder and Director of La MaMa E.T.C., the New York City theatre that began in October 1961 with the vision of nurturing and encouraging the creative endeavors of new generations of artists. To this day, La MaMa remains true to this founding vision, and has presented more than 1,800 productions. Its resident theatre troupe has performed throughout the world, and Ms. Stewart was instrumental in introducing to America some of the world's most influential artists including Andrei Serban, Thaddeus Kantor, Peter Brook, Jerzy Grotowski, Ryszard Cieslak and Ludwig Flazen among many others. She is a visiting professor of the Institute of Drama in South Korea and is a long-standing member of the Seoul International Theatre Institute. Ms. Stewart is the recipient of numerous Honorary Doctorates and awards, including the MacArthur "Genius" Award and the National Endowment for Arts and Culture. She was appointed an "Officer" in the "Odre Des Arts Et Letters" of the Republic of France, and recently received the Les Kurbas Award for "Distinguished Services to Art and Culture" from the Ukraine. In January 1993, Ellen Stewart was inducted into the "Broadway Theatre Hall of Fame," becoming the first Off-Broadway Artist to ever receive this honor. In December 1994, Ellen Stewart was awarded the "Order of the Sacred Treasure, Gold Rays with Rosette" by the Emperor of Japan.

MUNA TSENG is a celebrated dancer and choreographer acclaimed for her seamless fusion of Asian sensibilities and Western abstract forms. Born and raised in Hong Kong, her family immigrated to Vancouver, Canada in 1966. Ms. Tseng has been based in New York since 1978, and has performed throughout the world. In 1986 she founded her own company, Muna Tseng Dance Projects, and has presented many acclaimed productions over the past decade including SLUTFORART (1999), an homage to the life and art of photographer Tseng Kwong Chi (in collaboration with director Ping Chong), AFTER SORROW (1997, in collaboration with Ping Chong and composer Josef Fung), and THE IDEA OF EAST (1996, with composer Tan Dun, pianists Margaret Leng Tan, SouHon Cheung and architect Billie Tsien), among many others.

Ms. Tseng has received fellowships from the National Endowment for the Arts, the New York Foundation on the Arts, five commissions from New York State Council on the Arts and was honored as a "Chinese American Cultural Pioneer" for Distinguished Services in the Arts" in 1993 by New York City Council President Andrew Stein and named "Artist of National Merit" at Washington's Smithsonian Institute.

COPYRIGHTS | PHOTO CREDITS

Tokens? The NYC Asian American Experience On Stage
edited by Alvin Eng

The *NuyorAsian Anthology: Asian American Writings About New York City*
edited by Bino A. Realuyo

Watermark: Vietnamese American Poetry & Prose
edited by Barbra Tran, Monique T.D. Truong and Luu Khoi

Black Lightning: Poetry in Progress
by Eileen Tabios

Contours of the Heart: South Asians Map North America
Winner of the 1997 American Book Award
edited by Sunaina Maira and Rajini Srikanth

Flippin': Filipinos on America
edited by Luis Francia and Eric Gamalinda

Quiet Fire: A Historical Anthology of Asian American Poetry, 1892-1970
edited by Juliana Chang

For more information about the activities and programs of The Asian American Writers' Workshop,
please contact us at:

• 37 St. Mark's Place, Suite B, New York, NY 10003-7801
Tel | 212.228.6718
Fax | 212.228.7718
e-mail desk@aaww.org *web* www.aaww.org

To purchase any of these books, please contact Temple University Press,

• 1601 N.Broad Street, USB 305, Philadelphia, PA 19122
Call toll-free 1.800.447-1656 | Fax 215.204.1128
or visit us on the web at www.temple.edu/tempress